THE HIGHLIGHTS

THE HIGHLIGHTS

Frank Keating

Edited by Matthew Engel

First published in 2014
by Faber and Faber Limited
Bloomsbury House
74–77 Great Russell Street
London WC1B 3DA

Published with Guardian Books
Guardian Books is an imprint of Guardian Newspapers Ltd

Typeset by seagulls.net
Printed in England by CPI Group (UK) Ltd, Croydon, Surrey CR0 4YY

The article from Wisden Cricketers' Almanack 2001 is reproduced
by kind permission of John Wisden & Co Ltd

The article *Who killed Desmond Marsh?* is reproduced by kind permission of *Punch*

Extracts from the poems *Cheltenham*, *Uffington* and *Seaside Golf* by John Betjeman
are reproduced by kind permission of John Murray Publishers

A CIP record for this book
is available from the British Library

ISBN 9781783350193

FSC
www.fsc.org
MIX
Paper from
responsible sources
FSC® C008047

2 4 6 8 10 9 7 5 3 1

To the Keating family,
especially Jane, Paddy and Tess

The world is not amazed with prodigies of excellence, but when Wit tramples upon Rules, and Magnanimity breaks the chains of Prudence.

Dr Johnson

CONTENTS

INTRODUCTION

The death of a newspaperman, especially one well past the peak of his celebrity, does not normally attract much public grief. But when Frank Keating died in January 2013 it was different. One experienced colleague called it 'an outpouring of something a bit more than respect and affection, more like gratitude and love'.

His funeral, on a chill winter's day, caused a spike in the number of passengers on the sluggardly line between Paddington and Hereford. On a summer's night six months later a full house crammed into a hall at London University to celebrate his life. Many old friends were there, but most of that crowd had never met Frank. They were readers, mainly *Guardian* readers. They felt they knew him simply by reading his columns over the years.

Keating's sports writing in the *Guardian* spanned half a century, from 1962 to 2012. His first article was an anonymous hockey report, commissioned from him as the nearest keen young journalist on hand in Slough. There is still a little more to come: a couple of obituaries commissioned in advance still lurk in the *Guardian* computer system, awaiting their day.

For 40 years he kept writing: not far off 3000 *Guardian* articles, maybe two and a half million words. There were 14 books and well over 1000 magazine pieces: at different times he had regular columns in *Punch*, the *Spectator* and the *Oldie*. His last few newspaper pieces, before his final illness, appeared not in the *Guardian*, but its Sunday sister the *Observer*.

Journalistically he was a late developer: Keating was in his late 30s by the time he sprang into the *Guardian* sports pages and emerged, fully-fledged, as its star columnist. He began to lose his appetite for rushing around the planet after he moved back to Herefordshire in his 50s and his travelling tapered off rapidly after his health started to deteriorate in his early 60s. His rise was meteoric and in one sense he blazed across the sky, just like a meteor, only briefly.

But he packed a lot in. And the love affair between Frank and his readers was an enduring one. There were, I think, three reasons for his success. Firstly, there was his writing. It was only when I began to research this book that I began to understand that his truncated formal education was fundamental to his journalism. As Winston Churchill said of Harrow, his education was interrupted only by his schooling. And like Sir Neville Cardus 50 years before him, he marched into the *Guardian*, always a paper full of posh-university men, and, with barely an O-level to his name, wrote them under the table. He didn't seem to know how things weren't meant to be done.

His imagery was breathtaking and vocabulary audacious: he was indeed the 'onliest Frank'. This extended to his choice of subjects too. Daily journalists are essentially herd animals: contrary to popular belief, the main aim of a day's work is not the fraught business of scooping the opposition, but to avoid being scooped – editors get angry only if you miss something. But Frank would head in directions no one else had thought of: up in the morning to see Mother Teresa in Calcutta or the fortune teller in Bangalore; lunchtime with the French rugby team on Eurostar; late at night to watch Geoffrey Boycott, disc jockey. All recorded in these pages.

Secondly, there was his charm. He liked sportsmen (a rarer quality among sports journalists than you might think) and they took to him and trusted him. He made lasting friendships with them, often improbable ones: the convivial Frank hit it off with the stoical and abstemious Graham Gooch as he did with his more regular bar-companion, Ian Botham. It is true (and the great Cardus had a similar habit) that the quotes he extracted were inclined to sound a bit, well, Keatingesque. But I never heard anyone actually complain. He never misrepresented anyone's thoughts; he just made them more eloquent.

As Mike Atherton pointed out in a characteristically perceptive piece in the *Times*, this would be impossible nowadays. In the major sports, press and performers are rigidly segregated; there is minimal contact, controlled by public relations officers. The drivel that results, Mike might have added, is not just bland and boring, but – though accurately transcribed – inherently falser than Frank's cavalier interpretations.

The third and most important aspect is that his charm came across to the readers. They sensed that Frank was as starry-eyed and uncynical about sport as they were and shared their own delight in the personalities and their character. He was their representative at courtside, touchline and boundary's edge.

In all of that, he was the onliest. And it makes, I hope, the selection of his work that follows not just a compelling read, but also a unique record of our own sporting lifetimes.

I knew Frank for 40 years. I was his colleague on the *Guardian* for 25 of them and I was, by chance, his sort-of neighbour in Herefordshire (we lived at opposite ends of the county) for more than 20. He was a friend, something of a hero and to a large extent my mentor. His widow Jane kindly asked me to give the eulogy at his funeral. By public demand (well, a couple of people asked) this is reprinted at the back of the book, along with other tributes, in lieu of a fuller appraisal here.

Editing this anthology has been largely a pleasure, but it has posed particular challenges. At times I have felt like a scholar of Aramaic or Sanskrit, worrying away at the true meaning of some ancient fragment of text. Let me explain. To start with, Frank was not a precise every-comma-in-place kind of writer. He excelled at verbal pyrotechnics, which inevitably meant the odd damp squib (possible cause of error number one in this collection).

Most of his career took place using the old newspaper technology (not that he ever mastered computers). Newspaper reports were dictated by telephone to copy-takers, a profession now, alas, just about extinct. Nearly all were gloriously eccentric; some were brilliant, some were not. One on the *Guardian* was deaf (possible cause of error number two). Then there were the sub-editors, of whom I was once one. Mainly, we corrected the writer's errors of grammar or fact; being human, we sometimes added our own instead (3).

On the *Guardian*, the edited copy would be taken down to the basement by a chirpy Cockney messenger to be rekeyed into hot metal by a typesetter (4). The old Linotype machines did not allow the setters to correct mistakes; what was done was done. Of course, there were proofreaders to deal with this. But the *Guardian* printing presses were several streets away from the office and the corrections often failed to arrive in time (5), which is why the *Guardian* became infamous for its misprints and rechristened the *Grauniad*. Also, there was no precise means of assessing in advance whether the copy was the right length for the space available. If it was too long the metal type itself had to be cut by a compositor under the direction of a sub-editor, very, very fast. Both parties were capable of mistakes (6 and 7). Sometimes paragraphs would appear in the wrong place or transposed and a story might well end in the middle of a sentence for no apparent

Fast forward several decades. The technology has moved on so much that almost everything that ever appeared in the *Guardian* in the 180-odd years between its first edition and the arrival of the internet has been rescanned on to the web, an amazing resource available to anyone for a small fee. But scanning fading old pages can produce murky images (8). Furthermore, the result is in a format that does not allow one to cut and paste. So most of Frank's columns have had to be printed out and enlarged, not always very legibly, and rekeyed yet again by a typist who did wonderfully but nonetheless ... (9)

That provided a computer file for me to edit onscreen, giving me the opportunity to re-create errors that very possibly I myself introduced more than thirty years ago when I subbed the copy in the first place (10).

You get the picture? Normally, at this point of an introduction an author or editor thanks everyone who helped and then declares that any mistakes that have crept in are his own responsibility. I'm bloody well not going to say that in this case. The list of suspects is endless.

On selection, however, the buck does stop with me. A remarkable number of Frank's friends and colleagues responded to my plea for their favourite Keating column. As on the radio, not everyone can get their request played; editing an anthology involves delicate balancing acts. But I got in as many as I could, and I am very grateful to everyone who replied. The fact that several responders displayed signs of being able to go on to Mastermind – specialist subject: the Works of Frank Keating – is another tribute to Frank. Nearly all the pieces I have chosen are from the *Guardian*, which is where his best work was done.

I have re-edited the pieces a bit (11), mainly to cut topical references that make no sense at this distance, and the contractual-obligation factual bits that don't fit easily into an anthology. Real textual scholars and potential Mastermind contestants can hunt down the original cuttings if they want. In the main body of my book, the editor's interjections, intrusive in the first and last chapters but otherwise sparing, are in italics.

I would also like to thank Sara Montgomery, Laura Hassan, Lisa Darnell, Sophie Lazar, Andy Armitage and Helen May Kelleher at Guardian/Faber. Richard Nelsson, the *Guardian* information manager, was very useful as was, particularly, Frank's last sports editor, Matthew Hancock of the *Observer*. My own wife, Hilary, made many helpful suggestions. And Jane Keating was a constant source of books and cuttings from forgotten corners of Frank's library, plus encouragement, support and common sense.

And finally my thanks go to Frank Keating, for being so damn good.

Matthew Engel
Herefordshire, February 2014

6

TIMELINE

Born
Francis Vincent Keating, 4 October 1937, Hereford

Educated
Belmont Abbey; Douai School

Career
Reporter, local papers 1956–63 (*Stroud News, Hereford Times, Surrey Times, Bristol Evening World, Rhodesia Herald, Bulawayo Chronicle, Slough Observer*)
News sub-editor, *Guardian* 1963–4
Editor, Outside Broadcasts, Rediffusion Television 1964–8
Editor, Features, and Head of Special Programmes, Thames Television 1968–72
Sports sub-editor and occasional writer, *Guardian* 1972–6
Sports columnist, *Guardian* 1976–2012
Sports columnist, *Observer* 2012

Magazine columns
Punch 1979–90
Spectator 1990–6, 2004–8
Oldie 1997–2012

TV
Maestro, BBC 1981–5

Books
Caught by Keating 1979
Bowled Over 1980

Another Bloody Day in Paradise 1981
Up and Under 1983
Long Days, Late Nights 1984
High, Wide and Handsome 1986
Gents and Players 1986
Passing Shots 1988
Sportswriter's Eye 1989
Half-Time Whistle (autobiography) 1992
The Great Number Tens 1994
Gooch: My Autobiography 1995 (with Graham Gooch)
Band of Brothers 1996
Frank Keating's Sporting Century 1998

Family
Parents Bryan and Monica; sisters Clare and Ann

Married
(1) Sally Head 1975-80, divorced
(2) Jane Sinclair 1987-2013

Children
Paddy, born 1988; Tess, born 1989

Died
25 January 2013, Hereford

1

FLORID FLAM …

The name Frank Keating first appeared in the Manchester Guardian *in November 1927. Its owner had just failed to be elected to Heywood Borough Council in Lancashire as a Liberal candidate. It returned in May 1945, three days before VE Day, when Major-General Frank A. Keating, commander of the US 102nd Infantry Division, announced: 'On land, sea and in the air the Germans are thoroughly whipped and their only recourse is to surrender.'*

The Frank Keating of this book was not born until 1937, so these first entries in the paper's database represent intruders. His first bylines began to surface in local papers from the mid-1950s when he was starting out in local journalism, a time when he had not quite perfected his art. More a wanderer than minstrel, you might say: Stroud, Surrey, Salisbury (the one that's now Harare), Slough … On at least one of his early papers, the Surrey Times, *he was allowed considerable scope to express himself, but had not yet mastered the self-deprecation that would become his trademark. Unfortunately, this was the period when he was an aspiring theatre critic.*

'Had I been able to preface my visit to *Gilt and Gingerbread* at Guildford Theatre this week with a visit to some money-no-object hotel and a meal of seasonal game with full trimmings and the best bottle of claret, followed by a Martell and a Havana, I might have been smugly mellow enough to giggle cosily at its candy-floss, West End wit.

Two cups of tea and a boiled egg was my preface to the show, however, and it is the only account I can give to explain why all

9

around me were giggling cosily, while I could scarcely raise even a jaundiced smile throughout ...

By the middle of the first scene I started wondering how the dear old English theatre is going to survive when it turns out such laboured light-heartedness; and London's West End is full of it.

The time is bound to come when big theatre managements and promoters will discover that this sort of policy is stifling them. If they do not leave their awakening too late they will be forced to relax their cautious, parochial and avaricial [*sic*] grip on the reins and give the legions of young and eager theatrical thinkers their head ...'

Young thinkers like Frank, maybe. This was around 1958, the Angry Young Man era. Mercifully, he was not normally angry, and soon realised it was actresses that interested him more than the actual stage. However, there were hints of his ability to extract the telling quote. Once he made the front page splash under the byline Frank V. Keating (a name rather than a football fixture) with a story headed

1,400 FOREIGN STUDENTS IN GUILDFORD

Some Like Us – Some of Us Like Them

Not all, though. The Tunsgate Club in the High Street had banned the French contingent as troublemakers and, as Frank V. Keating reported:

Paul Frys, from Marseilles, who has been here nearly six weeks was definite; 'Guildford,' he declared, 'it stink.'

Keating was 25 when he first got a piece in the Guardian: *a short hockey report commissioned from him when he was in Slough in 1962, simply because the paper wanted a report and the local sports editor was a better bet than a random passer-by. There was no byline, not even a minor textual hint that this was the imperceptible and improbable beginning of half a century of* Guardian *history. But then, as Frank wrote many years later: 'They pitilessly cut all my florid flam about autumn leaves and Windsor Castle in the distance. But they actually printed the boring bits in between.' And how boring those bits were: a game with almost no spectator appeal reported in a flat tone, pedantic initials and all - exactly the kind of antique sports journalism that Frank would be partially responsible for demolishing. Keating's career lived up to his first* Guardian *headline.*

Surrey Slow to Find Form

Buckinghamshire 0 Surrey 4
October 18 1962

Surrey gained the anticipated easy victory over Buckinghamshire in the opening county championship hockey match of the season at Slough yesterday.

But the favourites made almost a hard task of it. Though they dominated the midfield approaches, their attacks disintegrated within striking distance because of over-anxious bunching in the circle, and a brave Bucks rear guard inspired by goalkeeper G.K. Bunnell. It was not until midway through the second half that Bunnell was first passed, R.B. Constable then shooting in from a short corner.

Thereafter, Surrey, having at last found the way, set about making the score line in some measure match their territorial superiority. S.D. Mayes shrugged off some flabby tackling before his well-angled shot went home. Bucks retorted with a rally in which they forced two corners, hit a post and won a penalty bully. But this was easily cleared to P. Austen, whose shot after a flashing run hit the bar, and P. Gent scored from the rebound. In the closing minutes, Constable for once got clear of I.L. Mitchell's close attention and beat Bunnell with a good drive.

When they finally got into their stride the Surrey forwards, encouraged by smooth service from behind, made grand use of the early, diagonal crossfield hit, and some sensible push and run passing. Bucks, in their sporadic offensives, relied overmuch on the predictable corner flag centre and the telegraphed through pass.

This report did not even make the Guardian *archive now available (for a small fee) on the internet. Presumably it appeared only in the London edition. In Manchester it was pushed out by only slightly more urgent news: the English table tennis rankings and the results of the 18-hole East Riding & District Alliance four-ball medal. It might have been lost to posterity – certainly its authorship would have remained unknown – had not Frank, characteristically, kept the cutting.*

That was eight and a half years before his reports would start appearing regularly. By that time he had joined the Guardian *as a sub-editor, but stayed only a year before being given the very grand title of Editor, Outside Broadcasts, at the London ITV station Associated-Rediffusion. His last major assignment as a TV man was the 1970 World Cup in Mexico when his activities including filing reports for the* Times, *encouraged by his friend David Miller. His World Cup reports included what purported to be an exclusive interview with the England manager; not, perhaps, even that famously reticent man's most revelatory remarks.*

From FRANK KEATING

GUADALAJARA: Sir Alf Ramsey told me yesterday evening that he would not announce the England team until the morning of the match.

This moonlighting appears to have been a factor in Frank having to skulk back to the Guardian *and a very ungrand job on the sports desk. His first reporting assignment must have felt a long way from Guadalajara. His report 'Littlechild gives Durham victory', dated 17 March 1971, was a rather dry account of a university rugby sevens tournament at Roehampton. One assumes there was a certain amount of florid flam in the original, excised by one of his colleagues.*

It took a while before the sports editor, John Samuel, realised that he had a special talent on his hands. It was even longer before the message got through to the Manchester office, which was still largely autonomous, and where the subs were very hard on flam. In that early period, when Frank was forging his reputation, he did more moonlighting – on Saturday afternoons. This was normal at the Guardian, *which did not have a Sunday edition, provided its sports writers used a pseudonym. Hence the brief life but ultimately sad death of 'Desmond Marsh'. Years later Frank told the story in* Punch.

The Millwall murder mystery
Who killed Desmond Marsh?
Punch 20 January 1989

A basic punter's rule of thumb is that the fifth-placed nag round Tattenham Corner goes on to win the Derby. As the leaders in English soccer's first division galloped into 1989's home straight this month, Liverpool were fifth, moving nice and easy, and coiled for the final furlong. Steady as she goes. You read it here first.

Arsenal led with a high-stepping, thoroughbred swank. Followed by Norwich City and Millwall. I'm sorry, I'll read that again. *Norwich and Millwall?* What the blazes is going on? Enough's enough. Joke's over, surely? Don't you be too certain. I have a very soft spot for these two hearty, heavily handicapped, homely old selling-platers, who are frolicking up the hill with the cream of the century. I served my apprenticeship at Norwich and Millwall. Or rather, Master Desmond Marsh did.

Seventeen years ago, as the coffin-like days of winter were hedging about turning into those of spring, my Saturday afternoon beat alternated for weeks between Millwall's dingy Den and Norwich's sword-sharp, Siberian sleet. And on successive Saturdays in April 1972, I saw them both promoted to the first division for the, till then, one and only time in their history. In Millwall's case, however, promotion that year lasted only eight minutes.

A kindly sports editor said he'd try me out at match reporting. They called me 'Desmond Marsh' of the *Sunday Telegraph*. Cadge a phone, and 400 breathless words 'on the whistle' – all for 11 guineas a time, plus travel warrant. Norwich and Millwall were neck-and-neck for promotion that season. The star writers steered clear, so I began to be considered the specialist in the respective second divvy charms of these two amiably unfashionable clubs. When I've popped in occasionally to either ground all these years later, old codgers who serve tea or Bovril, or dish out your free programme, still call me up in their ripely different accents, 'Allo, Des, boy, you got us again, then? All right, my son?' Bless them, they don't notice I'm not in short pants any more, nor have that ever-ready row of spare biros in my top pocket. To them, poor, dead Desmond still scribbles on.

My routine never changed all through that February, March and April. I've got most of the programmes still. Millwall one week, Norwich the next. The Den was an impenetrable black hole of mud-slimed field, tucked behind rain-glistening, rivulet-running, cobblestoned dockland lanes. My drill was to catch the Tube early to the Elephant about noon, then lazily loiter down Copperfield's old road to Kent. You had to be in the mood for Millwall.

I'd start with just one at the Thomas à Becket, where upstairs punchy old pugilists would puff and snort at the heavy bag; and, below, a raucous, peroxide blonde licensee would threaten to lay them out if they came downstairs and got out of turn. Then it would be time to amble on down to the public library, to go through the morning's tabloids and the local rag to see how they perceived the match; and, to end up, a final swift half at that scruffy pub on the main road corner, all effing and blinding and fist-fight scuffles as tensions grew before kick-off.

Norwich the next week made a very different day out for 'Desmond'. For one thing, the *Telegraph's* 11 guineas was a particularly paltry sum if you met a *hic* of fellow hacks on the 10.30 travel-warrant buffet-car from Liverpool Street. Certainly, you'd be out of pocket for the return journey by the time, awash with aperitifs, you stepped unsteadily out of the ritzy dining room of the – was it called *The Nelson Hotel?* – just opposite the station. By now, the earlier leisurely throng would have cranked on the extra scurry to their gait as 3pm approached – though they'd still have the agricultural roll accentuated by their heavy jackets of rusty tweed or lovat-check, all with leather reinforcements sewn into the elbows. Us London mob would roll along for different reasons.

Someone wrote a pained letter to the *Guardian* the other day pointing out that he'd never read a report of a Norwich match at Carrow Road this season without the word 'homely' cropping up at least a couple of times. It was difficult to resist the adjective in my day, too. Why, it was the only league ground with a pub, The Nest, built into the very grandstand itself. With all the new laws for soccer sobriety flying about, I wonder if it's still there?

On the penultimate Saturday of that romantic 1972 season, Norwich ensured their first-time promotion to the first division championship, and set up a heck of an unlikely East Anglian carnival hullabaloo. Their star turn Dave Stringer, by the way, is Norfolk through and through, and appropriately he is the club's manager in this present *annus mirabilis*.

Down the Old Kent Road the following Saturday (29 April 1972) Millwall had to beat Preston North End to go up into the ultimate big-time with Norwich – providing Birmingham City lost, as they surely would, at Sheffield Wednesday the same afternoon. Millwall were winning at a nervous enough canter, by 2-0 – Possee and Bridges the scorers – when raging bushfire whispers began to be spread though the multitude with five minutes to go.

Someone had heard on the BBC radio that Birmingham had lost 2-1 at Hillsborough. The knees-up started from the corner with the wireless, like that modern, billowing Mexican wave. At the final whistle, the jubilant thousands swarmed over the field. The overjoyed Millwall players happily had the white shirts torn off their backs for souvenirs before being hoisted aloft on shoulders and chaired to the milling touchline. Glorious bedlam. Kisses sweeter than wine. They had done it.

Up in the cramped little knee-crushing pressbox, 'Desmond Marsh', having cadged his early phone, dictated his 400 frantic words of purple praise to the Lillywhite Lions and their dramatic elevation to the highest division in the game. Then he thought he'd be even more smartly professional, and, within five minutes of the final whistle, was hotfooting it back up the Old Kent Road before the crowds had done with their glee.

Off he nipped, smartish as I say, and didn't tarry until he'd hit West London for a couple of quenching pints at opening time. Certainly it was a good couple of hours before he hit the home fire. The *Sunday Telegraph* were on the line. And not best pleased. It was *Birmingham* who had won at Sheffield by 2-1. Millwall had not been promoted. A crucial edition had been missed. No, I would not make a reporter. I learned later that a loudspeaker announcement giving Birmingham's correct score had been made just eight minutes after the final whistle at the Den. The party had stopped abruptly. But I was well on my way.

Desmond Marsh never wrote another line. In fact, that was the day he died. Murdered at Millwall.

2
PEOPLE

In the four decades after the demise of Desmond, much of Frank's best and most evocative writing for the Guardian *would be his profiles of and interviews with the sporting – and sometimes non-sporting – figures he admired most. He was able to write about them affectionately, tellingly, often teasingly, in a way that defied the conventions of journalism. These were completely idiosyncratic, yet often definitive.*

A question of living a little, my dear
Alec Stock
2 May 1975

Focus sharply on Alec Stock – deaf, wheezily asthmatic and 60 next birthday – when he leads out Fulham at the FA Cup final tomorrow. The straight-backed carriage of the old soldier at the head of his troops will represent, surely, the most touching moment of a pleasant but pretty ordinary old season. It couldn't be happening to a nicer bloke. Certainly he rabbits on (and on) about the old-time courtesies of first-class soccer; and he shouts because he's deaf; and like all ill people he likes talking about his illnesses – though it's apparently true that he might have died if the Fulham physiotherapist, Ron Woolnough, hadn't injected him after the tensions of the drawn semi-final against Birmingham.

The grey backpage eminences sip their Complan o'nights and lipcurl at Stock's fossilised approach to the game. But it's a long time that he's been liking the romance as much as the result; in fact, as he says, he's only presuming a Fulham victory tomorrow because he's a romantic. Even 'Fulham for the Cup', as his parting shot this week, seemed bathed in some sort of necessary philosophical Eureka.

The old stagers in his team, Bobby Moore and Alan Mullery, comparative chickens, have been subject to all the crowing of late. But the old cockerel ahead of them tomorrow is entitled to the most prancing strut of all. He's been so long around, and now at last he's arrived. Win or lose, his war is over tomorrow – to which he replies 'Long live the war'.

Stock's Wembley walk will also be the clincher that clears the family name with the Football Association; would that skeleton please come out of the cupboard at once? For Alec Stock reckons he is the first manager to lead his team out for an FA Cup final who still owns (and loves) a relative who has been banned from playing anywhere, in any country administered by FIFA, for the whole of his mortal life.

His brother-in-law – sensible, doe-eyed, agricultural Donald – was sentenced thus, *sine die*, by the North Somerset disciplinary commission, sitting magisterially in Shepton Mallet years ago. No evidence was offered in defence of the charge that after being sent off in a match between Shoscombe and Bath Rovers, Donald determinedly picked his jacket off the hedge, walked a mile back to his farm, revved his tractor back up the hill and with a maniacal Fordson vroom-vroom, chased the referee from the field of play and over the stile: a dodgem after a spindly bantam. Two weeks later a letter to the *Bath Chronicle* from a local referee complained that the sentence was far too light 'for a would-be murderer'.

But if gentle Donald, his one aberration enough to muse on warmly for life, could serenely live without any more soccer, it is certain that his brother-in-law couldn't.

When people are told there are coal mines in Somerset, they take the news with the disbelief of those who hear of Welsh in Patagonia, music in Manchester, prostitution in Cheltenham, split infinitives in the *Times*. And, sure, it's hard to twig that under the lazy Mendip green of cidrous Midsomer Norton, Radstock, Peasedown or Stratton-on-the-Fosse there are men with black-speckled faces and lamps clamped to their foreheads, pickaxe-pixies deep down under Camelot; sweaty, swearing, hewing black-and-white men 2,000 feet below the docile, chewing black and white Friesians.

Alec Stock's dad was a Somerset miner. And like all other miners, his time off centred around sport: cricket in those lovely shirts-off western weekend summers, soccer in the crispy blanketed, banked-fire winters. On Saturdays they'd bag the 4am shift so they could be up by noon for the Match – 'out of the pit cage they'd come, cagebirds liberated by a hooter,' remembers Stock. The whole area was made up of either big miners, smallholders, or the unemployed.

'We were professionals in as much as half the village would play the other half for a price – a Woodbine a man.'

The times were tether's end for parents: though up above fields were green as ever, the seams weren't showing any more. Many children had to be evacuated. Alec Stock's cousin was sent to Dartford; the whole family followed; old miner became Kentish sand shifter at a stroke – and young Stock found himself first at a rugby school, then apprenticed to a London bank.

But the old Western Woodbine days had taken root. He stuck to his soccer and after setting off as a fizzy inside forward with the Wilmington Total Abstainers, he started turning up to amateur practice games at Tottenham Hotspur. There Jimmy Seed watched him on the quiet one evening and talked him into signing for Charlton Athletic – as long as his father could also have a job cementing the terracing at The Valley. Two years later, in 1938, he was bought by Queen's Park Rangers ('I've still got the receipt, I was worth £500 body and soul; it didn't do much for the old ego').

The rude interruption that followed proved some sort of blessing in as much as it offered yet another bright cloth-cap youngster an explosive chance for development and responsibility, a chance that the haywire education system denied. Starting as a private, Stock was to become an expert in infantry tactics by 1942; he was a captain of tanks, and ended up a major. By the time his eardrums had become irreparably damaged and his body peppered with shrapnel at Caen he had determined to return to Somerset as, perhaps, a smallholder, or better still, a country auctioneer and estate agent. It was enough anyway to be going back to roots.

Then Yeovil Town, southern league dozers snuggling down in the balmy Blackmore Vale, advertised: £10 a week, full-time coach, trainer, player, captain, secretary, manager, preferably a goalscoring forward with knowledge of first aid. Major Stock couldn't resist. It was a fearful slog. The only other fellow on the staff was the groundsman at 30 bob a week. He says he was mentally numb by the time Saturdays came round: he was invariably sick in the dressing room during his half-time pep talks.

Then, in the 1948 season, Yeovil painstakingly, amazingly, won through to the third round proper of the FA Cup. They were drawn against Bury, who were the second division leaders. On a dull Thursday 10 days before the game, Jack Milligan, of the *Daily Graphic*, drifted back from Peel's in Fleet Street after lunch to do the first edition, throwaway Soccer Bits. Anything for an intro, and luckily Enquiries didn't take long to get him Yeovil Town's number. For something to say, Stock told him that Bury should really be bothered about Yeovil's incredible sloping pitch.

Though Milligan didn't know it, Yeovil's pitch was the flattest by far in the area; it was a good enough angle for a quiet sports desk day. Stock's quotes ran in all editions: 'We'll keep banging the ball up the slope to our winger on the side. He'll just blow his crosses over. It's hard work for our men on the bottom side but I can assure them that it'll be a lot harder for Bury if they don't grasp the idea.'

It was the perfect con. Bury by no means grasped it. Yeovil won easily into the fourth round and a home draw against the stars and stripes from Sunderland – Watson, Shackleton, Elliott, Ramsden, Daniel and all, the most expansive and expensive line-up of all time. Stock's near-invention of his slope and all the trumpeting follow-ups to Milligan's story made Sunderland hesitate: daily, it seemed, Stock was photographed on his centre-circle with a spirit level; he had the local brewery ring the ground with tiered terracing in the form of beer crates, not only to let 17,500 of Yeovil's 23,000 population see the game but to help cramp the Sunderland forwards. He even persuaded his Casterbridge-type grain merchant directors to put up his team of part-timers in a hotel for the week before the match.

And sure enough on 29 January, 1949, Sunderland went to bits. Stock himself scored a beauty, a 20-yard left-foot volley on the half-hour, Sunderland equalised on instinct, as it were, then settled back into a right old flap. Yeovil went ahead again and set about kicking everything out of sight – 'over the grandstand and into the allotments,' recalls Stock. When Stock hoofed one clearance into Devon with two minutes left, the immortal Shack complained to him, 'Come on, old matey, don't spoil a good game.' But they did, and they were through to Manchester United, played at Maine Road. 81,000 people, no slope and an 8-1 drubbing in the fifth round. And when Matt Busby came to the visitors' dressing room afterwards to say sorry about the volume of goals, Stock told him, 'Don't worry, my dear, at least we've lived a little.'

Stock and Yeovil (the club made £5,000 from the run, during which time the total players' wage-bill was £69 and 10 shillings) became a coupled byword for the times: Bevin and Bevan, Matthews and Mortensen, Jock and Snowy, Hutton and Washbrook, Granger and Lockwood, Stock and Yeovil. Anyway Pathé Pictorial just wouldn't stop filming them.

A few months later another journalist rang Yeovil. Bernard Joy, of the London *Evening Standard*, had been asked to sound out Stock about a move to Leyton Orient, who were in the old Third Division South. He moved, still pretty much in charge of everything, and within three years Orient were promoted. Stock was booked for the big time: Arsenal took him as assistant and heir to the ailing Tom Whitaker; he was poised for one of the most celebrated jobs in British club management.

But he never felt at ease, never felt fully occupied in so swish an outfit. Nevertheless, he joined when they were third from bottom of the first division, and they were sixth from top four months later. Then, one Saturday evening by a gorgeous fluke, Arsenal and Orient both travelled back on the same train. Orient's chairman, Harry Zussman, sensed Stock's unease in the big-time and offered him his old job back. He accepted with relief.

There was to be just one more flirtation with the bright lights. In 1957 AS Roma, the Italian club, fluttered their eyelids at him and he went. In his 16 weeks as team manager they lost only one of 11 games. But he spoke no Italian – his half-time pep-talks were translated by a 16-year-old who'd learnt English on summer holidays in North Wales. He could not cope with the dressing room intrigues. One of his best memories of Rome was the Sunday mornings when the English first editions arrived at Termini station: they had reports of all the West Country village matches – Radstock vs Peasedown Miners Welfare, Welton vs Paulton and all. When the Rome rumours reached England, the phone at once rang in the Stocks' lovely flat near the Vatican. Come back to Orient, said Harry Zussman. And back he went to the London editions.

Stock has carefully stayed in warm little ponds ever since. He likes being a father-fish. From Orient he moved to Queen's Park Rangers and stayed 10 years, an early two spent badgering Vic Buckingham, down the road at Fulham, to sell his eccentric teenage soloist Rodney Marsh. Buckingham finally did, for a desultory £15,000: Stock built a team around the nipper and Rodney repaid Stock by making him the only living manager to have taken a team from the third to the first division in successive seasons. He won him the league cup too, on that golden day in 1967 after giving West Brom a two-goal start. The Shepherd's Bush bonfire night went memorably into the early morning, ever accompanied by that haunting, chorused anthem to the lad: 'Rod-nee, Rod-nee' a descending major third of homage.

The deaf Stock, alas, never heard it: he was ill with asthma too; once Rangers got to the first division his doctor advised him to take six weeks off. The day he returned he was fired. He was incurable, said the board. He took up his bed and went back to the third division, to little Luton, to build another team. And what a side – he again conned Fulham into selling him a limited left-back for just £18,000, and turned him in a weekend into Malcolm Macdonald, England's five-goal centre forward. He also bought Givens, Nicholl and Anderson.

Luton won the third division straight off – and looked unquestionable favourites to go straight up to the first again. But the club was horribly tied up with Tony Hunt and his V and G insurance combine and, when the company crashed with an almighty clang, Stock had to sell all his jewels to keep the club solvent ... Macdonald went to Newcastle, Rioch and Nicholl to Villa, Givens to QPR.

Three years ago he came to Fulham and started building yet another new team. Mullery he bought for £60,000, Moore for £25,000, two old has-beens who are very much still-ares. And now they've got Stock to the FA Cup at Wembley, 26 years after he first set out in that third qualifying round with Yeovil. Moore was quoted this week: 'When we line up at the mouth of the tunnel on Saturday, Alec'll be at the front waiting. He'll give us the nod to go, then he'll be off striding out ahead in his collar and tie. We'll have to run to keep up with him. He loves it, does old Alec.'

If you notice Stock talking to Ron Greenwood of West Ham on the way, I bet he'll be trying to convince him that there's a sudden and terrible slope on the Wembley pitch. And also that, win or lose, he'll say to him afterwards, just like that day in February 1949, 'Never mind, my dear, at least we lived a little.'

West Ham beat Fulham 2-0 in the final. Alec Stock died, aged 84, in 2001. And until he himself died, Frank Keating called everyone 'm'dear'. I like to think it was listening to Stock that persuaded him it was not unmanly.

The greatest showmen on earth
Ali and Pele
1 October 1977

As the grey fingers of dawn groped their way up over the river yesterday morning, an amiable tramp-like chap accosts me in Piccadilly. He doesn't of course say 'Who won?' but 'How did *he* get on?' He's relieved when you tell him, and he smiles and for just one moment you can see he's up on his luck. 'What a geezer!' he mutters, shakes his head in wonder and shuffles on into the morning.

What a geezer indeed! A full drained house of us had just come bleary from the Odeon, Leicester Square, where we had watched, surely, two of the most heroic final rounds in the long history of the organised world heavyweight boxing championship. First Mohammad Ali looked dead ... then honest Earnie Shavers ... then Ali again ... then Shavers even more so ... For fully five minutes it was gruesomely, barbarically riveting as they traded swipe for grievous swipe like slow-motion ping-pong players with intent to kill. In the end, it was the older man, the nonpareil, who was able to dig deepest into his great heart and almost pull out a truly dramatic knockout at the very bell. Ali can box clever; but, by Allah! he can fist fight as well.

For long minutes at the finish he lay on the ropes, retching for breath. Bundini Brown, faithful Oddjob, was crying; for fear had turned to relief. Then Ali called for a comb and did his hair in front of Madison Square Garden and 60 million live viewers around planet Earth. And then he was saying 'I'm tired, I'm tired. That's it: the End.' And 60 million were glad.

After wash and brush up and bruises balmed, apparently he told the press, 'Well yes, 10 million dollars might well force me to turn out again, just one more time next year against Ken Norton.' One can only hope he doesn't. He'll be 36 by then – and the finest of all time nearly lost to Earnie Shavers, plodding labourer.

This finale had been set up. Hadn't the Madison Avenue men trumpeted this fight as Ali's last? They had – if only to tie in with a razzle-dazzling double-bill for their city – for another one-only, Pele, plays his final soccer match there tonight.

Mind, you Ali and Pele have been into the Definitely Last Public Appearance thing for some time now. That's showbiz. And the two of them have long time been Outrageous Showbiz. Almost as an afterthought nowadays is the certain realisation that the both of them are the finest athlete-operators ever. Even their adopted names represent the adman's spare syllables of the saleable international product in any language – like Esso, Mars or Coke. They are both black, both ballet-beautiful in grace of movement. Both came from a deprived background fostered in a system dominated economically by whites ...

I saw them both perform countless times – though only as an ogling child of the first television age. But, listen to this, I saw them in the flesh and spoke to them, on one occasion each. That will be enough to dine on in my dotage.

Can it be over 14 years ago that Ali first came to England, when I jostled for a glimpse of him in mufti outside the Piccadilly Hotel but (madness!) preferred to touch a forgotten girlfriend than see the hats at Wembley kite into the air when our bloodied Henry bowled him briefly on to his back? Can it be 13 years since I saw him for the first time live on television take on and take out the apparently unbeatable Liston?

Liston! Deafened by the defiant speech 'I am the Greatest', we did not think then for a moment that it might be true. But it was.

And it is 11 years gone since I huddled into that backroom snug with a whole French village, from tiny tots to grandmas, and we watched him flog and taunt poor Ernie Terrell for fully 15 rounds just because Terrell still called him Cassius Clay? After every cruel lash, Ali would sneer 'What's my name?' so at the sad end I fancied that the humiliated Terrell was asking his seconds, 'Never mind his name, what's mine?'

Then there was Vietnam and Black Power and the *Parkinson* show and his angelic way with kids and old men ... and the first Frazier fight at the Odeon, Kensington – Oh! His courage then! – and the Dominion, Tottenham Court Road, when the lights went up at dawn and even scarred punchies with cauliflower ears could scarce forbear to wipe away a tear ...

There were a few hankies about yesterday morning too in Leicester Square. As the Shavers match continued, we could see all of his life flashing in front of our man: first he had fooled, he had danced a bit for old time's sake, lain on the ropes too, then fooled some more, then danced or lain again – ever spurting out the licking jabs and weighty rights, mind you, to get well ahead on points. But still, at the last, he was fighting for his life, for his reputation. For us. And by golly, how he had to battle in the end.

I met Ali in the flesh only in Munich last year. He had passed his prime by then. But I shook hands with Pele at his very peak. I was at Guadalajara when Brazil were preparing for the World Cup of 1970. They were training at a private country club, behind Stalag wire and guarded by swarthy uniformed goons. On the third day of asking they let me in to watch.

What I saw remains one of my enduring memories. Pele and his Brazilians spent the better part of their afternoon dancing. Dancing! Making their own voice music too, as they did their non-stop hand-held routines into the evening, a sort of Ipi Tombi chain-gang cha-cha-cha, if you like. I was mesmerised.

I thought top soccer training was lapping the track at Highbury for an hour or so, practising running over the ball at free-kicks and then going to pot pink at the Locarno.

After an hour or so of *A Chorus Line*, Pele alone dropped out. He lay dozing on the grass. His own Oddjob, Americo, threw across an ice cube for him to suck. It landed fractionally out of Pele's stretch. He ignored it, so Americo, like a courtier, had to walk all of 50 yards to pick it up and deliver it to Pele's palm. Easy, man, easy, lies the head that wears the crown.

I saw him again in the final against Italy: that exultant opening header; that Cresta-skid that nearly tucked home Rivellino's ferocious cross; and best and last of all, his pass at the end, when he looked left, and all of Italy followed his gaze and did not notice his perfect pass to Carlos Alberto seaming unmarked all down the right ...

I felt it, too, about Ali last night: that at least I saw the Kings alive. Long Live the Kings.

Muhammad Ali had four more fights after beating Shavers: he lost three of them. The blows he took from Larry Holmes in 1980 are thought to have caused his brain damage.

For services to England ...
Alec Bedser
12 August 1981

By chance, we had lunch in an olde Englishe place not far from Lincoln's Inn Fields where he started work as a solicitor's office boy at the age of 14 in 1932. The ageing, aproned English waiters recognised him, which was nice. He didn't even look at the menu but simply ordered the roast beef and greens.

For a split second I even fancied he hummed a snatch of Gilbert and Sullivan ... 'When I was a boy I served a term as office boy to an attorney's firm ...' The Englishness of it all was appropriate. Alec Bedser, at 63, may be a successful something-in-the-city now, but he is still the great big-eared English yeoman of a long and ancient and trustworthy line. He bowled his boots off for England. He hung them up 21 years ago. In 1962 he became a Test selector and for the last nine years he has been Chairman. Peter May is to succeed him.

I had thought that the England team at Old Trafford tomorrow was effectively the last one to be picked by Bedser, and that May would be co-opted to help choose the side for the last Test and the tour of India. Not a bit of it. Alec's team list will be the touring team – 'And anyway,' he says, 'I dare say they'll ask me to help 'em out again soon enough.' So it meant I couldn't get any secrets out of him, though I did sniff the teeniest, accidental hint that Keith Fletcher will be the touring captain. We will see.

I met a young first-class cricketer the other day who honestly did not know even that his chairman of selectors had himself played for England. He just presumed Bedser was one of 'them' up there at Lord's. 'I dunno,' moans Alec. 'These youngsters today ...' and he shakes his head and his eyes colour a sad grey-blue and he is at a loss for words till another, 'I dunno, they don't know how lucky they are.' He loves a good moan does Alec.

You sometimes think he blames it all on school meals. Well, he and his identical twin Eric had to walk four miles a day to and from the Monument Hill Central School, Woking, didn't they, with sandwiches in the satchel and just a cup of water in the lunch hour. This lot don't know how lucky they are ...

At 14 he and Eric would get the train to London at 7.30 in the morning and get home at eight that night – at 10 on the three evenings a week they studied shorthand and book-keeping at night school. Their father was a bricklayer. He died at 89 three years ago. The two beloved bachelor boys still live with Mum, 88 last birthday, in the little house at Woking that the family built, brick by brick, in 1932, the boys labouring and Dad laying.

Eric was born first by a few minutes. If they are not quite identical now, Eric being slightly plumper, there's scarcely a wrinkle in it. John Woodcock, the editor of *Wisden*, once played golf with them at Worplesdon. Same outfits, same shot off the first tee with identical No 2 woods and identical short swing; the two balls ended up on the fairway kissing each other – 'Eggs in the same nest'.

They both joined the Surgery ground staff in 1938. They served together throughout the war, long, dusty, dangerous days in Africa, and wetter ones in Italy. On the resumption of fun Alec started taking wickets by the hatful. At once he played in the 1946 Test trial and though he had damaged a thigh he secretly strapped it up in the lavatory. 'Where d'you field?' said BH Valentine. 'Slip,' lied Alec. Then he winced, took a deep breath, got out Hammond and Hutton and was chosen for the first Test against India.

The great big boy walked to Woking station with his great big cricket bag. He took the tube from Waterloo to Baker Street, then a bus to Lord's. Wally Hammond gruffed 'Good luck'. He took 11 wickets in the match ... then another 11 in the next one. In all, he was to take a record 236 wickets for England. On Hammond's tour of Australia he toiled heroically for more than 500 overs. It lasted from 31 August, 1946, to 17 April, 1947; he was paid £295, plus 25 bob a week spending money. At Adelaide in 104 degrees he had to go off to be sick, then bowled Bradman with a ball that the Don still says was the best that ever got him. 'Yeah, and I bowled a lot more like it since,' mutters Alec, tucking into his greens.

He loves Australia. It's just that he likes England better. He still writes very regularly to Bradman, Arthur Morris, Ron Archer and Keith Miller. 'Keith has never replied, but always rings me first thing whenever he arrives in England.'

Brown's next tour of Australia: 'We could have won easy, but old Freddie stupidly wanted to be surrounded by youngsters.'

29

The end came in terms of the big time, for the second Test of his third tour, led by Len Hutton. Alec had shingles and should never have played in the first match. England were slaughtered. Alec, sickly, took one for 131 ('seven catches dropped, mind you'). So they let the Typhoon loose. 'No sour grapes, Tyson got plenty, sure, but I would have got a hundred wickets on those pitches. Arthur Morris put us in 'cos he didn't want to face me that first morning.'

But when the captain pinned up the team in the dressing room Bedser was not on it. Hutton had not even said a word. Alec felt humiliated. 'Funny bloke, Len. Do you know, when I was ill on that tour, I was in bed for a fortnight. He was in the next room, but never once did he pop in to visit.'

He is a more kindly selector. Either he or the captain is always in touch with the team on the phone. Alec's first chairman of selectors was the late RWV Robins – Snobby Robby. 'We would meet at his flat on a Sunday morning. He never really watched any cricket. Just went on what he read in the papers or heard from his cronies. He would turn up to the first day of a Test, but on the second day, after lunch, he'd sometimes clear off and go to the pictures.'

Boycott has loomed large over Alec's own chairmanship. The self-imposed exile started around the time Geoffrey kept getting out to the Indian, Solkar: 'a real toffee apple bowler'. Then he sulked something rotten when Mike Denness was made captain. At the beginning of every season Bedser would ring Boycott. The rum Yorkshireman was convinced 'public school blokes at Lord's had it in for him'. Alec would patiently tell him that the selectors, Bedser, Barrington, Hutton, and Elliott had all been to elementary school. When Geoffrey telephoned that he might be ready to return in 1977, he was playing at Northampton. Alec said he'd come and see him. 'No,' said Geoffrey, 'not here at the ground, man!' 'All right,' said Alec, 'I'll see you after the game in the corner of the foyer at the Grand Hotel, Northampton.'

'No,' insisted Geoffrey, 'I'll be in the car park at the Watford Gap service station. No, not in the snack bar, in the car park. We mustn't be seen together.' They sat there, side by side, for two hours. 'At least he was on time,' mutters Alec. The truce was worked out and the glorious comeback determined.

To have to coerce a man into playing for England must have been extremely distasteful to Alec. It was probably something, he thought, to do with free school meals. 'I dunno,' and he shakes his head and his eyes cloud over. 'I dunno ... These young blokes today ...'

Good meets wicket
Mother Teresa
5 January 1982

CALCUTTA: It was rest-day morning and the remainder of Keith Fletcher's England team was still dreaming dreams of run rates and declarations, when a couple of us crept out of the Grand Hotel at dawn. We went to the slums to see Mother Teresa at work. In her line of business you've got to get up early.

The Convent of the Sisters of Charity is down an alleyway off Calcutta's north circular road. Outside are a group of urchins with empty tummies and, when you put an arm around them for a cuddle, wide, white smiles. You knock on the door of No. 54A. Inside, seemingly some hundred nuns are bustling, washing, working, to prepare their day.

In the small room open to this courtyard there is a smiling portrait of the good Pope from Poland as he bends to listen to a little old lady in white. There is also a simple crucifix and one or two amateurish pious posters framed with loving care and passe-partout. You don't hear her coming, but suddenly she's there.

'Cricket?' she says, 'is it played this way?' And she flaps a wrist in overarm mime. 'Or is it this way?' and her arms essay a baseball swipe. You're not in awe any more, you are laughing with her and want to call her 'luv'. Without the slightest corniness, Mother Teresa of Calcutta and the world tells Bob Taylor of Derbyshire and England, that she and he are both equally serving Christ. 'You must play this game of yours simply to the best of your ability, for if you are doing your best you are pleasing mankind and thus you too are doing God's work. And never forget to smile to show you are happy doing your work for God.'

Tomorrow, she said, was going to be the happiest of days for her. 'It will be exactly 52 years that I arrived in India.' Since then business has boomed. Today, for instance, she would be serving meals for 7,000 people. Her nuns are not allowed to beg. 'We have never once asked for gifts or money, but just relied on them to be given to us with love, for then they come from God.'

Only once did such faith flutter for a moment, only once in 52 years. 'One morning, just like this, my sister came to me and said "Mother, we have no food today, no food at all." I knew we could only wait. And then a lorry arrived. And then another. They were both from heaven. They were both full of bread. Just for that day, for some reason, the government had suddenly shut down all the schools. They brought us their bread. There was so much bread, oh dear, all Calcutta ate bread for two days.'

Asked by the world record-breaking wicket-keeper: 'Mother, why do you smile so?' the Nobel Peace Prize winner replied: 'Because a smiling face is an integral part of Christian love. You should know that, you are a sporting man whose job is to give people pleasure. Remember how St Francis and his friars laughed so? In every clown there is a saint and in every saint there is a clown.'

And up the road, in her hospice for the dying, we saw she had taught old mortal men in ultimate agony to smile serenely. And in her orphanage too there seemed just as many smiles as empty stomachs. So we went back, refreshed, to the Grand Hotel for a slap-up Western-style breakfast.

Last of the vintage wine
The cricketers of yore
24 September 1982

There can have been no more satisfactory or romantic finale to any cricket season than the clamorous curtain call staged by the Oval last weekend.

On Saturday the last shafts of a summer sun beamed down as a congregation of 13,000 West Indians and Ian Botham celebrated a Caribbean carnival: on Sunday in the misty, still opaque damp of an English autumn, middle-aged men became for a brief hour or two once more the champions of childhood. Time for olde tyme! Those, indeed, were the days.

As Sir Garfield Sobers walked back after a superlative innings – admittedly against avuncular bowling – there was, somehow, an echo of lamentation and desolation rising from the fond and heartfelt tribute.

Everyone sensed that we would never see him bat again; never see that lissom tread, that jungle-cat's mix of jaunty, relaxed serenity and purposeful, businesslike intent; never see again the cavalier's smile fringed by the upturned collar, the pure arc of his golfer's follow-through after the cover-drive, or on-drive, or that genuflecting, exhilarating front-foot square-cut played late and cleanly murderous.

And in the evening drizzle, Ray Lindwall bowled. I had never seen him before. The nearest I got was the firm promise of a schoolmaster-monk to be taken to Worcestershire for the Australian's opening match of 1948. Then, on the eve of the trip, something came up and the black-cowled swine reneged.

I wondered on Sunday whether, even at the age of 61, Lindwall could muster just a glimmer, a sense of the outline and structure of what old men still say was the most perfect bowling action of all. He did too, though the arm was low and the run was short and sciatic. But I'd seen Lindwall bowl at last.

33

At the evening celebrations, four Aussies seemed very pleased to be back. They sat contentedly with their wives and well-wishers. There was Bobby Simpson, patient bat and supreme snaffle of the slips; Neil Harvey, boy wonder who confirmed his promise a hundredfold, and now in dark glasses, still smiling, and looking forward to a touring holiday in Devon and Cornwall. Also Lindwall, strong blue eyes and strong squared shoulders and off next day for a Continental holiday; and Sobers, now with a whispy grey mandarin goatee under his gap-toothed smile. He now has Australian citizenship, but not an Australian accent.

Lindwall and Sobers just overlapped. At the end of January, 1955, Lindwall and Miller having laid waste the West Indian batting in the previous three, came the fourth Test at Barbados. A slim 19-year-old, who had been picked as a left-arm spinner, was sent in as a stopgap to open the batting with JK Holt. Lindwall and Miller paced out their runs. Said a West Indian supporter on the jam-packed corrugated roof: 'Ooh'dear, dey feedin' de poor boy to de two tiger-cats to slacken off dey appetite!'

Lindwall admits he and his black-maned mate didn't know what, literally, hit them. Sobers hit six sumptuous boundaries in his first 25. In half an hour the boy had scored a breathtaking 43 and seen off the dreaded duo before Johnson had him caught. 'We were punch-drunk,' admits Lindwall, still shaking his head at the memory. Across the table, Sobers grins: still the sheepish grin of a found-out schoolboy.

Seven years before, at the Oval, Lindwall had, quite simply, demolished England. They were swept away: 52 all out; Hutton 30; Lindwall six for 20. It was the catching that was responsible, he says, recalling blinders by Tallon and Hassett and Morris. With gentle modesty, he explains that earlier in the week it had been rainy and the pitch was underprepared and damp ... 'England's batsmen were distrustful of the pitch and expected the ball to fly from a length. Actually it went through at a uniform height. At least four of them were bowled by yorkers.' Hutton had played wonderfully well – 'first in, last out, caught by Don Tallon off a genuine leg-glance.'

Hutton was the great, and admired, foe. Once Lindwall gave Hutton a lift from the Sydney Cricket Ground to the England team's hotel ... 'We didn't speak a word to each other, apart from saying "good night!". By actions in the middle we had told each other a good deal about each other's play. What was there to say after all that?'

At the Oval in 1948, Lindwall clean-bowled England's three tailenders, Evans, Bedser and Young. He does not condone present habits of bumping non-batsmen. 'If a fast bowler cannot bowl out numbers nine, ten and eleven without resorting to intimidation then he ought not to be wearing Australia's colours.'

Sobers hates the use of batsmen's helmets. He, like Viv Richards today, would never have worn one. 'The point of cricket is to protect yourself with the bat, man.' He says that if they had been worn in his day, 'there would have been no point in bowling at the likes of Kenny Barrington or Slasher Mackay: we'd have taken months to get them out, man; years, probably.'

Sir Garfield, you'd fancy, had a massive regard for Barrington's dogged, stoic fidelity to his cause. Of the great quartet of post-war English batsmen, May and Cowdrey, Dexter and Graveney, you feel he admired, and warmed to, the latter brace far more.

Of the bowlers, Fred Trueman – 'What hostility! What a trier!' – was his sort of fellow, and also India's mesmerising leg-spinner of the 50s, Subhash Gupte, who seemed to be as inventive and experimental and as accurate as the Pakistani who both enchanted and bamboozled the English this summer, Abdul 'the Bulbul' Qadir.

Sobers leaves. Lindwall nods goodbye. There is a sudden, awed hush in the room as Sir Garfield eases his way out, down the stairs, and across the Oval concourse for, perhaps, the very last time. The lights go out. It is, in fact, the end of many, many summers.

A man who set his cap at the world
Duncan Goodhew
3 December 1983

Today's national club gala at Leeds represents the British swimmers' opening plunge in the six months run-up to the Olympic Games. The endless shuttle length-upon-length of bleary, dreary dip at dawn, is nearly over for the children. Their parents can now summon just one last fierce, despairing shove, then it is up to the selectors.

Some of the toddling dolphins will sink without trace and with a sigh. It will be a crowded plughole. Those who remain afloat guarantee us months and months of fast-moving froth all the way to LA. Red-eyed, teeth chattering little mites who might. In TV terms, we are in for weeks and weeks of Weeks.

At the Leeds poolside today, watch out for one ex-mite who did. You cannot miss Duncan Goodhew. He's the one in the city suit and without a hair on his head. He won the Olympic Gold Medal in Moscow in 1980. Today he will be wearing a cap, not *the* cap.

The engaging enthusiast Goodhew resents my dismissive tease of 'moving froth'. He says: 'Competitive swimming is unique. It is the most psychological physical sport known to mankind. You dive into an alien environment; you can't hear anything, you can't see anything, you are all alone. In athletics Coe can see and hear Ovett on his shoulder; he can react. Swimmers have no such audio-visual awareness for the challenge. It is eerie. It is tremendous sport.'

Goodhew, now 26, is a remarkable young man. Since larking about at five with his flippers in the family pool in Sussex, there has been more than water pressing down on his shoulders. He was dyslexic and, as a presumed dimwit, the butt of every school joke – far more so when, after Tarzan-tumbling from a tree at ten, all his hair fell out inside a year.

Only his eyelashes have grown back. 'Wonderful incredible things are eyelashes. I can't tell you how vital they are: they field every bit of fluff, dust and sweat. I used to see flies coming straight at me, straight at my eyeballs and couldn't do a thing to stop them. Terrible.'

The wretched, sorry-for-himself, over-aggressive oddball at whom they jeered 'Kojak' supposes he must have found some sort of lonely solace in swimming. It helped him get to Millfield. 'I suppose I had a raw talent – like two arms and two legs.' Millfield was co-ed. 'I'd arrived there as a broken person. They helped put the pieces back together.'

But was a girl ever going to look at – or at any rate not stare at – a gawk with no hair, and who couldn't even read, and kept wanting to write from right to left? One day, just 10 years ago, he walked into the common room wearing his blonde wig with the middle parting. 'A fellow pupil was in there, one of the most marvellous people I have ever met. He'd had polio, he had a club foot and a hook for a hand, and he just looked up at me and smiled, "What's your problem, Dunc?" That question was a crucial turning point.'

He was 16 then. It was the year his father died of a stroke. Those second-generation eyelashes momentarily moisten. 'It's not that I miss him, for his presence is always with me. Yes, he'd occasionally turn up for my early competitive swims. I think he was a bit embarrassed at my devotion for him. He didn't talk much but once, in the very trough of my despair and torments, he said to me "My boy, just remember your name is Goodhew and be proud of it." That was another momentous occasion.'

Six years later he was swimming in the European Championships. 'The night before the race, I dreamed Dad was there in the crowd watching me win. And he was smiling. When I woke up there on the chair by my bed was Dad's old cloth cap. It was the only thing I ever had of his. I put it on. My Dad was a God to me.' He wore the cap at the Moscow Olympics two years later. I was in the crowd. The place was seething for the breaststroke final. The Russian or East German would surely win. The swimmers paraded round the pool like brooding boxers in their dressing gowns. Duncan wore his Dad's old cloth cap. The tension eased as the throng laughed. The gladiators disrobed. Duncan reverently placed the cap behind his block.

'In the heats I had brainwashed myself to pile on the pressure; to go for a psychological advantage; to make the Russians watch me and worry. For the final I decided on a new tactic. I decided to relax because this time I was going for the world record too, wasn't I?'

Silence, a bang, six splashes sound as one. Shrill screams pierce the hall. 'Twenty-five metres out I realised my plan wasn't working. I forced my will to concentrate as it had in the heats. I had an unbelievable turn. Even the Russians said it was unbelievable. But that was a big mistake.

'I thought the turn had won it for me. Out of it, the water suddenly ripped; you must never tear the water: I did: it left bubbles behind my fingers and made me spin terribly, like an outboard motor just out of the water; it could have been fatal. For 20 metres I couldn't get it under control. I screamed at myself "Duncan, if you're not going to get it under control, you're not going to win!"' But he did. He climbed out of the pool and, gilded at the breast, refused to doff his Dad's old cloth cap even for a victorious happy and glorious national anthem. Then, mysteriously, he lost the hat. It is still somewhere in Moscow. But it had done its stuff.

Three years on he is at Leeds not only as a bald, beaming beacon, a totem for the tyros in the tank, but as British swimming's most remarkable young professional entrepreneur. He is putting his university degree in business studies to good use with charm, appeal and originality. He still stammers and stumbles if he has to read a speech in public: 'but without notes I can rabbit on for hours.'

Competitive swimming, he says, receives a lot of stick because it's such a 'young' sport. Children are so good at it if, he concedes, some parents and coaches drive them too hard. 'Youngsters take it up, work tremendously hard, but then finish by the time they are 20.'

'There are three basic ways of succeeding – an unquestionable belief in your own ability, an unquestionable belief in your coach's ability, and an understanding of the whole philosophy of the drive and motivation of competition. In swimming, most wholly trust in the second method, a few in the first – but most of them are too young to go for the third.'

'Up to a point it is the same in other sports. Like that amazing man David Wilkie. Ask him why he's great and he'll just say "I suppose I was blessed with some talent." Seb Coe will say the same. I don't know what someone like Steve Ovett would answer, but it would certainly be something different. There has to be a philosophy behind what he does and has achieved. It might be so personal he won't let it go to anyone.'

There is no doubt about it, he says: everyone, 'even the dumbest of dyslexic dropouts', has to be good at something. 'I must be statistically right. Well, just think of all the possible things there are in the world that someone could be good at. A billion billion things. The luck is discovering what you're good at. Then the most crucial thing is recognising that you've found it. Me? I was just lucky.' For my part, I'll be looking differently at moving froth in future.

As he approached his 57th birthday in 2014, Goodhew – co-author with Victoria Hislop of Fix Your Life Now! *– was a motivational speaker and president of the Swimathon Foundation.*

The voice at 70
John Arlott
25 February 1984

His wife, Pat, brings him a cup of tea at 7am and on comes Radio 4's *Today* programme. By 8.15, in his bottle-green corduroy bags and anorak over the great blanket of a Swedish sweater, he is having his first solemn, plodding constitutional 'over the top' on the hillocks. Such is the minuscule one-mile-by-three rocky blob of Alderney that at most places you can see the choppy Channel fuming and frothing on the rocks at every point of the compass.

Later in the morning he will turn in the other direction from his wide, bright white house and this time the parade takes him up and down the cobbled little doll's-house main street. 'Mornin' George!' 'Mornin' Margot!' 'Mornin' David!' They all reply with a hoot and a wave and a smile. First call is to the post office for the wad of letters and pile of parcels. 'Ahh,' comes the satisfied, familiar old growl, 'I do like my post.' It remains one of the most enduring, endearing, evocative voices known to Britain and beyond.

The telephone never stops. Indeed the volume of Alderney Telecom business that obviously increased the moment John Arlott retired to the Channel Islands gives absolute lie to the very idea of 'retirement'. It was only day-in, day-out cricket reporting for this newspaper and the BBC that ended with such wrenching finality in the early autumn of 1980. 'I can't sunbathe or sit in the garden or go on cruises. Not that I'm trying to build a career, I've come as far as I can. But I still love writing. Now I'm just coasting, not downhill, but just coasting along on a lovely level.'

There are strong hints that he is to embark, at last, on an autobiography. He has already decided on the first sentence: 'It was a fat baby of seven pounds that Nelly Arlott gave birth to at the Old Cemetery Lodge, Basingstoke, at 4am on the morning of 25 February 1914 ...' Exactly 70 years on and the birthday is celebrated today with a family party for his wife, his two surviving sons and their women – and his favourite friend and cricketer, Leo Harrison, the former Hampshire wicket-keeper. And tomorrow at noon it seems that half the island will be popping in to raise the hairs from the dog with a further bracer or two. 'Mornin' George!' 'Mornin' Margot!'

This week, the old spaniel soft-boiled eyes still shining bright, the birthday boy showed me round his green-grey granitey island. We sat in a picture window watching spectacular waves snap and fret at the sea wall. It was like the royal fireworks. 'Ooh, look at that one!' 'Golly, there's a beauty for you. Wow!' It was calmer up the cobbled street. I had, of course, to be introduced to the bearded young man who kept the DIY shop and who last season scored 216 off 51 balls on the island's little cricket pitch. 'Even Frindall says Jessop never matched that!'

After a pre-lunch bracer in the Albert – fino sherry in tomato juice – back home for cold meats and the accompanying myriad of honest bottles – reds, whites, rosés all the way from France and Germany and California, from Spain, Lebanon, New Zealand and even England. We tasted in slugs large and small and long. On the whole I think wine correspondent might be a better job than cricket correspondent. The newspapers have arrived from the mainland. He goes straight to the *Times* obituaries. Then to the *Guardian* sports pages. 'Good God! Lillee's put Miandad in hospital. In a benefit match, too. The bastard!'

Then an afternoon's work. He taps at his typewriter, sometimes dictates to Pat. 'I'd go mad if I didn't work.' He first discovered Alderney some 30 years ago. 'It is the most beautiful place I know. So quiet. You can only realistically arrive by air. We enjoyed many family holidays here when my late son and wife were alive.' His eldest son was killed in a motor accident. The sorrow of his loss still pains him intensely.

The isle is full of silence and the house full of treasures. In the hall is a grand and ancient old wireless set – it belonged to Haley when he was BBC's Director-General. There are watercolours of Winchester and needlework of Worcester. In the kitchen is Toynbee's lively and glorious oil of *The Nets*, drawings of Hardy and Dylan Thomas and a striking portrait of Elizabeth David. In the Long Room there are the first editions – Hardy, Hazlitt, Betjeman and all – and on the walls Lowry and Rowlandson, Lancaster and Beerbohm.

John Arlott's beloved father, Jack, ended up keeping the graveyard neat at Basingstoke. He wanted the boy simply to get a job with a pension. He began in local government and then in the police force. When the young man started making his name with the BBC, father and son embraced, 'and cried together at the wonder of it all'. His third cricket book, on the Australians of 1948, was dedicated 'To my father who knows nothing about cricket and cares less but who wos werry good to me'. The last sentence in that book reads: 'Is there, I wonder, anywhere in the world such a human, generous, unenvious, shop-talking, enthusiastic, mellow, craft-versed sporting community as English cricket professionals?'

He still loves his cricket, though since that famous day at Lord's when the ground and players stood to him in farewell he has only seen one day's play – at Taunton when Somerset made him a life member. Hampshire have not done him similar justice. And of course he still loves cricketers. 'Of all of them over the years I think I have only known four bad ones. Yes, only four.'

Supper, beautifully cooked by Pat, is served with another swill and clink of honest bottles. You start with sherry to brace up the soup. And the stories and opinions keep coming. You ask about Yorkshire cricket. 'The only thing that can sort them out is five tonnes of napalm!'

You wonder if you will be steady up the stairs. You leave, early to bed, and John solemnly munching and dictating to Pat his cheese column to be typed on the morrow. You stagger upstairs and below the old voice is gravelly dictating: 'A deep, intense nose ... pungent taste ... but deep, creamy and satisfying ...'

And in the morning he will be up far earlier than you to greet the day. 'Mornin' George! Mornin' Margot!' Happy Birthday, John.

Blast from the fast

E McDonald Bailey
25 August 1984

Allowing 15 seconds for each of his three long jumps and adding that to his sprint times, Carl Lewis was in working action for just 165 seconds in the Olympic Games. Most conservative estimates reckon his four gold medals will have made him £1 million by Christmas. That's more than £350,000 a minute. Nice work.

Whatever the ins and outs and small print in his Nike shoe contract, Lewis is said to have demanded – and received – £19,000 for his 100-metre dash at Geneva on Wednesday; £2,000 a second. He says he runs only for himself and God. Ask and ye shall receive.

Lewis does not even hold the world 100 metres record. Between 1951 and 1956 it was held for Britain by E McDonald Bailey. There's a name to conjure with! Mac agreed to lend his name to some sprinters' starting blocks marketed by Lillywhites of Piccadilly in the early 50s. He would get a tiny royalty on each sold, if any. The Amateur Athletic Association turned purple in collective apoplexy. The runner was suspended, *sine die*, from ever performing again. Out came the civil libertarians: Tom Driberg asked questions in the House, Frank Soskice rose in impassioned oratory for the fast underdog; there were indications that Lady Huggins, wife of the Governor of Jamaica, might even raise the matter with the Queen.

Thirty years on, and the memory of that pioneering hoo-ha makes E (for Emmanuel) McDonald Bailey throw back his grey head and let out a great big belly laugh. He still looks as fit as a flea and is still always smiling.

By coincidence, as Carl Lewis arrived last week for his European business trip, Britain's long-ago Olympian whizz was leaving Port of Spain for his month's summer holiday in England. He is now Sports Co-ordinator for the National Energy Corporation of Trinidad. When I last met him, he and his wife had been running one of the Caribbean's best soul-food restaurants à la Creole. Their recipes, he reckons, were part of the 'secret weapon' of Clive Lloyd and his men. Another laugh.

He was fascinated to meet Lewis two years ago. 'Now he is worth his millions, he might have changed. But I was very impressed not only by his lithe athleticism but by the boy's calm determination. He seems sensible and mature. He certainly knew what he wanted and look how soon it has come to pass.' There is not an iota of jealousy in the man who was the world's fastest for five years after his 10.2 in Belgrade in 1951. Besides that, he held a further 14 sprint records between 1946 and 1953. 'My medals are still jinglin' in my office: I look at them often and always with pride.'

Lewis came into Heathrow last week with a big bang on Concorde. Bailey was a bewildered 18-year old boy when he first arrived in Plymouth from Trinidad in a German banana boat after a choppy two-week voyage. He had been sent over to run in the AAA Championships at White City. He did nothing in the 100 yards but made the semis in the 220.

Four years later he was back in Britain with the RAF and after the war, along with such other heroes in demob suits as Denis Compton, Reg Harris and Bruce Woodcock, his was a household name. The first athletics picture I ever cut out for my scrapbook was from the *News Chronicle* of the 100 metres finish in the 1948 London Olympics – Dillard, Ewell, LaBeach, McCorquodale, Patton ... Britain's McDonald Bailey was last and the nation sighed ...

'Getting into that final was a triumph, honestly. With three weeks to go my thigh went as flat as a pancake. We sorted that out, then with 10 days left I got an abscess under my arm,

44

and then, would you believe it, laryngitis?' Could it have been psychological? 'No, alas, it was all genuine: I was very run down,' and he laughed at the memory.

Four years later, in the Helsinki Olympics, he was hot favourite. He won the bronze. 'I must admit there was enormous pressure being favourite. It was wet and miserable, and stupidly, I got upset at the lane draw for the final. When the gun went I simply tensed. I ran half that race coiled up with tension. Ridiculous! If it had been 105 metres do you know I might just have made it.' The American Remigino and McKenley of Jamaica took the first two places ... and Eddie Waring signed him for rugby league with Leigh.

In 1980 he sent Allan Wells a telegram of congratulations on his 100 metres gold medal in Moscow. Wells, I remember, was decidedly chuffed when he opened it. Mac did not send a cable to the leading sprinter of this month's Olympics. It would, after all, have only been read by one of the office staff in the conglomerate known as Carl Lewis Inc.

McDonald Bailey died in December 2013, aged 93.

Howard's Way
Trevor Howard
7 October 1986

Knock, knock, who's there? Still, answer came there none.

It was the second time you'd bashed the door of the tranquil white-washed country house and only the startled birds of greenbelt, russet Herts had made any sort of answer around the eaves.

Check again: right address, right time, right date. Definitely you had arranged to turn up the morning after his 70th birthday. 'We'll have a few delightful drinks to celebrate, old boy,' he had said on the telephone the week before. Damn, I supposed he'd forgotten. Famous film stars can. Or had last night's party continued into the bright-lit dawn of this blissful autumn morning?

It was promising to be less than a brief encounter. Give him five minutes, one more clattering knock, then call it a day. You kick your heels then attack the door-knocker again until the ancient sign above rattles. It says, 'No Children, Pets or Actors.'

You have one last squint through the letterbox. Hang on a tick ... Is that a movement in the darkness at the top of the stairs? Just the flutter of a shadow? 'Anyone at home?' you shout through the slit with quite appalling rudeness. Caught red-handed, the shadow takes cringing shape and is forced to grope down the stairs. Bleary, bloodshot and bearded like the bard, and in slippered pantaloons which are blue pyjama bottoms. St Michael brand. Nothing else.

A man plays many parts, but here was the lot of them in one unsteady entrance. The Outcast of the Islands. The tortured wreckage of Scobie the day after deciding the deed in Greeneland. Poor old Tusker after staying on too long at the Pankot Club. Captain Bligh swaying down the rope ladder. Morel the miner, surfacing and blinking into daylight. It is indeed all of those, and a hundred others – and now all of them are finding great difficulty in turning the doorknob the right way.

'My dear fellow. How sorry. I'm shamed. Forgive me. What day is it? Tuesday! Is it really? 11.30, you say? In the morning, or evening? Morning? Is that so? Well, I really am most awfully sorry, old boy.'

The shafts of sunlight now arrow through the hallway. The birds are content. The very idea of it turning out OK in the end in a mellow-yellow Indian summer in good old England goes perfectly well with Trevor Howard – especially as the day before he posted his three-score-and-ten, on the day they published his biography. It is subtitled *A Gentleman and a Player*.

'What will you have to drink? A quick one here, then we'll go down to the pub. Lots to tell you. Just a short stroll. They understand me there. I love them. No need for money. I settle up every Christmas.'

Outside, a crunch of gravel on the drive, a slammed door, and a red-headed bustle as his beloved Mrs Howard of 42 years, Helen Cherry, scampers in from the shops to sort out the disarray. 'Why didn't you ring me?' she says, 'he's hopeless at dates'; and, yes, there was some good cause for some happy celebrations yesterday, though he's been very good lately and done very little roistering, certainly not like he used to ...

'Hennie, the fellow wants a drink,' he says. Not until you're up and put your pyjama top on, she says, and your new dressing-gown. He goes up obediently, pointing from the staircase: 'Have you seen that?' and there in the very pride of place in the hallway is a large, framed action portrait of the Australian all-rounder Keith Miller, inscribed 'To Trev, my old mate ...'

Another good, full day had begun.

Seventy years ago to the very morning, one-day-old Trevor Wallace Howard-Smith was probably wrapped in swaddling clothes in Kent, and his mother began to prepare for the long sea journey to present her firstborn to his father, who was the Lloyds of London man in Ceylon. Seven years later, the colonial mite made the return journey – to be turned into a gent and a player at Clifton College.

In summers, he made stacks of runs, bowled fizzing off-breaks and watched young Hammond blossoming for Gloucestershire. In winters, he boxed, played rugby and occasional truant from the dorm to see Frank Benson's touring company of thespians. A tiny bug bit – though when he left school he first considered pro cricket, then salesmanship for Harrods ('Wanted to send me to sell umbrellas in Argentina: didn't think it rained there, so saw no future in it'), and failed the medical at the fledgling RAF college at Cranwell ('That morning I had bloodshot eyes as well as a boil on the bum').

His doting mother, as colonial mothers did, came over for the annual Clifton v. Tonbridge match at Lord's (RIP), where his English master, Mr Garrett, told her of a classroom declamation by the young man that had reverberated round all of the Avon Gorge – Marullus in *Julius Caesar*, 'Wherefore rejoice? What conquest brings him home ... ?' – and suggested to an astonished Mum that her son should try for RADA. It was not a career for chaps in the 1930s – 'there were five fellows and 25 girls: if you turned up in a suit they took you on without a murmur.'

By 1936, just 20, he was in the West End smash *French Without Tears*, and till war broke out was off and running ... square-chinned, prow-nosed, natural, totally unaffected, and working on that thunderous moose-bellow that was to announce his presence on film locations round the world, not to mention adjoining public bars, late-night cafes – and, it must be said, police stations.

On demob, he was his generation's finest Petruchio, and a memorable Recruiting Officer Plume (where Helen signed him up for life). Then *Brief Encounter* made him a worldwide film star. He was paid £500, and has never made a penny more from its million worldwide repeats ...

But such talk bores him: if the drift continues he threatens to go back to bed. Another large tonic water. 'Now answer my question. I can tell you're a Botham man. Good, so am I. Now there's a *performer* for you!' and the word rumbles up from his chest and explodes with such glee that the birds outside the window start chirruping again in alarm, 'But good riddance to that bloody Boycott, what? Can you possibly like a fellow who takes two hours, 18 minutes to score 23 runs? Course you can't.'

He saw Hammond bat, you see. And Woolley. 'Remember, darling' – Helen at that moment was trying to say what a marvellous Macbeth Howard might have made in his prime, but he doesn't want any of that – 'remember the day we sat behind old Woolley, in his Homburg hat, and watched the South African Pollock batting. A revelation. Like peas in a pod, but generations apart ... who was that other South African left-hander darling ...?' – it was on the tip of his tongue. 'You know, lovely fellow. Drove him down from Trent Bridge after the war. Was that in the Alvis? No, got the Alvis with the loot from *Golden Salamander*. So must have had the Wolseley then. What *was* his name? Left-armer. Specs.'

Tufty Mann, I suggest. 'TUFTY MANN!' comes the great thunder-and-lightning roar of the legend, and you fancy windows have shattered at Hertford, a dozen miles' distant.

Watch out for your crockery when he plays Lear on the radio next month. 'Blow winds and crack your cheeks!' Touchingly, he grew his beard to play the demented old lion. Must be the nearest he's ever got to the Method school of acting. 'Bugger that!' he growls. 'Is Astaire expected to "explain" his dancing, or a jazz player his rhythm?' And in her engaging, often racy, and always allowably star-struck new biog, Vivienne Knight says, 'He has never felt the need to act like a bowl of soup or to go up a mountain and shout God Save the Queen for the sake of his voice ... nor get up to tricks with false noses or any facial props, because for him it all comes from inside.'

She quotes the critic Dilys Powell: 'His acting has qualities that the so-called "greatest" lack. He has a huge range, yet he can depict grief, misery, sadness, defeat – as well, of course, happiness and joy – without the need to contort his face. It is a very peculiar quality, and perhaps not really recognised. Even in the smallest part you just don't want him to leave the screen.' Robert Mitchum said the same on television the other day – 'You've never actually caught him acting.'

Howard has a huge affection for Mitchum. And Errol Flynn too – 'born to be soulmates'. Of all his leading ladies, from starting with her in *Brief Encounter* to the two left behind by the Raj in *Staying On*, he has to give the palm to Celia Johnson. 'She looked like the secretary of the WI but there was a real trouper underneath.'

Sure, he liked Orson. 'Lovely man. He'd say, "let's work out this scene together." Then we'd do it his way. Usually it was better. Orson claims to have discovered Anton Karas, the zither fellow from *The Third Man*. Well, I did. Came back humming him, didn't I darling? Woke you up to hum to you. Dum-de-dum-deeda-deeda. I'd found him busking outside a restaurant in Vienna. Carol Reed put him in the picture and next time we went back he owned the restaurant.'

The old Gent dislikes talking about Players you know he thinks are shits. Mr Fletcher Christian Brando – 'Really he should be pitied ...' Anyway, bugger him and his mumbling, where was he before he was interrupted? 'Oh yes, cars. The Alvis, the Wolseley ...' They have been in many adventures together.

His second driving charge came in the early 1950s, on the day England won the Ashes. His producer, Euan Lloyd, was called for the defence: 'Your Worship, Mr Howard and I were driving along Piccadilly with the car wireless on. It all depended on two final runs. When finally someone hit a four which won the game, Mr Howard jumped out of the car in front of Fortnum and Mason's, danced on the pavement, let out a roar, then jumped on to the bonnet, peered at me through the windscreen and yelled, "We've done it! We've done it!"' Case dismissed.

But another time at Middlesex Sessions, Mr Ewen Montagu banned him from driving for eight years (cut only on appeal), and on another famous Hollywood occasion he had to pay all his fees for the war-film *Morituri* after trying to extricate Holden's car from the parking lot following a pretty decent party – 'he went forward into one in the driveway, backed into another, shunted the next two in line both fore and aft, before Michael Wilding took charge, and also arranged for the substantial repairs to be made. The bill was his exact fee for the film,' says Helen.

'He's not interested in all that ...' the grand old bear interrupts. 'D'you know, I once took six for two before lunch with my off-breaks ...' I want to know about *The Heart of the Matter*, and the classic *Catholics* that had been on television last week, and he's still rabbiting on about cricket when Helen returns after rummaging for a letter.

It's from Graham Greene. 'My Dear Trevor, I can't describe how moved I was by your performance in *Catholics*: there were tears in my eyes at the end and I had to take a pill to sleep. For me it was one of the two finest performances I have ever seen on the screen or the stage – and I write "one of the two" only because otherwise you mightn't believe me. I write this with the cold wisdom of next morning, not in the flush of first enthusiasm. Affectionately, Graham.'

Dead silence. Then, plaintively, 'Look if you don't want to hear about my six for two, before lunch too, then can I please go back to bed?' Silence.

'Okay, have you ever been kidnapped?'

'I have. In Italy. I let out a roar and they ran.'

'Have you run the bulls in Pamplona?'

'I have. I once woke up in the back of a fast car in Panama and said, "Hey, this isn't the Barnet road!"'

Okay, if not cricket, he'll talk about prison. He's had the odd night there in various ones round the world. 'Quite pleasant really,' and Lear's quote rumbles up:

'Come let's away to prison;
We two alone will sing like birds i' the cage ...
And pray and sing and tell old tales and laugh ...
Who loses and who wins; who's in, who's out.'

'Now, darling, can I go back to bed, please?' He has a long day tomorrow. Off to make a new film in Toronto with Loretta Young. Has he ever played opposite her before? 'No, and I can't wait, old boy', and by far the grandest and most compelling of our un-knighted actors rolls his merry blue-grey eyes, and climbs the stairs for bed. The Player and the Gent.

Trevor Howard died little more than a year after this glorious interview was published, aged 74. The article was under-noticed at the time because it appeared on the day the Guardian's *new daily rival,* The Independent, *was first published, to great initial acclaim.*

Squire of the county still in the hunt
Ian Botham
16 May 1992

With a proprietorial attention to detail, the squire with the raffish moustache inspects his estate. He is wearing a multi-pocketed, yew-green poacher's jacket and battered, grey-kneed jeans tucked into tall leather boots. He looks very much the part: he could be a young Tory knight of the shires just biding his time organising the family acres before the inevitable call comes from the local constituency for him to take his rightful place as the voice of his people at Westminster.

This could yet come about. If Seb Coe can charm votes out of faraway Cornwall, could not Ian Botham do the same in his very own rustic neck of the north Yorkshire woods?

It is a sparkling springtime morning of timeless renewal and contentment: buds and blossom and birds on the bough. There is no cricketing today but, with Tigger the busily snuffling boxer at his heel, the young landowner could not tarry on his rounds.

There is another sport to play after a check on the lake, well stocked with brown and rainbow trout, a threatening glance upwards at the circling jackdaws as they beady-eye from on high the chirrupping clusters of newly hatched goslings at the lakeside, a thwacking morning pat and fond nuzzle for the horses and, in one of the evocative old stone barns, a brief surveillance as father-in-law supervises the preparation of the great iron salmon-smoker.

Then, all creatures great and small present and correct, his sometime foe and good friend, the Australian bat and equally new Durham debutant Dean Jones arrives – and off go the two dauntless, bold Lochinvars for a round of golf on top of a Yorkshire moor.

In 19 summers this with Durham is to all intents only Botham's third as a 'home' player. After his very first championship curtsey (8 May 1974, vs Lancashire, c D Lloyd b Hughes 13, and nought for 15 in three overs), he played only two seasons for Somerset before he and Kathy, a Yorkshire girl, married and set up house in her home county.

With Somerset and Worcestershire Botham rented cottages and lived out of (very large) suitcases. 'Now, at last, home games really feel like home,' he says with relish. 'It's wonderful having him home with us all at the start of a summer,' says Kath, adding with a giggle, 'although ask me again in six or seven weeks and I might give you a different answer.'

Hotfoot from the beanstalk and Bournemouth's pantomime boards, Botham played his 100th Test at Wellington in February. In the World Cup he was, after Wasim Akram, the competition's most successful bowler (16 at 19). His Test tally is now 5,192 runs, 383 wickets and 118 catches. Three more catches and he will overtake Sir Colin Cowdrey's England record of 120 (in 114 Tests), an astonishing figure, for the new knight of Lord's was able to pouch his from both ends, not being required to bowl the 21,561 Test deliveries which Botham has – more than any other Englishman except Derek Underwood's 21,862, another record certain to fall to Botham if he plays this summer.

So are there one or two challenges left? 'Well, to play for England is challenge enough, and always has been. I love it, and will always keep trying to get selected for as long as I'm physically able. Blimey, I'm only 36, why do you always keep writing me off? It's up to the selectors, of course, but if I make it my priority to do really well for Durham, well that goes hand-in-hand with my chances of playing for England, doesn't it?'

After beating Australia almost single-handedly in the World Cup, the final itself was an anti-climax. Launching England's innings, he was given caught behind at once, though even a fuzzy satellite picture still showed a wide shaft of floodlight between his bat and the ball. His immediate, but obviously seething, departure from the crease was accompanied by the strident suggestion from Pakistan's impudent and long-memoried little Sohail, at short-leg, that Botham should 'next time send out your mother-in-law to bat'. Botham once suggested Pakistan was a place best suited for exiling one's mother-in-law.

Touché – and now the seen-it-all old warrior can laugh merrily at the cheek of Pakistan's young blood. The mother-in-law in question, by the way, was in the kitchen helping Kathy make cakes. The two girls, Sarah and Becky, are whizzing around outside, pretending to help the gardener mow the lawns.

The eldest child at 14, son-and-heir Liam, is in from his early shotgun patrol round the estate and now preparing to return to school at Rossall. The tall, tousled, engaging teenager is a chip off the old block; Liam is looking forward to the new season, too – last year he became the youngest ever to play for Rossall's first XI – after a brilliant winter for the school at rugby (full back or fly half).

Not far away the glorious, babbling, deep-gullied Greta flows into the Tees – small fry for Botham the angler, who has just bought a £50,000 timeshare for a stretch of the real McKay on the Tay. There Turner painted *The Meeting of the Waters* and, for good measure, Scott wrote *Rokeby*.

In the inn at Greta Bridge, Dickens stayed when he was researching *Nicholas Nickleby* and the horrendous Yorkshire board schools. As we strolled through his own acres, the young squire of cricket was surprised to be reminded of his own education at 'Dotheboys Hall'.

Twenty years ago this month Botham set off with gangling bravura from Yeovil to be a groundstaff lad at Lord's. He sold scorecards, cleaned the Long Room windows, worked the scoreboard, bowled interminably to snooty MCC members in the nets and wheeled the covers on, and off, and on again. The two grizzled old coaches, Harry Sharp and Len Muncer, winced fondly enough at the boy's lusty confidence, but not much else, and they thought at very best the kid might make a fair-to-middling, lower-order county professional for a season or three. Then what? A carpet-layer perhaps or a corner shop?

The two, sage metropolitan coaches could not have remotely thought their rustic and rumbustious pupil would first break every all-rounders' Test record that was going; resurrect the game as a sport of, and for, the people; and end up ushering in a brand-new county championship team as an estate-owning squire with columns framing the front-door steps, trout in the lake, horses in the stables, farm workers in the yard and a Mercedes on the gravel.

And still, he insists, there is a lot of cricket in him. 'I didn't think I could enjoy it more than my time with Worcester, which was great, and I thank them for it. But, who knows, why can't I still be playing for Durham when Liam makes his county debut? That's something to aim at, isn't it?'

And he laughs that relishable and wolfish laugh that has never been far away through the two decades in which he has played his game with the whole man of him, body and soul, spirit and skill, and especially that bold courage which Chesterton defined as almost a contradiction in terms – 'courage displaying a strong desire to live, taking the form of a carefree readiness to die'.

The much-travelled young squire sniffs a new summer with satisfaction. He has come home at last.

Not for the only time, Frank erred on the optimistic side. Durham finished bottom in their first two seasons; Botham was to play only two more Tests before losing his place, and retired from cricket the following year. He equalled Cowdrey's record but finished 47 balls short of Underwood's. Liam Botham did play three first-class matches for Hampshire, after his dad retired, and had a more successful career in both rugby codes. Ian still has time to stand for parliament but – perhaps mercifully – has not done so.

A long look back with the lionheart
Harold Larwood
24 April 1993

SYDNEY: An Australian cricket side arrives tomorrow to resume the ancient challenge. 1993 is a notorious jubilee year in Ashes legend. Sixty years ago today an England team was making the same journey from the Antipodes – homeward bound on the high seas and celebrating the cruel capture of the tiny urn at the end of still the most infamous rubber of the whole sequence: the bodyline tour. The shipboard celebrations took six weeks and the MCC team did not disembark from the *Duchess of Atholl* until 6 May 1933 at Greenock.

'Aye,' remembers the still surviving chief protagonist of that whole infamous shooting-match, 'we got home on 6 May after near eight months away, had one night with our wives and then were off next day playing for Notts at Worcester or wherever.'

He was to play for Nottinghamshire for five more summers but after he had won, almost single-handedly and immortally, the Ashes in that bodyline series, the establishment turned their back on Harold Larwood, who was never again picked for England.

By gorgeous quirk of paradox, this now wizened elder – as small and sharp as a sparrow, blind and 90 next year – whose skills 60 years ago so stirred colonial passions and hatreds, has been settled happily in Australia for the past two-score years. Happily and almost anonymously, except that his surname more than any other remains an eponym for venomously hostile fast bowling.

Larwood lives with Lois, his devoted wife of 65 years, in a tidy trim Sydney street of splintery, sentry-neat colonial bungalows. You ring at the porch door. The bell plays an upbeat 'John Brown's Body'. The inside door opens a fraction. The eye which looks up at you may be blind but still manages a beady aggressiveness. 'I'm not talking cricket – and I'm certainly not talking bodyline,' he says. The accent is still ripely Nottingham. It goes on: 'Ask me one question about either and you're out. I can't remember a thing about the old days, and can't see a thing, so I know nothing about the present.'

You plead softly: 'I only bring greetings from England, sir . . .' The door opens wider.

'Don't "sir" me, I'm plain Harold, one-time coal miner and one-time professional cricketer.'

'Sorry, sir.'

'Well, I can tell you're from England all right. I suppose you'd better come in – but no cricket questions, mind, and certainly no bodyline.'

How can this tiny ancient have been the most feared in history – patron saint and forerunner of Lillee and Lindwall, Ambrose and Holding and Waqar? If he was scarcely 5ft 9in in his pomp, he is 5ft 6in in his dotage, but still proudly straight-backed. He and Lois brought five bonny daughters to Australia; now they have 13 grandchildren and 'five or six, I think' great-grandchildren.

The walls of his spotless little sitting-room are dotted with framed photographs – heroes in sepia. He hears you hum with pleasure and recognition, and you know he is suddenly glad that you do. Photos fade faster than fame. 'You can have a quick look at my pictures if you want,' he says.

He stands by each one, like a museum guide – which, in a way, he is. He cannot see them any more but he knows exactly which is which and, in detail, who is who. Percy Chapman's happy 1928–9 MCC team in Australia gaze confidently at the camera. Sixteen of the 17 are dead. Now Les Ames has gone, he is the only one left. 'Me, Les and Wally Hammond were the babies on that trip. Les remained my best chum and dear pal. He asked me over, all expenses paid, for his 80th birthday. Couldn't go, of course. Wally was always a funny fellow. Moods, you know. On tours, us kids would knock about together. One day you'd say, "Coming out tonight, Wally?" and he'd say, "Course I am", and be the life and soul. Next day we'd say, "What about tonight,

Wally?" And he wouldn't even answer you. Funny fellow, Wally. Hell of a bat, mind.'

The bright southern sun from the window illuminates the little shrine. The blind man is unaware of it as he steers you proudly to a framed, faded, official scroll. It marks a long-ago appreciation for his cricketing feats from fellow members of his Miners' Union at Nuncargate, the mining village where he was born in 1904.

'I left school at 13, down the pit at 14, driving a pony. Oh yes, lots of crawling along them tunnels. "Old Joe" Hardstaff lived in our village. When I was around 17, he said I should go down to Nottingham for a trial. I didn't want to go, I was quite happy mining. In the end my dad took me on the bus. They set me to bowl at Art Staples and Ben Lilley. After a bit I went over to dad and said, "I'm no good at this lark, dad, let's go home."

'Just then they sent over to say I was wanted in the committee room. Mr Dixon was the president. He owned half Nottingham, didn't he? He says, "Look here, Larwood, how much are you getting down the pit?" I tell him, "32 bob a week, sir." He says: "Right, that's settled, you can join the groundstaff at 32 shillings a week."

'Outside, dad was fair livid I hadn't asked for more, especially when the secretary gave him a list as long as your arm for stuff I'd need like a bat, flannels, new boots and all. It came to £9, a hell of a lot for us, and on the way home I said, "Dad, if I make the grade I'll make it right with you."'

Late one Friday night, in the midsummer of 1925, the 20-year-old received a telegram at home: 'Proceed to Sheffield. Be prepared to play – Carr.' The county's long-time and autocratic captain was AW Carr. 'They put me at square leg and Yorkshire's Edgar Oldroyd kept playing the ball towards me and feinting to run, you know "kidding the new kid" sort of thing, teasing me.

'Any road, he tries it a fifth time or so, and I'm in on it fast and let fly – and knock all three down from square leg. He's out by a mile. Mr Carr walks over slowly and says, "Good throw, sonny, but never ever do that again."

'"Why not, sir," I say, "he's on his way, isn't he?" "Because," he says, "try it nine more times out of 10, you'll miss and it'll be four overthrows." He were right, too.'

In that last half-summer of 1925 he took 73 wickets at 18 each, and word was around that a gale was blowing. The following June England blooded him at Lord's. His first Test wicket was Macartney's. For the Oval Test England recalled the 49-year-old Wilfred Rhodes.

The old man blindly shuffles a hand around in a drawer and pulls out a parchmenty old newspaper cutting. 'Is this the right one?' he asks. It is – from a *Sunday Express* of August 1926, the headline exclaiming 'Larwood Too Young, Rhodes Too Old'. Now he directs you to a framed scorecard on another wall ... the Ashes were clinched, Rhodes took six in the match and so did young Larwood.

'Rhodes were pure genius. I got Woodfull for a duck and after a bit Rhodes came on. That Ponsford was a vicious cutter of the ball, vicious. I was at point but Rhodes keeps signalling me closer to the bat. Still fetching me up till I'm almost standing on Ponsford's crease. Sure I'm a bit scared. Rhodes comes up, just two paces from behind the umpire. But he stops dead, and stares at me.

'I'd involuntarily taken a pace back from Ponsford's crease. He fetches me in again. First ball nips through and smacks into Struddy's gloves. Second ball breaks back – and Ponsford, surprised, pops it up and I jump across and catch it left-handed. Rhodes walks down the pitch to me and says softly, "You can go back a bit now, sonny, we got him."'

On the mantelpiece is a small silver ashtray. I tap my pipe out on it. The old man hears the clink. 'I think you've just emptied your ash in my most treasured possession,' he says, though without any trace of admonition. 'Read what it says,' he orders.

You read: 'To Harold. For The Ashes. From a Grateful Skipper.'

The blind eyes mist over and stare at the wall in a reverie. 'Mr Jardine gave me that when we came back. His inscription still means an awful lot to me. He was a real leader of men. I'd bowl two or three overs for him on that tour and he'd come up and say, "Anything in this wicket for you, Harold?" and I'd perhaps say, "Yes, quite lively, skipper."

'Sometimes he might wait for Bradman to come in, then he'd clap his hands and everyone would move over and suddenly my field would be Les, at wicket standing back, not a slip, just a short gully to stop the sort of jump and jab, then a mid-off, and every one of the rest in a leg-trap ring. I just used to watch Bradman's feet as I bowled. If he shuffled slightly to leg I'd follow him, if he moved across his stumps I'd follow him there. No, the barrackers never got at me, just at Jardine. They detested him. "Sardine" they called him.'

Larwood came into the final Test at Sydney, the Ashes already well won thanks to his 32 wickets at 19 apiece. 'Bradman comes in. At once my foot went and I'm collapsed in agony. Jardine picks me up and says I must finish the over. "I can't, skipper, I'm finished." He orders me. So I do, in terrible pain.

'"Can I go off now, skip?" I say. "No," he whispers, nodding towards Bradman, "not until the little bastard's gone. Let him think you can come back for another spell any time. I want you to stand at short cover-point and just stare at him." So Hedley Verity comes on at my end and that's where Bradman loses his head, thinking to cash in while I was "resting". He dashes out at Hedley's second ball, head up, and it bowls him. At once Mr Jardine signals me off. He'd done the trick – and Bradman and I walk off beside one another and neither of us spoke a word.'

Larwood never played for England again. 'Well, I wasn't about to apologise, was I? I had nothing to apologise for, did I? To tell the truth, from the moment we got home from that tour I've been fed up to the back teeth with the word "bodyline". Still am all these years later.

'Vow never to talk about it – except for a little chat like this. Well, you're from England, aren't you? Not many from over there comes to see me now. Well, I'm totally forgotten now, aren't I?'

Another time, another planet

The fly-halves

From The Great Number Tens, 1993

For England there was Stoop, there was Davies, there was Sharp. More often down the century, as the admired Alan Watkins put it once with such typically perfect fine-tuning in his unmissable column in the *Independent*, 'There are in England usually three or four players who are more or less up to the job, and the selectors cannot make up their minds whom to choose. In Wales, by contrast, a period of competition between two players or, alternatively, of cosmic confusion is succeeded by the emergence of one usually great outside half.'

Thus the uncertainty about whether to choose Billy Cleaver or Glyn Davies was succeeded by the domination of Cliff Morgan. The reign of Morgan was followed by baronial wars, until the succession descended on David Watkins, who, after a brief struggle, gave way to the mightiest sovereign of all, Barry John. He abdicated, however, when he was only 27, in favour of Phil Bennett, who, after a successful reign – with the brief interregnum of the late John Bevan – transferred the crown to Gareth Davies. Unhappily the reign of Davies was marred towards its close by the preference for Malcolm Dacey evinced by Bevan (by now a power behind the throne). Davies abdicated in disgust. But the throne left empty by him was not filled by the usurper Dacey. Another Davies, Jonathan, had appeared in the kingdom. 'Lo, we have another king,' the simple folk of Wales cried in exultation and relief.

Alan Watkins, of our certain generation, I'm sure hosannahs with us all that, lo, on the contrary, there could never be another king. (I'm aware it is crass to use words like 'king': but, well, this little guy *was* a monarch.) Barry John came upon Wales, and then the world, like a ghost in the night first to delight and then to enrapture totally. He was an insouciant natural sprite with a pale presence and a frail one (although with deceptively strong hips and thighs). Sometimes, as the gilded spirit glided through ferociously hulking enemies, he made it seem they were actually mesmerised by his presence – that, or they were careering into unseen glass walls down there. He was generous and chivalrous; there was a gaiety about him, and he ran like an elfin Puck, and kicked like a dream, particularly out of hand – garryowens or artful bobblers, great raking things, inch-perfect at the corner-flag; or snake-spitting grubbers, or one-bounce off-spinners (or leggers) which tantalised and cruelly taunted end-of-tether full backs to distraction (and, in one or two cases, to retirement there and then).

Or rather, no, John did not 'cruelly taunt'. Angels made in heaven do not 'cruelly taunt'.

He was from Cefneithin in the west, a mining village shadowed by Mynydd Mawr (the 'great mountain') and triangled by Llanelli, Swansea and Carmarthen. Barry was one of four boys, and the back door of the family's terraced council house opened on to the village rec, a scrubby stretch of land which became 'our Wembley, or Arms Park or, in the summers, Lord's'.

His uncles were miners and so was his father, 'with blue scars on their hands and dust in their lungs to show for it', Barry remembers. How could he ever forget. 'In the winter sometimes, Dad wouldn't see daylight till the third day. The lovely thing about the village was that all his mates knew he had six mouths to feed – eight in all – so when the chance came they'd give him their turn for a 'dubbla' [a double-shift], saying 'Here, Will, you need the extra pound more than us.' And when he was on dubbla, we boys would take it in turns to run to the pit with his extra sandwiches for the morning.'

At the village school – 'no, not academic, me, if the passmark was 50 I'd get 51 in everything; none of this 70-80 lark for me; I'd just clear the crossbar. Why not, still get your three points, eh?'

Soccer was the impromptu game at school. 'The best game to develop skills for rugby, anyway. In a way, I think all fly halves are frustrated inside forwards anyway, fantasising about being at Old Trafford or Anfield or the Maracaná – because in both positions you have to be born with the balance, the touch, the decisiveness, the boldness.'

Do not read that and think, 'Blimey, what a swank'. There is not an ounce of conceit in John, nor, they say, has there ever been.

At Gwendraeth Grammar School, he made the under-15s at 12. By 16 he was playing village rugby for Cefneithin, 'the green-and-golds'. Across the rec from the John household lived a man who played for Llanelli, a few miles down the hill. He was a fly half, too. And had played for Wales. His name was Carwyn James. At solitary practice sometimes on the rec, little Barry would field the balls for Carwyn. And on Saturdays, 'the whole village would go down to Stradey for the match. Can you imagine, Stradey full to bursting, hundreds of us boys on the "tanner bank" clustered together; it was our Mecca, total heaven. And of all of us, I had the bigger bond with Stradey, with the team, the "Scarlets" – because of Carwyn. Because Carwyn called me Barry and I called him Carwyn. Oh, that lovely bond ... that almost blood relationship ... And in time, I got to standing by myself, just concentrating on Carwyn's play, making little sort-of binoculars with my thumb and forefinger and my hands ...'

And in time, as the gods had obviously long decreed, John succeeded to Stradey's scarlet mantle. And, by Jove, what rugby they were playing, too. In 1966 Australia toured. Early on, they played Llanelli at Stradey. A filthy day. John was 21, a student at Trinity College, Carmarthen. I have just replayed a murky videotape, black-and-white, fuzzy little monochrome figures flittering in the gloaming. The once and former crown prince, Cliff Morgan, was at the commentary microphone: '... This is Barry John again ... going for the break ... oh, no ... can't make it this time ... yes, he can ... he's broken one tackle ... he's broken two ... he's inside again ... is he clear? ... 10 yards to go ... can he get there? ... what a try!'

On the following Sunday, the old maestro centre (outside them all from Jones to Morgan), Bleddyn Williams, now a journalist, wrote in the *People*: 'A new fly-half star has been born in Wales ...'

The best game Barry John ever played in was the one where Wales confirmed the Grand Slam in 1971. It was a tumultuous collision, and a voluptuous one. Power and glory. Passion and pride. 'The French that day were superb. Wales were superb. When France attacked, Lux was going this way and that, Bertranne all over the shop, Villepreux chipping here, there and everywhere, Berot the fly half doing daft things, the Spanghero brothers smashing through the middle ... it was crazy, beautiful, great rugby. We defended, tackled everything – even me, believe it if you dare, when that rock-hard Dauga rolled on me at the corner flag and broke my nose. I was back on in no time.

'Then we started to play a bit... Back and forth ... it was the most perfect game of rugby... skill and honesty and sportsmanship; muscle, blood and bone, and flights of fantasy ... the lot.'

It was settled, at the last, by Barry John, lightest and slightest man on the field. There was a set scrum just outside France's 25, midfield-right. Young, the hooker, struck against the head, Edwards spun to John, going left, who intuitively sensed Berot (expecting a French heel) was a yard off the pace. John ran straight at the inside centre, Bertranne, who brought the shimmy of a dummy to Dawes. An imperceptible change of gear did for full back Villepreux and, in spite of Berot's lightning recovery, Barry was over, halfway between posts and corner. The Grand Slam was won. 'I felt Berot's fingernails running down my back as I crossed the line ... it was the most important try of my life.'

In the victors' changing-room afterwards, Barry kept repeating, 'It was not my try, it was Jeff Young's over there who won the ball against the head. The rest was the easy bit.'

Passing gems show foppy, soppy Betjers loved sport

John Betjeman

5 September 2006

The Beeb's gone bonkers on Betjers. As well as the broadcasters, publishing and the public prints – two biogs, feature pages, arts reviews, even the sex sections – have been bursting their banks and budgets on the centenary of Sir John Betjeman's birth. Before Saturday's stellar gala in London's West End rounds off the revels I reckon, as a devoted fan, it right and proper that sport should dip its oar in tribute.

Mind you, Betjeman would have shuddered with distaste at most of the professional sport dished up daily on these pages. Yet he clearly valued sport's relationship with, and its place in, Britain's cultural fabric. Whether or not the complicated old Laureate was your particular cup of Twinings – was he a minor major poet or a major minor poet? – his vast output in verse and prose threw up no end of passing gems to illustrate how, well, on the ball he was.

Sure he was slow to sport; very. A weedy, bullied idler at school at Marlborough, 'the greatest dread of all was dread of games'. On family hols in Cornwall, his sports-loving father disdainfully scoffed at the callow drip's fondness for bicycling all over to various local parish churches – 'Boy! It's no good sulking: listen here, you caddy for me on the morning round/This afternoon you'll help me dig for bait.' Up at Magdalen, poetry soirées were rudely, regularly raided by despised and boisterous rugger-buggers or oarsmen hearties – 'types in tweeds, shouting, drinking beer' – and talking 'of sport and makes of cars/In various bogus Tudor bars/And daren't look up and see the stars/But belch instead.'

Tennis turned the tide. Mixed tennis. 'Tennis was where one's heart sang, and mine particularly if I had Biddie Walsham as partner, with her straight gold hair and her laughing uselessness

65

at the game which equalled mine.' Half the English-speaking world knows how dotingly drooling was the foppy, soppy young JB when six-loved by 'great big mountainous sportsgirls' whizzing them over the net. 'Fair tigress of the tennis courts,/So short in sleeve and strong in shorts.' He squirmed for Pam and 'the size of her thighs, the pout of her lips, and see the strength of her arm, as firm and hairy as Hendren's'. Of course, Patsy Hendren was London's sturdy cricket hero of the 1920s.

Another JB cricket reference I've long and lovingly hoarded is a darling quatrain in the poem 'Cheltenham', which hints that Betjeman as a boy might even once have watched (and supported) 'Glawse' when the county played Sussex at my own dear old Cheltenham Festival:

I composed these lines when a summer wind
Was blowing the elm trees dry,
And we were seventy-six for seven
And they had CB Fry.

And any cricketer who hasn't must rush to read the epic 'Cricket Master', JB's gloriously hilarious attempt, post-Oxford, at being a prep school games teacher and his revenge on a 'hearty' colleague, 'the beastly, brutal, thick Devonian, Barnstaple'. It is a poem snug in my all-time top-ten treasure trove.

Golf – 'goff' to him – was 'it' in the end. In spite of his father's early despair, a love of the game did seep in and stay; links golf, that is, in his beloved Cornwall. Just as tennis to Betjeman could never mean the loathsome claptrap of Wimbledon and its grunting, self-absorbed obsessives, nor could he possibly relate golf to the zealots of blinkered concentration who play at the Open. John may have been a pretty hapless potterer at the game, but who has more ravishingly relished, and written down, the intrinsic, timeless essence of golf? 'It is a beautiful game. It tests the nerves and then soothes them. It can be played alone (which is how I like playing it best) when the player can quietly cheat to himself. It encourages an eye for landscape. It turns a dreary stretch of clay or the coniferous aridity of some sandy waste into an enchanted kingdom of contours, hazards and distances.'

Perfect. A couple of summers ago, on a voluptuously wild poet's day, we made a fond pilgrimage to Betjeman's grave at his beloved seaside course at St Enodoc and then, letting the kids lark about, I pootled around in a reverie, pitching and putting and slicing and shanking, with an old hickory club. And spouting, alone and aloud, the good old boy's rhapsodic lovesong to the seaside swipe:

> *He loved each corner of the links,*
> *The stream at the eleventh,*
> *The grey-green bents, the pale sea-pinks,*
> *The prospect from the seventh;*
>
> *To the ninth tee the uphill climb,*
> *A grass and sandy stairway,*
> *And at the top the scent of thyme*
> *And long extent of fairway.*

Yep. That's heaven.

PS
12 September 2006

Immediate retort last week on Sir John Betjeman's golf. How dare I call him 'a hapless potterer'? Did I ever see him play? His devoted daughter Candida, diligent editor of his prose and letters, wrote: 'While being hopeless at every other outdoor game (except perhaps croquet), he remained a dab hand at golf until well into his 50s.' Mea culpa. My evidence had been Sir John's fabled air-shot on the first tee at Moor Park in the imperishable BBC film *Metroland*, and the toast proposed to him, six years after his death, by Sir Robin Butler at the centenary dinner of his St Enodoc Golf Club in 1990.

Butler fondly parodied JB's famous verse in 'Seaside Golf' – changing

> *And so I did. It lay content*
> *Two paces from the pin;*
> *A steady putt and then it went*
> *Oh, most securely in.*
> *The very turf rejoiced to see*
> *The quite unprecedented three*

to (far more likely, he said):

> *And so it did. I chipped it low*
> *And thinned it past the pin*
> *And to and fro and to and fro*
> *I tried to get it in;*
> *Until, intoning oaths obscene,*
> *I holed it out in seventeen.*

3

A YOUNG MAN'S GAME

Some of Britain's most successful sports columnists – Ian Wooldridge was a prime example – have managed to have wonderfully successful careers while giving Britain's most popular sport a wide berth. Frank Keating soon opted out of the reality of modern English football. Neither the hooligans of the 80s nor the pampered stars of the Premier League fitted his idea of a column. In any case, the Guardian *could allow him to evade it – the brilliant football correspondent David Lacey (Lace the Ace) neither needed nor cared for the presence of a columnist alongside him. But the romance of the game, its misty past, his early idols – ah, those were different. When I asked colleagues for their favourite Keating piece, this one, about the old days at Craven Cottage, was by far the one most often mentioned. Written just before the 1975 semi-final, it forms a pair with the profile of Alec Stock, above. These were the pieces that alerted the* Guardian *readership to the wayward – Fulhamesque, even – talent that had landed on their newspaper.*

Moments of Pure Tosh
4 April 1975

Johnny Haynes was England's captain and unquestionably Fulham's finest footballer. But he was never what we reckoned to be your actual Fulham-type player. For one thing, he was far, far too good. For another, he wasn't half eccentric enough. Haynes suffered 18 glorious, exasperated years for Fulham, carpeting out the world's most sumptuous passes to a motley crew of single-jointed unappreciative nuts; a Brylcreemed Schweitzer among the pygmies.

Going down to Fulham on Saturdays when Chelsea were playing away was part of the corduroy scene in the 1950s and early 1960s. They were, as John Moynihan said in his joyous chronicle of the times *Soccer Syndrome*, 'a Saturday afternoon team, offering a feeling of animated recreation rather than solid professionalism ... a side of happy, sometimes comic, triers watched by garrulous actors, serious actors, pantomime players, band-leaders, stuntmen, starlets, tweeds, black leather, green leather, pink ankle-length knickers, baggy overcoats over armour-plated suede, cheroots between thumb and first finger'. They were days when a joint was a jazz cellar, LSD was a couple of Friday fivers, a trip was a moonlight bedsit flit – and dope, more often than not, was Bedford Jezzard's latest signing from the Hellenic League.

Liquid lunch, long walk alongside the cemetery past tiny, prim houses called 'Hazeldene' to marvel in wonder at Haynes, and to groan and wring our hands with him when the little men forgot to run on to – or even ran away from – those lancing, expansive long passes. He was too good for us, too; and really we turned up to love the fellows who forgot. What a litany: that loping trier, Maurice Cook, who could never quite fathom what Johnny was at: it was like Laurel and Hardy. Every resigned dismissive shrug by Haynes made Maurice simper with inferiority. And could it have been Maurice who ran out one afternoon with that high-stepping dressage I'll-show-'em swank – and promptly doubled-up with a hamstring injury and was stretchered off even before the kick-off?

Over the years they came and went. But mostly came and stayed: Arthur Stevens, grizzle-haired wingman, who'd be wound up at the start to run the full 90 minutes – but only in straight lines. 'They Also Swerve' we used to plain-chant at him. Arthur was the original subject of the legendary theatre-bill joke – 'This will run and run' – F Cashin, *Daily Sketch*. Then there was Jimmy ('Give it to the Rabbi') Hill – who, of course, we still know and love. Jim to be sure, scored many thousands of outstanding goals – but on double-checked reasoning he also muffed about 971 sitters (plus two half-chances). One now famous actor said on the terraces that Jim only patented that piratical growth on his chin because he thought it might make him play like Charlie Buchan (don't strain yourself working it out, corny humour's changed too).

And what about Killer Keetch? Blond and butch, fancy in his pointed Eyetie patents, but a devil in boots, no shinpad had an earthly. Horrors, we even loved him that afternoon he got stuck into Bobby Charlton. He'd be jeaned and conspicuously casual down the Portobello on a Saturday morning – after a casual canter down Rotten Row – sniffing out bargains for his junk shop (sorry, high class antiques emporium), outstanding headscarfed brunette snuggling into his armpit; at 2.30 (unless stated) he'd wickedly set about some unsuspecting and innocent No.9 shirt; by 6.30 he'd be downing a few swifties at the Queen's Elm, setting himself up for 10-ish and eyeball-to-eyeball confrontation with outstanding blonde over candles and white tablecloths of L'Ecu de France or some such gracious nosherie. (Why didn't Parky write a book on Keetch, for heaven's sake?)

Earlier, there was Eddie Lowe, the statutory baldy-ass wing half alleged to have lost all his hair overnight, through the shock of reading one of Walter Winterbottom's coaching pamphlets on peripheral vision. Or Jim Langley, bow-legged back with convict's crew-cut who, astonishingly, played for England and didn't let us down (though we were terribly worried for him) and then taught that tubby antelope George Cohen all he knew about overlapping and George became the best in the biz.

Our last great joy at Craven Cottage was the young Rodney. In a way Marsh was more of a genius then, simply because he hadn't yet realised it; only we nobodies were telling him and he, sheepish then, thought we were taking the mickey. For one season, just about the final one of those lovely winters, we'd go and watch Marsh in the reserves. Once, the goalkeeper was injured and Rodney excitedly bagged the polo-neck and gloves for himself, but when the first corner came over the dear nut tried to tip it over the top with a flying bicycle kick. Own goal.

Rodney, as a teenager, rated self-education. His bible was *Pears' Cyclopaedia*. He carried it with him everywhere and learned pages by heart. On away train trips George Cohen would solemnly have to hear him – 'Right, ready: World's Longest Rivers. Ready?' – and he'd close his eyes and recite 'Amazon 28 billion yards,' or whatever, 'Limpopo 19 billion ...' right down to the blooming Arno. When Rodney went deaf and almost had to pack up completely after he had nutted the crossbar with an almighty clang, it was sad, era's end – but it was also pure, undiluted Fulham.

But of all of them, most pure and undiluted Fulham was Tosh Chamberlain, winger supreme. It was Tosh who refused to get up after a hard tackle, saying he'd sit the game out 'until that bleeding ref apologises'. It was Tosh who once snapped the flag clean in two when he mistimed a corner kick (if the stick had carried we all bet that Maurice would have nodded it home). It was Tosh who once broke the ribs of his own goalkeeper, Tony Macedo, with a ferocious back-pass. Tosh was the only one who'd audibly swear back at Haynes – indeed once the referee, Mervyn Griffiths, Bethesda Chapel and all that, almost booked him for it.

The team's much slicker now. And there's an impressive grandstand covering the bank from where we used to watch the Boat Race – and invariably miss Fulham's one goal of the month. And they've got two ex-England captains now instead of one. But Tom Trinder, great stand-up comic, still sits down in the directors' box; and the thing to remember about all the foregoing list of loves is that, for all the memory of endearing incompetence, those sides were, more often than not, in the first division – or rather, they were *quite* often there, and once in, it must be said, they spent all their time frenziedly trying to stay there. (Someone once tried to get a new nickname going for them, the Fokker Wolves – 'bloody miraculous how they stay up'.) But they finished 10th in the first division once, in

1960. And they're no newts to FA Cup semi-finals. They lost in a replay in 1962, and in 1958 when Manchester United, rebuilt by Jimmy Murphy after the Munich crash, beat them by 5-3 with all the world praying for a Fulham defeat. The atmosphere was too much for Macedo, whose fine talent in goal had been instrumental with Haynes, in getting them that far, but on the day he flapped and fumbled like a schoolgirl.

By and by, and hopefully not relevantly, Fulham's present goalkeeper, Peter Mellor, has done more than most to get them to Hillsborough for the semi-final tomorrow; but he has been living with a reputation throughout his career as being prone to the most appalling gaffes – his colleagues cheerfully admit to calling him Teflon (non-stick) or Daffodil (he only comes out once a year). But he played a marvellous game in the sixth round, apparently, and if he catches everything tomorrow he will scotch the sniggering murmurs for ever. For himself. And for Fulham.

And if they do get to Wembley, unbelievable thought, the 1950s mob must have a reunion: laughter and memories. Who wouldn't pay a paypacket to hear J Haynes rollicking Maurice again? Or Tosh showing Les Barrett how to take a right-foot away, swinging corner from the left with the outside of his boot: 'The damn trouble is, lad, the damn flagpole makes it so damn difficult.'

Melanie's dad joins the red pilgrimage
25 May 1977

ROME: The high spot of our day was going to the airport to meet the Liverpool team in the late afternoon. Till then we were happy to fill in the time hanging around St Peter's making friendly Scouse jokes about the Pope and splashing boorishly around the fountains both to cool off in the sweltering heat as well as to annoy the thousands of tourists who, when they planned their pilgrimage, hadn't banked on having their Rosary upset by anthems and arias from the New Kirkby Hymnal.

The ancient old Bellini pillars that perfectly ring St Peter's Square have been witness to many a good and heartfelt tune over the centuries but none before, I warrant, that accompanied this sort of lyric:

We say to you Eyeties, give up your ice cream
Throw it away and come see our team
If you don't bring your Pope
We won't bring you our Queen
Just come and give 'cheers' to our beautiful team
We know you'll admit it's a side very rare
And if you need another cathedral
We've got one to spare.

That was sung by a clutch of about 30 red and white Koppites, aged from 12 to 50, yesterday lunchtime. And all day more have been arriving. So far there's scarce been a German to be seen. The Italians, meanwhile, continue with warnings about the terrors of the English soccer hooligan. We shall see. Certainly yesterday the whole temper of the visitors, while ultimately becoming a bit of a bore, never went further than that displayed by only slightly over-exuberant Blackpool day-trippers. The Romans can't see it like that, though. Apparently tomorrow the police at the Olympic Stadium promise more snapping dogs than Battersea could ever dream of. Over 30,000 tickets have been sold in Italy for the European Cup final and we are promised that, to a man, they will be supporting Borussia Mönchengladbach.

To the airport to meet the team. On the way, halfway up the Spanish Steps a young red was sleeping off the night before, but his banner still fluttered his message: Heighway Sells More Dummies than Mothercare.

And later, plans were being made to spend the evening encamped outside the players' hotel. Just to be near them. Young Joey Jones seems the new Kop favourite. 'D'you know,' said one fellow in the bar alongside St Mary Maggiore, 'he's been a Koppite since he was eight; he had LFC tattooed on his right arm when he was 13. You ask him to show you.'

In the same bar, two older men grew misty-eyed. They see tomorrow night as a culmination of Liverpool's 12-year run in European competitions. They had travelled to the 1965 European Cup semi-final against Inter-Milan. Liverpool had won the first leg easily but Milan had gone through after walloping them in the San Siro. They still remembered every detail. 'It was sheer bloody robbery. Their first goal came with a free kick, indirect, which they scored from direct. Their second was a blatant foul on poor Tommy Lawrence. But their third, Facchetti scored it, made me burst into tears. Never, ever, did that through the war. Do you know, truth, when I got back home I never spoke to my Judy for three weeks ... not one bleeding word for 21 whole days.'

Both of them had a great love for Liverpool's two present veterans, Smith and Callaghan. They were playing on that maudlin night in Milan. Both will be on duty tomorrow evening a dozen glorious years on. 'I only hope we can do it, not for me, not for any of us, but just for those two. Cally and old Smithy.' Not to mention, thought I, for his Judy.

Supporters paying their £100 and more range from retired dockers to Kirkby dole queuers to a pretty 25-year-old Lewisham schoolteacher. Three hopefuls are due to arrive tomorrow morning after driving all the way in a Bedford van they only bought last Thursday for £70.

One man, 20 years in exile, usually hitchhikes to Liverpool's games in England from his home in Brighton. He told me about his family: 'My first son's called Ian St John. When our daughter was being born, I was there in the waiting room at the Royal Sussex. Nurse comes out and says "It's a girl." I had me two bob ready. I telephoned Anfield. I said: "I know Shanks's old lady's called Nessie, but what's her baptismal name?" The secretary said she couldn't divulge it. The pips went so I said to the secretary: "What's your name then?" "Melanie," she says. So that's why my daughter's called Melanie isn't it?'

The following day Liverpool became the second English club to win the European Cup (after Manchester United) when they beat Borussia Mönchengladbach 3-1.

Bridge of sighs
17 October 1978

Don't worry, they said, about the English national team. They don't reflect the strength and skill of our national game. Go on any Saturday to the English first division to convince yourself that it remains the most competitive, the most attractive. It is still the envy of the world, they said. I took my biro to Stamford Bridge, but nobody asked for an adjective. Chelsea vs Middlesbrough, Young Lions vs Old Hands.

The first needless back pass to the goalkeeper came after 38 seconds. Thereafter the end-to-end ding-dong clash went something like this;

Needless back passes: Chelsea 10, Middlesbrough 16.
Aimless goalies' pass punts to centre circle: Chelsea 12, Mbo 23.
Inaccurate passes less than 22 yards: Chelsea 32, Mbo 18.
Accurate passes over 40 yards: Chelsea 4, Mbo 16.
Noticeable time wasting: Chelsea 10, Mbo 16.
Diagonal centres pumped hopefully into penalty area: Chelsea 33, Mbo 16.
Obviously considered ploys inside area: Chelsea 3, Mbo 6.
Free kicks pumped hopefully into area: Chelsea 14, Mbo 6.
Jersey pulling: Chelsea 14, Mbo 17.
Professional fouls: Chelsea 5, Mbo 9.
Amateurish fouls: Chelsea 10, Mbo 7.

Goalkeepers slightly extended (i.e., not fielding back passes or
    catching said diagonal centres): Bonetti 2, Platt 3.
Triers: Langley, Ashcroft.
Talent submerged in mediocrity: Wilkins, Souness.
Terrace songs without noticeable swear words: 1.
Terrace songs with noticeable swearwords: 6.
Crowd: 21,000.
Break-even crowd necessary to balance book: 28,000.
Duration: 92 minutes.
Result: Chelsea 0, Middlesbrough 0.
Quotes: Neal – 'We were worse against Derby.' Shellito – 'We
    don't believe in ourselves.'
Television title: MATCH OF THE DAY.

Wednesday night and Thursday morning
1 June 1979

MUNICH: Two years ago in Rome, the Liverpool celebrations
lasted into the early hours. The night they ran out of champagne,
da di, dai di, dai di ... !

I even seem to remember doing the Gay Gordons with Bob
Paisley. Well, you don't win the European Cup every day of the
week, do you? I took my tuxedo to Munich in expectation of
another red-eyed jingle-jangle Alka Seltzer job ...

Some hopes. Nottingham Forest do things differently. After they
had beaten Malmö in this year's final, Munich Airport reopened for
night flights to get rid of the supporters smartish. The players did a
lap of honour, and were off for a bedtime cup of cocoa at their wives'
hotel within the hour. They flew for home at crack of dawn. Brian
Clough, that rum manager, did his own imperial promenade round
the perimeter of the stadium and managed to be rude again to the
foreign press before resuming his own rudely-interrupted holiday in
Crete – and we left with a night to kill moping around looking for
late night pizza and chips. Ah well, you can't win them all.

But Forest did, and that's what really matters these days, especially if you're saving up to pay for a new grandstand and a new side. Though for the life of me I don't understand why, if you manage to do something truly outstanding in your life, you can't pause a moment to show that you are enjoying and savouring the moment.

It would have been nice, for instance, to bear witness as the full realisation of their triumph sank into the noddles of those who Clough in various ways has brought back from the dead. Such fellows as Frank Clark, approaching middle age, who was given the dreaded free transfer to oblivion by Newcastle four years ago, or Garry Birtles, who might so keenly have gone to Aldershot for £15,000 nine months ago, or Larry Lloyd, who has proved the exception to the rule that established first division players leave Liverpool at their peril, or to learn what John McGovern said to Archie Gemmell as he fought his way at the whistle to the substitute's bench to embrace his old Derby pal. It was McGovern's very first instinct.

Or even what Trevor Francis thought now he's in the charge of a man who intends to make him a genuine all-round super footballer, not just a glamourguts pontificating over 10 acolytes (apparently Francis desperately wanted Coventry to cough up the £1 million for him, until Ron Greenwood insisted that Clough and Forest would make him an infinitely better international player). The packed press conference ('My God, it's like being on trial' – Clough) pleaded with the manager to send up Francis for interview. Not only that, but he would send four players, said the manager. In came Woodcock, Anderson, Birtles and Bowyer. No Francis; Clough's sides have no high priests. But there's no disputing Clough's sides are teams.

It takes a team to make a team. Clough and Taylor have been together now for 21 years, more than half Clough's life. They met when Taylor was transferred from Coventry to be Middlesbrough's first team goalkeeper, and immediately twigged that a raw reserve, just out of National Service, was making his palms sting something terrible during practice. Taylor was the only person who persuaded the young centre forward that he had a future. Clough usually asked for a transfer every other day: on every other day Taylor would calm him down.

When Clough went to Hartlepool as manager 14 years ago, bells ringing for the first time, he went cap in hand to pubs and clubs to raise the money to persuade the forgotten manager of faraway Burton Albion to become his assistant. That man was Peter Taylor. They did split up once. Clough went to Leeds too soon. Taylor stayed at Brighton. Three years ago I was in Southampton to report the humdrum second division game against Forest. Aye-aye, I thought, why was Peter Taylor waiting at the railway station to greet Clough? I dismissed the possibility of a little scoop by thinking it was just a lunch-time drink between old friends. Taylor rejoined Clough a fortnight later. Since when the Notts nuts have won promotion, the championship, two league cups – and now the grandest prize of all.

It has been an outstanding 36 months. The Nottingham public are still doped and dazed by it (all this and Derek Randall, too!) More than 20,000 made the journey to Munich. Hours after the game it obviously still had not sunk in as little knots of red-decked stragglers shuffled around the city looking for all the world like those Alan Sillitoe Notthingham anti-heroes of the 60s, glaze-eyed because they'd just heard their girlfriend's got pregnant and the only satisfactory cure was a night on the beer, being sick behind the sofa, and creeping contentedly and with a burp out the back door. Wednesday night and Thursday morning.

I saw a little troop of them in the Odeonsplatz yesterday. Trying to be funny by goose-stepping in front of little grey-haired old ladies and doing the stiff-armed Heil Hitler statute. But then, I thought, nor had Brian Clough been amusing when he turned up over an hour late for his press conference on Tuesday and blamed his German driver for losing the way. 'No wonder you guys lost the war,' he grated at his hosts. 'Doubtless this chap was head of your transport command.'

It was meant to raise a laugh. It didn't. But you've got to hand it to Forest's Führer. As I say, he's a rum emperor. But an emperor, nevertheless.

The day the fan trampled the flag
11 September 1981

OSLO: The Norwegians tidied up quickly the morning after the night before. Some 30 lardy-faced visiting laddoes had spent the night in the cells and were due to appear in court yesterday afternoon – but before midday the magistrate decided to press no charges and sent them back pronto. 'Why should they be a burden on our tax-payers?' he asked.

One policeman was still in hospital after being hit on the head, but in fact the day had been less bad than any English league match. The fans had filed away from the ground in resigned and sullen groups. They knew this England team had not remotely deserved to win, not remotely deserved even their support. Simply, one felt they had been humiliated by the lamentable performance of their hollow heroes, whose names will nevertheless probably remain as big as their bank balances.

You did not dare look poor Ron Greenwood in the eye. The bereaved uncle. There was one defiant tableau in grotesque mime when, during Greenwood's press conference after the match in the gymnasium below the little grandstand, a teenager was seen through the long windows to unfurl the Union Jack blanket from his shoulders, throw it to the ground and repeatedly stamp on it while mouthing an obscenity through the plate glass like the man gone berserk in the Flora margarine TV ads.

The players looked suitably sheepish for a bit, then they showered and changed and most of them settled down for a few drinks and a few in-jokes in the hotel nightclub. 'Ah well, you win some, you lose some. What's your poison, mate?' At the time you are inclined to say 'Arsenic'. It's all water under the bridge, innit?

And they would be home soon, snug in the bosom of their clubs – and there was an important match coming up this Saturday, wasn't there? You fancied they felt it would not take long to forget England's match in Oslo in 1981, the night England lost a World Cup qualifier 2-1 to Norway. Norway!

They are wrong. It will take an awful long time. I know hindsight is easy, but my mind keeps pulling me back to Tuesday morning's training session, when half of it was conducted by the team's business agent, the bewhiskered, sharp-eyed, diminutive Harry Swales. He orchestrated the photocall for the adverts that were going to make them lovely money out of the World Cup. Not a ball was kicked or a toe was touched till the bouffant hair-styles and smiles of 'cheese!' were just-so for the photographer and Harry announced he was satisfied. Somebody wondered yesterday if a World Cup loss was tax-deductible.

You wake in the morning and, thank heavens, what you recall most is the gleeful shrillness of the beautifully mannered Norwegian crowd as they revelled in the victory. Dammit, you are pleased that you are so delighted still for them. At the end I had scurried off down the tunnel with the English team. They were followed by the solemn-faced, slow-marching military band.

As soon as they were in the tunnel and out of vision the bandsmen put down their bugles and drums, took off their frowns and twirled their feather hats – and embraced each other with laughter and tears of joy – they had beaten England!

And if England's overblown superstars are not at the 1982 World Cup, well having slept on it, so what, who really cares? Business agents and publishers and TV moguls? Well, to them this lovely game is actually a different game, isn't it? After breakfast in private the snappily-dressed pride of England blearily climbed into the airport bus past the newspaper placards that said 'Miracle!' in Norwegian and 'Tragedy' in English.

And off they went into the Scandinavian-grey day, back to fame and fortune and adulation, and the stern pine forests looked down as they drove past all the little wooden houses freshly painted in white and ochre and rusty red where life was already getting back to normal the morning after the famous night they beat the English at football for the first time.

Modern-day curse of plastic footballs
18 April 1983

The abiding impression that Bill Nicholson gave you over the years was one of dourness – honest, unapproachable Yorkshire dourness. In 17 years he built and dismantled three fine, expressive, articulate and singular football sides at Tottenham Hotspur, yet you seldom saw a smile.

Nicholson retired eight seasons ago and is now the club's star scout. He never had a contract and on Sunday afternoon Spurs' testimonial match for him against West Ham will be prefaced by an exhibition game between some of his golden oldies, the legendary likes of Greaves and Jones and Gilzean and Blanchflower.

The Yorkshire gravity discouraged any sort of flippant rapport. Win or lose, his reaction always seemed to be pouting and pudgy deadpan as the years rolled by. The few stories that seeped out were regurgitated down the grapevine: that he worked so assiduously that he wept at his daughter's wedding – 'I never saw her grow up'; that he didn't tell his wife for days that he had been promoted from trainer to manager in 1958; that he lived in the same tiny terrace house next to the ground that was loaned to him by the club in his playing days; that he cried off from his second England appearance because he felt his priority duty was to get fit not for his country but for Tottenham who paid his wages.

In fact and reality, Bill Nicholson is not at all in the gruff image he portrayed in those interminable monosyllabic interviews he put us all through for all those seasons after the match in

Tottenham's dreary, drizzled-on car park. 'Well, at least it was a private car park!' he said, laughing fit to bust. In retirement he is hale and healthy and glistening in the pink.

He puts the whole decline of soccer today down to one thing – the lack of a little rubber ball. His dad was a driver of a horse-drawn cab that clopped along the front at Scarborough. Baby Bill would follow him, dribbling his little rubber ball. Not a tennis ball, you understand, but a rubber, sorbo job that bounced and needed a delicate touch to control.

And when he joined Tottenham for £2 a week in 1935 the only time in two years that apprentices would have a game, except for an hour on Tuesdays and Thursdays, was with their little rubber ball under the stands when they had finished painting the girders. 'The biggest setback to our game – and I'm not joking – has been the mass manufacture for children of plastic footballs,' he says. 'You're not going to learn the skills unless you learn them from birth with a little rubber ball against a wall.'

'Matthew and Finney had a little rubber ball. So did I. A whole encyclopaedia of skills can be learned with a little rubber ball against a wall. My grandsons won't dream of playing unless they have one of these great big plastic jobs. Come to think of it, the nearest my seven-year-old grandson gets to a football is on his computer.

'Football to him is nothing to do with a little rubber ball, it is a computerised game, programmed for 16 leading teams; he can buy himself players and each one has a predetermined skill factor. It's just numbers to him but he cries his eyes out when his team gets beat.'

Bill reckons he had the best times. 'After the war for a decade or two must have been the best period of all for a player and a manager. I remember even when we were in the second division they'd have to close the gates for matches. What an atmosphere!

'The game has become tense and bound with fears. Everyone's trying to catch sparrows. Arthur Rowe told me: "The simple gospel: make it plain and accurate and quick – especially quick."

First-time passing is the secret; it doesn't look it but it is the greatest skill still. And then you've got to have vision. I still say to every player today, "When not in possession get into position." No question about it, the man without the ball makes the play.

'Next to Tottenham, Liverpool have been my favourite side. They too, have the simple philosophy.' It all stems from learning with that obsolete but bouncy little ball.

Why Uncle Roy is drawing a veil
30 January 1988

Just like the old days, it's a cup tie Saturday in the Potteries. Us versus Them, or, as we are allowed to say on these occasions, minnows and giants. Port Vale versus Tottenham Hotspur, the people against the gentry. Such matches were made for men called Sproson to get stuck in and do what a man has to do.

Phil Sproson, six-foot bulwark of Port Vale's defence today against the strolling players of Spurs, is a one-club man, answering over 400 league and cup calls to the colours. But that's not half the matches his Uncle Roy managed in a playing career that, almost unbelievably, spanned 1950 to 1971.

While the passionate oohs and aahs and cheers and sighs this afternoon swirl all around nephew Phil in the muddy slop and slap and siege of the penalty area, some of them will be carried down on the chill winds from the bleak ridge of Burslem's Vale Park and be heard most certainly by Uncle Roy as he administers one of his three newsagent's shops down the hill. Roy Sproson will pretend not to hear, intimating in his affable, bluff and comradely manner that he doesn't give a fig for football any more.

When Roy Sproson was sacked as Port Vale's manager after serving the club, man and boy, for 25 years, he vowed never to set foot in the place again, never even to glance up at the tumbledown old arena as he passes it time and again each day. He has kept his resolution. This afternoon it will be tested severely, I fancy. Roy is

in his greying middle-50s now, still a strapping man, as successful
in business as he was down the years in his own half of a football
field – more so, for when he drove away from Vale Park for the
last time it was in a Cortina. Now he cruises about in a Mercedes.

'I never even looked back in the driving mirror. I'd worked
there a quarter of a century. I've never set foot in the place from
that day to this, and never will. I just can't, don't know why really.
Other than Phil, I couldn't even tell you this Saturday's team.

'A manager can smell the end of his time, you know. The whole
club reeks with an imminent sacking. Not that they actually say
"you're bloody fired". It's all innuendo and muttering, you know,
"things not going too well are they?". But you know they're
after your blood and if truth was told you already had your bags
packed for weeks.'

C'mon, surely when you get up at five o'clock for the papers
this Saturday morning, you'll make your cup of tea, look at the
weather and think 'a good day for the Cup, eh?' and just get a
bit misty-eyed and the old brain box will shuffle through a few
of the memories?

'No, I won't.'

Bet you will.

'I won't, promise.'

I don't believe you, not even 1954 when Vale got to the
semi-final?

'No, all behind me now, that.'

Get away with you, fourth round of the Cup, 34 years ago to
the very Saturday. Vale vs cup-holders Blackpool, all the stars and
Stan Matthews back at the Potteries?

The grin gets broader. 'Oh yes, OK, if you force me, I can't
forget that.'

The eyes glaze over. 'I was marking Ernie Taylor. No disrespect,
but he was arrogant, jibing at me all through. When we looked
like winning, I started getting back at him, "Come and watch me
in the next round, Mr Taylor." I was only a cocky kid then. At the

end, Taylor just walked off, wouldn't shake hands. Stanley took it very well though, but I bet he was mad inside.'

When he was a sprog at Oakhill School before the war, Roy used to wait every day at the bus stop at Trent Vale for a sight of his hero going to Stoke for training. Once Matthews had got on the bus, the boy would hare up to school. When he grew up he played against him in the cup tie against Blackpool.

'Stan was even more of a genius close to. I fancied myself as a tackler. Suddenly, he's coming at me down the touchline, jockeying, shimmying, his classic situation. Lo and behold he goes and shoves the ball too far in front of him: he's given it me. I smile to myself and think "watch this, folks, I'm bloody taking the ball off Matthews."

'Then bloody hell, unbelievable. Just as my toe was an eighth of an inch from the ball, he's found another gear, two ruddy gears, and his toe comes and sniffs it past me and he's skipping over my sliding leg and is away. I didn't just think I had him, I knew I had him – and now here I was flat on my backside realising genius is really genius, and the crowd all laughing.'

We were in one of his shops at Cobridge. A few hundred yards away is Arnold Bennett's old house in Waterloo Road. A few doors along is a mosque. Vale Park and its pylons look damply forlorn, plucking up courage for Saturday. Outside sit the sponsored cars emblazoned with the players' names. Phil is now the big man at the back. Twenty years ago or so, he first went to watch his uncle play.

'It was against Brentford. I was so proud of him. Nobody believed he was my uncle till he came and tapped me on the head to prove it at the end. No, it's no matter he doesn't watch us now, he gives me advice whenever I've needed it.'

The home dressing-room is friendly: comfortable chairs and a carpet even. The visitors' room is like a barn. Cheerless, cold tiles, a slim bench round the walls, and one large ancient bathtub. 'This room's our secret weapon for Spurs,' says Phil, 'not forgetting their luke-warm pot of tea for half-time.'

His uncle chortles when I pass on the tactic. 'With any luck, Spurs might be in for a culture shock: out of their stockbroker houses and warm snug luxury coach – straight into that huge cold room. There are omens too this week from that Blackpool match. It has rained all week, and our rain can chill the marrow.

'It chilled Blackpool. We'd spent days drying out the pitch with coal sacks, wringing them with mangles, even shovelling water off, then forking and rolling so it looked quite reasonable till you trod on it and you'd sink in well over the top of your boots. Might be like that this Saturday.

'Then we'd soaked the leather ball in water for 24 hours – filling one of those screw-lid buckets, with warm water down into it for a day. After lunch on Saturday, out it comes, dry off the surface water, and then a coat of dubbin so it looked all right. But it weighed more than a canon-ball. Then for the kick-in we gave Blackpool a few old balls, dry and light and pumped up like balloons. After that they could hardly kick the match ball off the deck.'

So there you are, Roy, you see it took me no time to get you back in the mood for football?

He grins some more and nods acknowledgement. 'Phil's a good stopper, more defensive than me perhaps, I started off as a wing half of course, a left-sider who could run all day. People complain about the players today, but they're all right, pretty good. But no, you still won't get me up there even to see that Waddle or Ardiles. Can't really explain why, but I'll never go again.

'It was already a young man's game when I packed up at 41. But it had been a real good life. I came out of National Service and was suddenly earning £8 a week and £4 more in the summers. That was more than my brother, Phil's dad, was getting as a skilled engineer.'

He played 761 league games. Only beaten narrowly by Trollope of Swindon, (770), and Dickinson (764) of Portsmouth. 'Might have beaten them: one season I was off injured for 21 games.' At

41 he tossed his muddy kit into the laundry skip and tried life in a collar and tie as the manager. 'Any manager in football with a streak of reality or reason knows that sooner or later he's going to be crucified.

'I couldn't have been one of those blokes, good friends of mine too, you see at these annual get-togethers who just can't leave football alone. It's in their bloodstream like inky fingers are on newsagents' hands, and they scrimp and save for jobs scouting on wet Wednesdays in the Cheshire League and go round touching forelocks and cringing in front of directors. It's sad and pathetic, and there's an awful lot of them about, I'm afraid.'

He will be up at five this morning and, OK, if you press him he might have a squint to see what the papers say about Port Vale's chances. By 9.30 he will be back home till the afternoon. Then, around four o'clock, he'll be driving back to organise the evening rush.

Won't he even glance up at the windswept paddock?

'I doubt it.'

Not even switch on the radio for the half-time score?

'Yes I suppose I will, blast it,' and he laughs at himself for his cussedness.

'Deep down, I really hope they do OK. I can't explain really why I couldn't bring myself to go, but like Arnold Bennett himself said somewhere, didn't he, "most things are to do with nothing, but in its way football is to do with everything."'

Vale beat Spurs 2-1 and then lost to Watford only after a replay. It was the year Wimbledon beat Liverpool in the final. Roy Sproson died in 1997, aged just 66. There is now a Roy Sproson Way by the stadium, and a statue. 'The very spirit of Port Vale ran through this unique man,' says the inscription.

The debt football owes to Jimmy Hill
15 January 2001

'Wasn't it Queen Mary Tudor who had "Calais 1558" written on her heart?' asks Jimmy Hill. 'Well, when they finally open me up, they'll find "Ministry of Labour, January 18, 1961" carved on mine.'

The good old boy, 73 this summer, still juts his anteater's jaw at you to emphasise every earnest point and opinion – which flow in torrents – and, after each one, he breaks into the merry chortles that have always engagingly speckled his sporting progress from £7-a-week Brentford inside forward to broadcasting eminence.

On the steps of the ministry that Wednesday evening 40 years ago, in time to be lead story for the BBC Home Service's seven o'clock Radio Newsreel, the bearded young chairman of the Professional Footballers' Association announced that the footballers of England would call off their strike, having successfully won the abolition of the iniquitous maximum wage of £20 a week (£17 in the summer).

Hill made the patriarchal, cigar-chewing football league president Joe Richards shake hands with him – as well as the Minister of Labour, John Hare, and the chairman of the TUC, Ted Hill – and in no time the pictures of the workers' triumph were circling the world. Of course, it was not actually as simple as that. The distraught league management committee and its reactionary and apoplectic club chairmen spent the following months prevaricating and repatching the agreement, hedging their bets and going back on their word – but to all intents the slim, athletic (and unlikely) luminary of that cold January evening remained the working-class hero, returning to Fulham to be cheered every time he touched the ball.

By the start of the following season, even the combative league secretary Alan Hardaker was telling his remaining diehard chairmen to pipe down, for they had effectively been routed by Hill and the PFA's impressive realist of a secretary, Cliff Lloyd.

Hardaker admitted that Hill's public relations skills had swung the debate decisively a week before that 18 January meeting – and triggered the involvement of a government fearful of having an electorate with no pools coupons to fill in.

With 344 players from the northern clubs packing the ballroom at Manchester's Grand Hotel, Hill made a stirring call for industrial action on Saturday 21 January. Then, on the suggestion of the hawkish Blackburn winger and later Scotland manager, Ally MacLeod, he invited in around 50 waiting journalists to hear him demand: 'Is there any man in this room not prepared to strike on Saturday week?'

Remembers Hill, 40 years on: 'The unanimous NO could have come from the Kop at its loudest.' Rheumy eyes bright in reverie of his militant past, the slippered septuagenarian – four wives, five children, double-figures in grandchildren – is now an upright denizen of Surrey's stockbroker belt. He seems hardly to believe it himself.

'I was just a kid really. Of course, I was keen on working-class rights, but I wasn't really what you'd call a political animal. At Brentford I had been collecting the PFA's weekly subs, and when they transferred me to Fulham it coincided with their PFA rep Norman Smith giving up the game. So I continued collecting the subs. The only other thing you were expected to do was try and get to the AGM in the summer.

'The first one I attended was in 1956 and for some reason I found myself defending the rather loose-cannon methods of our then chairman, Jimmy Guthrie of Portsmouth. "If our opponents can't stand him he must be doing something right," I said. So as a penalty for not keeping my big trap shut, they promptly elected me to the eight-man committee of management.' Within a year, Guthrie had gone and Fulham's Hill was elected PFA chairman.

'I can safely say those extraordinary four years, 1957 to 1961, irrevocably changed my life. Suddenly I was having to argue my case in different parliaments, deal with the media as well as my fellow men in the most delicate matters. A university degree in politics and philosophy couldn't have been more rewarding; the PFA simply gave me a crash course in life and maturity.

'League football had been set in its feudal time warp. January 18 was the watershed, but even in their shellshock the league and its chairmen looked to overturn the agreement. They had spent generations looking down their noses at players and now, even at that meeting at the ministry, they presumed to treat us as inferior beings. Being totally in charge of us was ingrained into their culture. And to find me, not a venerable ex-player but a lad who was still actually playing for a club they controlled, must have been anathema to them.'

Not that the young founder of the feast was able to cash in on the PFA's triumph. Fulham's chairman was the comedian Tommy Trinder, who, as Hill's battles swirled around that winter, announced: 'Haynes is an entertainer like I am, and if the maximum wage is ever abolished, I will pay him what he is worth, which is £100 a week.'

The nation gasped – and, of course, after 18 January, Trinder had to fork out. From his home in Scotland, Haynes remembers with a strained smile: 'It was just a Trinder publicity stunt really, but when Jimmy had led the troops to victory, Trinder was lumbered. I was into his office with my pen and solicitor's sheet of paper, and a couple of journalists outside, before Trinder could gulp. He had to sign, but I suppose he had the last laugh because I may have been the first £100-a-week player but I played for Fulham another eight years and never got another rise. I was on £100 a week till I packed up.'

Hill stayed on £18 a week, not even the maximum. He did not play long enough even to negotiate a new contract that September. He had injured his right knee at Luton in January 1960 – when Fulham, lying second in the first division, had been leading 1-0. 'No substitutes then, and we lost 4-1. We finished tenth, Fulham's highest ever league position. And when my knee was patched up and after everything, I was happily back in the first team. But it was only going to be a matter of time.'

On 5 March 1961, the *Sunday Times* reported Fulham's 1-0 defeat against Everton: 'Brightest spot of the match was the effort of the bearded Hill. Tireless and covering acres of ground, he never gave up till two minutes from the end, trying to force an equaliser, he received a nasty knock.'

The 'knock' was a severely torn cartilage in the same knee. It was his last game as a professional. Fulham claimed £10,000 insurance compensation on his injury – and kept it – so, seeing as he had been bought from Brentford for £5,000 eight years before, the club made a £5,000 profit on Hill's 277 matches and 41 goals.

The football-mad Boys' Brigade cornet player from Balham, whose first job at 16 had been as a clerk for the London & Lancs insurance company, now prepared for an apprenticeship as a new-fangled 'sports agent' with the Bagenal Harvey organisation. That September, however, the clients, the England cricketer Jim Laker, introduced Hill to the chairman of third division sluggards Coventry City, Derrick Robins – who suggested lunch the next day.

Hill steered Coventry to the first division before, in 1967, becoming head of sport for London Weekend Television. Six years later, he was headhunted by the BBC, where he continued to point his chin at the nation and vibrantly pontificate on all matters football for more than a quarter of a century until the end of the 1998 World Cup when (like David Coleman) his contract expired and he left with not so much as a note of thanks, private or public. 'Perhaps they lost my address,' he says, 'but more likely, in terms of manners and common decency, the BBC hierarchy needs some serious tutoring.'

Sky Sports now employs the spritely ancient – he has given up riding to hounds but still plays a mean three-setter at tennis – and on Wednesday he can be seen chewing over his great political triumph. Perhaps Sky has located that sepia reel of film from the spring of 1961 of Hill's deadly adversary, Hardaker, indulging in his hobby, fishing for shark off the Cornish coast at Looe. He hauls in a hundred-pounder and the boatman gives the poor beast a vicious knobkerrie clout. 'Hit it again,' demands Hardaker. 'It's got a chin like Jimmy Hill.'

He chuckles at that. 'Hardaker was a tough opponent, all right. I took him out to supper a few years later and he reckoned they would have won easily if only his bosses had offered a deal of, say, a £10 rise and set a new maximum wage at £30. As it was, they let loose a free-for-all.

'Not that I've ever changed my beliefs. The battle we fought was for a player to be free to negotiate for what he was worth with no restrictions. That holds good in 2001, and is nothing to do with the David Beckhams of this world being overpaid – he justifies, earns and deserves his money because a super-wealthy club like Manchester United can happily afford him.

'The stupidity which is rife is that outside the top eight or 10 ultra-rich clubs, there are others demanding, and getting, ludicrous salaries when the clubs simply cannot afford them. Even some third division players are on £1,000 a week. For their clubs and directors that just means guaranteeing bank loans and consequent debt, debt, debt. Crazy.

'And then, doing their utmost, they get spat on by the fans for not spending more. I've been a director and chairman of three good, modest clubs – Coventry, Charlton and Fulham – and the abuse you get can be cruel and shameful. I've had a wonderful life, and wouldn't change a moment of it professionally – except that I should never have become a director.'

Nice: the old gamekeeper knows, deep down, he should never have jumped the fence; that he should have remained the militant poacher of his youth.

4

THE PROSPECT FROM THE SEVENTH

The bear with a sore head
11 July 1977

By absolute fluke, he actually sat next to me in the first of yesterday's early morning shuttle flights out of Glasgow. It was a jam-packed scrum; every man, woman and child for themselves. His son, Steve, was marooned in the last spare seat a couple of rows back; his wife, Barbara, was three rows up and immediately game for a chinwag with an unknown neighbour.

The big fellow didn't want to talk about it much. He had awakened the morning after the final round more disappointed than he had gone to sleep. 'Tom just played better ... yep, I think he's really getting it now ... but no, you cannot measure "greatness" in a sportsman till he figures a lot in the records – it's not technique or guts or flair, "greatness" can only have one yardstick and that's to be always winning, then winning some more. You can have a classic swing or the best competitive nature, but nobody remembers you if you haven't won anything, if you aren't in the records ...

'Now, will you excuse me, please, I must try to finish my book.' He said he would have rather gone to sleep, but he dug into his battered executive's case and flicked through the paperback *The Rhinemann Exchange* to find his place from last night in bed at the Turnberry Hotel. He was into it at once. About 60 pages to go.

The back cover screamed out the unattributed reviews ... 'All Intense Action ... Intriguing Suspense ... Nerve-Wrenching

International Thriller' – and no fellow hack could surely think of a better blurb for the drama that he himself had played out 15 hours before. Jack Nicklaus escaped into his book. Escaped from the day before. And I relaxed into awe.

In the row ahead of us three Scotsmen, oblivious, read their Sunday sports pages. One said WATSON MAKES HIS DREAM REALITY. Another was WATSON MUZZLES THE BEAR. The third JACK BLOWS UP AGAIN. He had looked at them, but hadn't seemed to read them. So he got into the book. About us, on this bleary pyjama flight, were men who had lost far more badly than Nicklaus. Though every one of them knew that he was the only loser. Eleven strokes ahead of the rest of the field, finishing with 65 and 66 but a shot behind a man who hit two 65s.

We crossed the Pennines ... then Manchester ... ahead of us was bleary Ballesteros, another doe-eyed youngster who snoozed the flight through. Mrs Nicklaus chattered charmingly on ... incidentally she's now a celebrity too. She does TV commercials, one for bicycles and another, nationwide, for Magic Chef ovens – 'Hi, I'm Barbara Nicklaus. I'm Magic. Buy me.'

And Mr Nicklaus read on. By London and seatbelts, he had 20 pages left. He said he was spellbound. I said *we* were, yesterday. That's the way it goes, he shrugged. 'I've never remembered shooting 65, 66 to finish and still losing. Tom played better that's all. He really did ... Yes, I'm still disappointed. Up to 17, I thought I was in, but apparently Tom was on heat. He said to his caddie "we've got him now" even before the last two holes. And he did get me.'

He made a generous and noble speech at the prizegiving. Eleven years ago he had won his first Open at Muirfield. He said then, 'Excuse me, friends, do you mind if I weep? You see, I just want to enjoy this moment.' And I know now he was near to tears on Saturday.

But a year later ...

Time for pandemonium, pomp and pride
17 July 1978

The end of the Open – once television has so suddenly left the high drama for the higher eyebrows and low camp of Angie's News – is touchingly poignant. Talking of tents, the hired heavies muscle in on every marquee the moment the final putt pops in.

All around might be pandemonium – scaffolding scattered, guys pulling guy ropes – but at the very nub of the thing is enacted the annual little scene in front of the clubhouse that brings timeless history into bold relief. The old silver jug is handed across to the victor ludorum with all the garden-party formality and mayoral pomp of a church fete in a snooty parish. The secretary looks fraught; the committee straightens its collective tie; there is lots of throat-clearing and reading of notes with shaky hand. And, of course, the microphone amplifier wheezes and whistles like bad sci-fi title music. I love it.

Saturday's climax, for sheer excitement, was not to compare with last year. Then, at Turnberry, everybody's cockles were drained by the consuming drama of the finish. This time, 1977's gracious and much-loved loser was 1978's gracious and much-loved winner. The big fellow had walked in solo state up the 18th garlanded with affection like an emperor home from a three-year war. The cheers rose so thick as to make a tangible proscenium over the vast open-air theatre. 'I understand their feelings for me,' said Nicklaus, 'and they know my feelings for them. They know my feelings for golf, for British golf, for the history of the game.'

After the Lord Mayor's show and all that ... Jack had to wait for Oostie and Watson to finish. I squashed my nose to the window of the scorer's hut. It was like a country solicitor's office in there – two precisely dressed and well-spoken clerks talking in a whisper. The emperor and his young adversary from New Zealand, Simon Owen, had to check their cards.

They slumped for fully five minutes alongside each other like students poring over an exam paper. The youngster studied his card, hole by hole, with biro poised. The new champion simply put his head in his hands and stared through a gap in his fingers at nothing. He was spent. He had done it. He was elated more than we can imagine, I fancy. At last he wrenched his hands away and stared at the plyboard wall about 12 inches from his dazed head at the wonder of it all. Suddenly, those blue Teuton eyes re-focused. He smiled a private little smile to himself before turning an expansive public one to Mr Marker as he signed the card and went out again, worldly-wise, to embrace first his wife, then the world.

Nicklaus had brought over an entourage of 57 family and friends to stay at a posh hotel. But he clapped like crazy when Peter McEvoy, an articled clerk from Warwickshire, was called up for the amateur's prize. McEvoy had been living the week in a borrowed caravan in a nearby car park.

Let's hear it for the still-bright Butten Boys
4 April 1988

Winter rules end here. All the world's golfers have Georgia on their mind this week, when green is the colour and the scent of azaleas and jacaranda seems to seep via satellite from Augusta to our late-night television screens. And, who knows, they might yet be raising a glass to the first British winner of the Masters. It would be the culmination of a plan lasting a quarter of a century.

In 1963, Ernest Butten, a wealthy London businessman and all-round vim merchant who loved golf, found himself so completely cheesed off at his native golfers' meekness in tournament play that he hand-picked a clutch of likely apprentices and set them up in a strict boarding school at stately Sundbridge Park with the express aim of winning a major or two within at least four years.

The engaging, get-up-and-go Butten was convinced that the youth of England had become milksops on account of, as he put it, 'lack of opportunity, know-how and effort', not to mention decent diet, manners, morale or anything like strong and manly wrists. He also reckoned that if you practised a 12-foot putt long enough you would eventually hole every one with your eyes shut, and ergo take the two Opens and Masters for year after year after year.

A quarter of a century ago this month, Butten assembled his fortunate corps of youthful 'cor-blimey'. Not that any won a major, but they have all been a fair credit to the game, and will all be back for the reunion next week – Tommy Horton, Brian Barnes and Mike Ingham leading in Jim McAlister (Haggs Castle), Sandy Wilson (Tytherington), Iain Clark (Ponteland), Tony Martin (Horsenden), and Alan Ibberson, the only one forced to give up the game, on account of two wonky ankles, and who is now mine host of the Salisbury Arms in Cambridge.

In 1963 the last Brit to have won an Open was Max Faulkner (in 1951), so Butten hired him as 'headmaster'. Also on the payroll were two dieticians, a weight-training specialist, an orthopaedic surgeon and senior coaches to the British Olympic team. Tommy Horton recalls: 'We even had dentists and eye surgeons. The body-builder, Oscar Heidenstam, taught us how to lift weights and do circuit training. We learned how to develop self-confidence, and mental concentration, and even how to speak in public. There never was a happier team of professional sportsmen. I look back on those days with great affection and pride.'

Butten paid them £20 a week, £5 extra for Ibberson, who was married. 'It was,' agrees Ibberson, 'a tremendously rewarding scheme. Every one of us tried very, very hard to live up to Mr Butten's ideas, and the lads simply gave everything he asked for. I can't wait to see them all again at the reunion.'

Ibberson says the game is now out of his system – 'I only miss it when I see the lads on TV or in the papers' – but he recalls his ankle injury as if it was yesterday. 'Little Aston, that par five, what is it, 12th or 13th? Anyway, the one with water up the left-hand side. I was pitching to the green; as I struck the ball I fell backwards, my ankle crumpled; as I hit the ground, so my ball slewed off into the water. Lost ball, lost ankle ...'

Ibberson says he remains 'immensely grateful' for Butten's regime, 'especially when I see some of our ragamuffin sportsmen today'. Butten's written orders – 'to be studied at least once a week' – included the following:

> DRESS: another factor in personal impact. On-course Kit: white sweater and shirt, navy blue trousers, navy blue or black socks, black shoes, hair neat and tidy, all items clean and neat i.e. shoes polished, trousers pressed. Each member of team to have enough clothing in first week to eliminate necessity to have clothes laundered; in second week one team member will be responsible for laundry, programming one afternoon when he will collect dirty clothes, and take them to the dry cleaner or laundrette, whichever is available and collect them at prescribed time.

Butten's widow, Jacqui, 80 next birthday and still bubbly, recalls one tournament when she joined the team for breakfast. 'Young Brian didn't stand up when I arrived at the table. Ooh, Mr B tore him off such a strip, I'll never forget it. Poor Brian! But Mr B was extremely fussy about that sort of thing, you know.' She still corresponds regularly with 'my boys', and will be guest of honour next Tuesday.

On rising, each boy would be given half-a-glass of orange juice, plus two teaspoons of glucose. He would then have to go through prescribed 'technique checks':

a) Check Grip in mirror and carry out following exercises for grip – 10 repetitions of shaft flexion exercises; 10 repetitions of grip tension exercises;
b) Check Stance in mirror, feet, legs, knees, hips, arms, shoulders, head – 10 repetitions of taking up stance.

c) Carry out Swing Components individually without club to 1-2 rhythm, i.e. correct foot and hip action x10; shoulder turn, hands on hips with club behind shoulders x10.

BREAKFAST, if pre-tournament play, will consist of only: Muesli, if like, otherwise porridge, plus milk and sugar; 1 egg, 2 pieces of crisp toast or wholemeal bread, 1 tea or coffee with milk, 1 Multivitamin Perihemin tablet ... and so on through the day, from 'mid-morning Refreshment, 2-3 wheatmeal-type biscuits' to 'Afternoon Refreshment, 'preferably chocolate biscuit unless considered too sickly', up to One multivitamin capsule, 7 Heptuna Plus, with Dinner Daily', and 'Fortified Milk Drink with Sweet Biscuits to help boys sleep.'

Through the day, a number of cups of 'Protein Food' were served, but there was a total ban on 'Ice Cold Drinks', which 'should NEVER be taken, otherwise Gastric Ulcers may result.'

... and so on ... sleep'. Through the day ... result.'

But the boys loved it. 'It was such an opportunity. We revelled in it,' said Ibberson. 'It is almost impossible to express the competitive spirit and sheer thrill of opportunity given us handful of working laddoes. We really felt we could take on the world, and Mr Butten and Max Faulkner really made us believe we could win.'

In 1967, Butten's scheme ended, his Boys sent out into the world to make their own way. He had, in the earlyish 1960s, also approached another young apprentice, little Anthony Jacklin, and though the two became good friends in time, the young man declined Butten's offer to enrol at his 'school', saying 'I think I'm too much of a loner, sir.' In 1969, of course, that same stocky little loner from Scunthorpe won the US Open by more shots than anyone had managed before, and in 1970 he hoisted Britain's ancient claret cup. There was no further need for Ernest Butten's expensive, expansive, patriotic crusade.

He died in 1985, the year that Europe wrestled back the Ryder Cup at last. Now there was only the Masters to go ...

That week did indeed produce Britain's first Masters champion: Sandy Lyle.

A sure-fire cure for the yips
23 September 1989

A couple of evenings ago I was mesmerised by Sam Torrance on the practice putting green. A crowd gathered, the sort who just stare numbly at a man mending a hole in the road. And to be sure, Torrance did look like the chap from Dyno-Rod, particularly with a cigarette butt behind one ear and his scorecard pencil planted behind the other.

In fact, all he was trying to do was tap a ball into a hole from about three feet, the sort of thing a five-year-old child might do six times out of a dozen. Yet here he was, pensive and pondering, and making a right palaver of coaxing the wretched thing into the cup by twining his body round a 50-inch stick like a constipated clematis, at the same time attempting to keep it steady with his chin. The men who designed this contraption put it on the market this week, at £75 a time, and have pledged Torrance a bonus of £20,000 if he again holes the winning putt in the Ryder Cup as he did on the 18th here at The Belfry four years ago.

Torrance, simply, is recuperating from the yips, the putter's twitch, the fiddler's elbow. A four-foot pole might be his answer, but the problem itself is much shorter. For as another sufferer, the great Bobby Jones, once observed: 'The width of any green, the length of any putt, or the height of any putter, is just five and a half inches – the space between your ears.'

Torrance's captain, Tony Jacklin, once tried a one-week Scientology course to cure the problem. He thinks it did him good, but he was never the same on the greens. For as Longhurst said of the yips, 'Once you've had 'em, you've got 'em.'

Another of Jacklin's team this weekend has been terribly afflicted, twice. Both times Bernhard Langer has ground out a cure on the practice green. The first time, he celebrated by daring to write a book, *Langer on Putting*; the second time he started putting one-handed, in effect 'splinting' one wrist by bracing the club shaft against his forearm. Each to his own. I once saw Nick Faldo play a poor putting round. He went straight, and grimly, to the practice green, threw down 50 balls and looked to pot them, alternately with his eyes tightly shut and with his eyes open, but neither way following the ball on its way towards the hole. 'Visual information,' he explained, 'can sometimes overpower the feeling in your hands and stance.'

Has ever such a mundane activity as rolling a ball into a hole from a handful of yards been invested with such mystique, awe and difficulty? To one, boldness is the friend. 'Never up, never in' is the old Scottish rule. To another, go gentle into this good fight. 'For safety, always let the putt die at the hole' is another definitive maxim.

So take your pick. Stand with your feet apart, or closed; put your weight on leading leg, or trailing leg; use the croquet-mallet style, or the Peter Willey French-cricket mode. Pretend you are just driving in a nail; no, closing a door softly, or sharply; putt like a pendulum, or like a slap on the wrist. Or, as an exasperated teaching pro once told me: 'Have you considered simply hitting the ball closer to the hole?'

Well, I might not have had that talent, but, unlike a few of this weekend's heroes, neither have I ever had the yips. Even Patrick Campbell, for my money the finest and funniest of them all on golf, got them: 'A six at the first, suddenly suffering that vertiginous feeling that my clubs had been shortened or the whole course lowered several inches by some outside agency during the night, so that even by striking sharply downwards I could reach only the top half of my ball.'

Then there is Doug Sanders, misser of the most famous last half-inch putt that ever lost an Open, on the 18th at St Andrews. He signed his card and emerged shaking from the hut. A radio man jabbed a mike at his quivering lip. Suddenly Doug smiled. 'Gimme some whisky first,' he ordered, 'and make it a very large pot of that Red Devil Eye.'

5

FIGHTERS

The donkey brays at 'stumblebum' Dunn
20 May 1976

MUNICH: What, when drunk, one sees in other showbiz self-promotions, one sees in Muhammad Ali sober. It's all too much. Take this morning. It wasn't true, but it was, even though we all knew it was all done to drum up ticket sales to this match here against Richard Dunn next Tuesday.

Champagne at the opening press conference. In comes Ali of the Universe, to meet Richard Dunn, of No.2 Northcote Terrace, Bradford, Yorkshire, for the first time. At once Ali tries out his strangling act. Straight for Dunn's throat.

Dunn is nervous but his script is to be uninterested. So Ali has a henchman (one of the 40 he has here in attendance and which are costing him £5,000 a day in hotel bills) to put on a children's green monster mask and, having made sure the photographers had snapped enough of him attacking it, looks up his notes and starts calling Dunn 'Igor' and 'Frankenstein' and then verbally setting about the champion of Europe, England and Bradford.

Stephen Potter put it perfectly in *Lifemanship*: 'If you have nothing to say, or rather something extremely stupid and obvious to say, say it in a plonking tone of voice, that is: roundly but hollowly and dogmatically.' Thus Ali yesterday. Spot on.

It got interesting only when Dunn, who, other than being sandy-haired and tattooed, is a cross between Fred Trueman and Harvey Smith, was asked for a comment on the antics. All he could say was that in Yorkshire he wouldn't stand for such unless he stopped himself by thinking that 'every donkey needs must hear himself bray'. And though the Germans and Japanese didn't understand and the interpreter asked him to repeat it, he still left it at that.

Afterwards, I asked Dunn – a nice man – if he wasn't already cheesed off by the publicity round that he is going through. 'Yeah, course I am, aren't you?' Surely he was a bit worried about the fight at least? 'I couldn't give a stuff. Let's get it over with. All I want is to get home next week. They've asked me for a packet of money to fly straight back to New York to appear on the telly but I just want to get shot of this lot and get home. The only thing that stirred me up today was the attack on the old man – that was a bit strong.'

For when Ali could get no rise out of Dunn this morning, he picked on his trainer and father-in-law Jimmy Deveney, a 60-year-old whose hobbies are bee-keeping and collecting butterflies near Bradford. 'Don't take no notice of that little fat man. What does he know about boxing?' he told Dunn. 'He don't know nothing about boxing. He just makes you into the dumb stumblebum that you are, my friend. I don't know why people keep listening to stumblebums in boxing – the only person they should listen to if they want to know how to box is me. Remember, my crown, brother, is too heavy for thy brow.'

Well, says Dunn's manager George Biddles, afterwards: 'That bloke is the most exploited man the world has ever known – all those men using him for religious purposes, for money, and God knows what, and he has to go and take it out on a nice old man like Jimmy Deveney.'

Brave Dunn turns the jeers into cheers
25 May 1976

MUNICH: In brutally efficient manner Muhammad Ali retained his world heavyweight boxing title at the Olympiahalle here in the early hours of this morning. Richard Dunn, the British and

European champion, lasted five rounds – which was four more than many of us had anticipated before the referee stopped the fight to save him further punishment. But the nature of Dunn's brave challenge did everyone the world of good, except himself.

Giving away a stone in weight, Dunn was floored six times, but to the last he was still tottering gamely to his feet and even if by then he was looking like a drunken matelot trying to take off his waders underwater, at least he was prepared to die well. Dunn had arrived in the ring to jeers from the surprisingly full house: he left it to cheers with his head high. Fair's fair: he had given it his absolute best.

I whipped back to Ali's dressing room at the end with Ferdie Pachecho, Ali's doctor: 'Lawdy, lawdy,' he said, 'what a brave, brave guy. If that Joe Bugner had half the guts and the courage of this Dunn, then what a fighter he could have been.' And it must be said that the honourable Dunn in five rounds landed more crisp and menacing blows – he even ruffled the nonpareil once or twice – than Joe Bugner managed in 27 rounds against Ali in two fights.

Afterwards Ali – usually he is gracious once the fight and ballyhoo is over – was as good as usual. 'Dunn's more good than Bugner, Dunn can hit. I'm proud and honoured to have fought a good fight with a good Englishman. He's a genuinely brave guy.' And Dunn was genuinely touched by this praise from Ali. 'I thank him very much. It's really nice to hear that. It's funny isn't it that the English press are meant to be on my side, but the one word of praise comes from an American who is also your opponent?

'I fought the only way I know how. I'm not a fancy-dan, know nowt about the noble art and all that. I just go out and fight, like I tried to do tonight. Ali talked to me in the clinches like, you know, goading me on, saying I couldn't punch, but I answered him back, you know, just idle chit-chat, socialising like.'

For three rounds Dunn had put up the fight of his chequered middle-of-the-bill provincial career. He lost the first two rounds, but not by all that much, and he probably won the third for his barnstorming bravery. Anyway, just as we were looking at each other and thinking about the impossible, the tough egg cracked asunder in the fourth and for the next five minutes was pouring all over the floor.

Ali might at first have been a touch flummoxed by the Northern southpaw and his rushes but now, instead of anybody else's textbook usual left-hook counter, Ali started turning full-on and flat-footed and letting go some fearful right-handed grenades: short, straight and programmed for the button on the lantern jaw. The lights started dimming at once. The stars came out. Our hitherto blue-eyed boy began hearing the chimes of midnight hours. But six times he struggled up and dived fearlessly back into the cannon's mouth – it was idiocy but truly heroic.

Even immediately before the fight, Dunn's composure, not to say confidence, never publicly wavered. He had been led into the ring by a bodyguard of four Red Berets from his beloved Parachute Regiment; and on his shorts he wore a para's insignia alongside the union jack. He fretted a bit through the preliminaries, asking 'Where's Janet?' and wasn't happy until he had located his wife's seat and blown her a kiss and continued flinging her carefree winks.

He and two unlikely attendant relatives, one very fat, one very thin, joined in the National Anthem lustily and at strict attention, but one couldn't help thinking that they still looked even more like refugees from a two-week Bavarian charabanc holiday who'd lost their way and their phrasebook, taken a wrong turn, and suddenly and accidentally ended up in the opposite corner to Muhammad Ali.

One-fisted Conteh should be thinking of retirement
31 March 1980

ATLANTIC CITY: John Conteh's fond hopes of regaining the world light-heavyweight title finally came to a sad and painful end.

Painfully sad. In the space of a minute, he went down five times, got up five times and then was helped to his corner to count his 366,975 dollars – the only time he used his right hand all night.

After a calm enough recovery period in his hotel bedroom, Conteh hit the town and this time he didn't miss. He drank the night away, getting moister with each bar he visited. His wife Veronica became hysterical at times as the beano went on, and by dawn the security guards on the sixth floor of his hotel were still being kept pretty busy as he drowned his sorrows. 'The booze really got to him,' said his business manager, Bobby Naidoo. In fairness, John had a lot of sorrows to drown.

Conteh managed none of the skill and spirit he had summoned here last August in his first challenge for Mathew Saad Muhammad's title. That day he had boxed so classically well for Queen and Queensberry that he was leading on points until the end of the 13th, when only the champion's barnstorming finale kept a grip on the championship.

The rematch was ordered, with Conteh awarded an extra slice of the purse, after Muhammad's seconds were found to have used unsporting unctions to stem the flow from his cut eyebrows. There was no such controversy this time. The champion came out fast, throwing long punches which landed with increasing regularity.

At first Conteh countered with one or two slinging left jabs that sent glistening little necklaces of the champion's sweat shooting into the arc lights – but never enough to call a halt to the menacing, almost carefree, advances of the young American. In the fourth a short right-hander was jabbed like a brick on to the side of Conteh's jaw – rendering one melting mandible accompanied by the faint tinkle of crystal like a chandelier caught in a Waterford breeze.

John's eyes came over all fuzzy like when a stone hits a windscreen and from then till the merciful end he was as dizzy in the vertical plane as a lift-boy in a department store. Thank you and good night. Not that our guy didn't fall well. Each time he collapsed he landed as dramatically flat as if he had been practising in a potato-packing factory for weeks.

John Conteh had just one more easy fight before he did retire. He is now available for after-dinner speaking, which is more than can be said for many ex-boxers. ('Brilliant sense of humour,' says his agent.)

Sweet, sharp Sugar takes all
18 September 1981

LAS VEGAS: It sure was one heck of a fistfight and at times it got near even to living up to the outrageous ballyhoo that preceded it. In fiscal terms Wednesday night's world welterweight fight was certainly the richest fight in history; it matched the boast well enough and deserved at least to be listed as the first 'Fight of the Century' of this young decade.

Sugar Ray Leonard, his pop-eyes closing all the time into weaselly slits, realised on exactly the right occasions when he had to be very, very good. And those were the times when Tommy Hearns, by comparison, seemed to me to be just slightly out of his depth.

When the referee stopped the fight halfway through the 14th round, with Hearns as laden with leather as a full cattle truck, the three judges announced Hearns slightly ahead on points. Well, as far as I was concerned, that meant each of them was as daffy as Don King's barber.

The third round will surely remain logged as one of the most awesome three minutes of world championship fighting. Fire answers fire! And the sixth and seventh were not short of gruesome excitement either. Longeurs set in through the middle areas – Hearns, where he could not throw his jackhammer right hand for fear of the quicksilver left-hook counter, and Leonard, while cockily throwing examples of his full repertoire, seemed content enough to pace himself through a chess match now rather than a manhunt.

Yet all the time Leonard's left eye – elbowed by a sparring partner in training – was getting uglier. His right cheekbone, too, was puffing up. Still Hearns remained tentative about mustering a concerted attack, just flicking out his temples like a stinging wet towel. By the 13th, as he admitted afterwards, Leonard had indeed just been circling the wagon, getting ever closer and twanging in the odd arrow or three. But then the burning faggots started flying and Hearns was a goner ... three minutes later the credits came up.

Self-taught King of the pre-fight verbals
18 July 1986

Remember the Norwegian football commentator a few years back who got so dramatically worked up at the final whistle – 'Norway has beaten England the home of the giants! Lord Nelson! Lord Beaverbrook! Sir Winston Churchill! Sir Anthony Eden! Clement Attlee! Henry Cooper! Lady Diana! Maggie Thatcher, can you hear me ... ?'

Well, the American boxing impresario Don King makes that fellow sound like Longhurst at the Open or Dimbleby in the Abbey. There is no one quite like Don King. He is the first to point this out.

Mr King likens British boxing's cauliflowered-eared corporate trio of Mickey Duff, Mike Barrett and Jarvis Astaire to 'Captain Nelson, Winnie Churchill and Madame Thatcher'. Where does that leave him? 'I am not a promoter. I am The Promoter. First there was the Prophet Isaiah, then that ol' forecastin' dude Nostrah-Dee-Muzz, yeah, then PT Barnum, then Mike Todd. Then there is me.'

When King arrived last week, ticket sales for Frank Bruno's Wembley challenge on Tim Witherspoon's third of the fragmented world heavyweight title were sluggish. King got out the big bass drum and with a well-planned series of impromptu happenings soon had both boxers – ordinarily nice big softies – snarling at each other for the benefit of the box office. Tickets have since gone like hot cakes – or as King would say, 'hot potatoes'. In all, including television rights, the show should gross $4 million. In professional boxing there is a winner and a loser. Promoters are seldom the latter.

First there's the hair. It is an almost frightening Friesian friz, a piebald mane that starts up from his scalp like he's a cartoon cat whose tail is caught in a light socket. Then there's the voice: it is like a tractor at work in a gravel pit, and comes equipped with a quite thrilling thesaurus of thoughts and ruminations culled from quotes books and bibles alike. The New Testament is as freshly-minted as the Old in Don's diatribes. He's also hot stuff on Shakespeare.

When you can drag your eyes from King's crimper's masterpiece, they are dazzled by his accessories: gold and diamonds, rings as big as matchboxes and a watch which is a bejewelled Big Ben. They could start *News At Ten* with a close-up of his wrist. But it's the words you really cower under. Out of his 24-carat mouth they flutter and zigzag round the hairstyle like a swarm of batty butterflies. Perhaps he thinks he's in Paris this week, because he keeps referring to 'the noble art of the Marquee de Queensberry'. Marie Antoinette ('Let them drink Coke') has been as regularly on his lips as Victor Hugo ('Popularity is glory's small change').

King got the geography together when he dedicated this, his 25th 'fight of the century' in the last 14 years 'to Prince Andrew and the Princess Fergie'. He has sent personal invitations to the couple to attend the ringside tomorrow night, and also extended invitations to the Queen and Mrs Thatcher – 'now there's another fighter, your Margaret, yeah.' But he is sorry to have to tell 'the very wonderful Thatcher' to get to her seat early, for Witherspoon is going to hit her Frank Bruno such a humdinger in the kisser as to KO the poor young man – but he will do it 'as her Captain Lord Nelson decreed, with grace, style and elegance'.

King swotted it all up, this torrent of borrowed wisdom, in the Ohio State Penitentiary, where he served four years after being charged with manslaughter. He started with the Bible, reading it, he says, from chinks of light under the door of the solitary cell – 'they that dwell in the land of the shadow of death, upon them doth the light shine – Isaiah, Chapter 9, Verse 2, yeah.'

Young Don's first job had been delivering crates of battery hens from Hymie's Chicken Shack to be decapitated at the Cleveland central abattoir. Inbuilt bravado and cunning and desperation to escape led him into the city's murky numbers game. The cops called it a racket. He was almost numero uno when he had a fist fight and one of his rival runners lay dead.

He has always maintained he did not deserve a jail sentence at all, that the police had pinned the numbers game on him. But in retrospect it was the making of him – in a manner of speaking. For after the Bible came 'Bill the Bard's' Complete Works, and after them it was downhill all the way, words-wise.

King and Norman Mailer apparently once compared reading lists, and the great author was amazed. 'My prison education included Freud. He almost blew my mind. Then Masters and Johnson, Kinsey and ...' He hesitated. 'Knee's itch, I read a lot of him.' Who? 'Knee's itch. Nigh zitch.' Nietzsche? 'Yeah.' But the error had him jiving for embarrassment. 'Yeah, cerebrum and cerebellum, you got to use them, that's what I learned from that man.'

What else did he read? 'Kant – *The Critique of Pure Reason*. That helped my head. And I read Sartre – fascinating! And then the guy who wrote that book on Hitler, Shirer, I read him. And Marx, I read Karl Marx, a cold motherfucker, Marx. But I learned a lot from him.'

King also made many millions for and from Muhammed Ali, and staged all his classic later fights. Incidentally, saddest of all this week's sombre spectacles has been the shambling presence of that once-beautiful genius. Undaunted by Ali's haunting hobble at his side, King of course has even found time to put up a remarkable quotation-laden defence of the 'Marquee de Queenberry's nobility' on the Jimmy Young show. All boxers, he said, simply adore each other when the final bell rings – 'though he slay me yet I love him: that's Job talkin' to the Lord, yeah.'

Beaten Bruno holds his bruised head high
21 July 1986

We scavengers for gruesome tittle tattle waited until almost dawn outside the famous dressing room at the end of that scruffy concrete corridor-ramp below the Wembley tunnel. From there generations of legendary footballers have marched up into the sunlight to make names for themselves in May.

This summer's night Frank Bruno, cowled like a monk in a rose-red habit, his doe eyes scarcely open and his cheekbone hideously out of alignment, shook off the concerned and kindly circle of comrades who had been cosseting and half-carrying him from this gallows to make the last 20 yards on his own after being stopped in the 11th round of his World Boxing Association heavyweight championship fight against the American, Tim Witherspoon.

Bruno had spied a waiting television camera and wanted to make the dressing room by himself, even on his still ropey legs. For the few necessary seconds the young man held his head courageously higher, then ducked into the dressing room and his friends slammed the door behind him.

The mayhem earlier, alas, followed predictable British patterns. For just over half an hour the contest had relentlessly dribbled away. And when he was left at the last like a crumpled, unstrung, chocolate marionette, and the referee, Isidro Rodriguez of Venezuela, had stopped the fight and had dragged the fighter's sleeping dead weight back across the ring to his corner, a section of the crowd, zapped up and misled by weeks of patriotic hype in tabloids and on TV, could not take their medicine. As the American champion left the ring he and his surrounding posse of policemen were pelted angrily by coins and not a few chairs.

When the dust had settled you realised how well Bruno had done. It was as though, having shown remarkable bright promise at his 11-plus, he was early sitting his O-levels, but when he turned up the examiner started doling out papers for an Oxbridge honours degree. In the event he furrowed his brow and gave it a most courageously honest, you might even say heroic, go.

Since March 1982, Witherspoon, an abrasively awkward, cussed, fussing customer, has fought 102 rounds in only 13 fights against all the world's leading roundhouse roughs. In that same period since he turned pro, Bruno has fought only 85 rounds against 29 mostly spoon-fed, falling-over no-hopers – boxing an average of only 2.64 rounds a fight.

Every gob that Witherspoon aimed at his spittoon was one in the eye for all those homesters who refused to believe his claim last week that fitness for boxing was nothing to do with fitness for weightlifting or marathon running. Yet, optimist that I am, I kept telling myself between rounds that one haymaker on the very button from Bruno could still turn the predictable pot-boiler into an epic. But in Witherspoon's every head-ringing cuff there was a jagged edge sawing away at the guy-ropes that were joining the young man's mind to his nerve and training, until there was only instinct left.

And so it ended with a little sleep on the referee's shoulder as he dragged the lumpen dead weight across the ring, and the promoter, Don King, imperiously allowed that Bruno had 'accredited himself with credit'.

Bugner takes money for old hope
26 October 1987

One of the longest goodbyes of all showbiz was mercifully concluded last night in the pokey little windowless referee's dungeon under the Tottenham Hotspur grandstand after Joe Bugner had gone in the eighth against Frank Bruno. 'Sorry about all the bullshit that's gone before, but you can take it I'll never fight again,' said the fat man on the bench as he dabbed with a towel at the grazes on his great squashed prow of a nose.

The official doctor had been first in, then the prize-fighter's devoted moll called Marlene, who had watched the one-sided bore from an 'executive box'. They embraced. He said to her: 'Sorry.' She said to him: 'We are very, very proud of you.'

The old white room was sparsely and eccentrically decorated in green and yellow streamers and those pointless little paper pompoms people put on present-parcels. By the time he had lumbered, steaming, out of the shower, two perfectly formed crescents under the big fellow's eyes were already turning into the same matching colour scheme. By this morning they would be a painful, purplish mauve. Cheap at the price of £250,000.

Equally well-defined crescents were above Marlene's eyes and, just as methodically, were also man-made. She arched them, crossed long voluptuous legs, smoothed the creases in her expensive sequiney-dress and her equally rich made-up face and said: 'Of course I was never worried. I had a definite pact with the corner men that at the first sign of the possibility of Joe being hurt they would throw in the towel. The end was sudden, so the towel came in. He was not hurt and I'm truly proud of the wonderful, wonderful job he did. He is a fine man, a great fighter and just listen at his chivalry in defeat.'

A caretaker-type wandered in and, stroking his chin, seemed to be considering the removal of the quaint wall decorations. He left them up while Joe, sitting under a strip of Elastoplast stuck to the wall with the word WIN written on it, was fingering his own messed-about mandible even more tenderly, took up his girl's cue for a last cheerio (he promised most sincerely) to his 'public', mixing magnanimity with, as he put it, 'the end of this last bit of bullshit'.

Rather like the first of Richard Nixon's many goodbyes – 'you won't have Nixon to kick around any more' – Joe said he had been fired to stay on his feet only because he 'wanted to stick it to you Fleet Street guys'. He said the ultimate fall (only the third in 70-odd contests) must surely 'have marked the end of a great era as far as the legends of all boxing are concerned, for I go back to the fabulous era of Ali and Liston and Quarry, and all those people out there must surely realise that tonight was the end of an era for Britain and the world.'

Before he left to resume Marlene's efforts at buttonholing the casting directors of the Australian film industry (a visit to his mother first this week) he paid generous tribute to young Bruno. 'In the end I have to say he impressed me. Honestly he did.

'Age doesn't come into it. I don't regret my age; I don't regret my weight; I don't regret anything – even if the referee was an idiot tonight at the end letting him hit me like that. I don't regret anything. Life goes on, thank God.' Spoken like the nice man he really is, and Marlene, who had by now stopped arching her eyebrows, looked at him with love, re-smoothed her dress for the umpteenth time, uncrossed her legs, and simply purred. The car was ready, she nodded the order, and off they went to re-read the cheque.

The last heavyweight sportsman to be flattened by anyone other than Dave Mackay on the centre-circle at White Hart Lane was Jack London by Bruce Woodcock on Saturday 17 July, 1945. That took six rounds. Many more, 38,000, watched it. Woodcock took home £995 to Doncaster and the fishmonger-promoter, Jack Solomons, admitted a profit of just £400.

And, just like 32 years later, everyone went home happy. It was the result they wanted. Marlene and Joe included – unless the cheque bounces, it's goodbye from him and goodbye from her.

Not quite. Bugner was still fighting professionally, and even winning, in Australian seaside resorts until the late 1990s, when he was approaching his 50th birthday.

6

THE HEART OF THE SCRUM

Wales sink beneath a boiling sea of style
England 34 Wales 6
19 February 1990

Before this, England's largest winning margin against Wales was 25-0 at Blackheath in 1896. They then went up to old Hampden Park where Scotland beat them roundly by 11-0 on March 17, the very day of this year's clincher. Omens everywhere.

On Saturday's form, however, you would not expect England to give a fig for soothsayers. It was blazing stuff, a radiantly flaring team effort from first whistle to last. No side I have seen from the British Isles have played with such a sustained, invigorating, bonny presumption and panache since the Welsh team's grandeur nearly two decades ago. It was a golden afternoon for a crowd so long fed on dross.

There is a touch of Sir Alf Ramsey in the public pronouncements of England's manager, Geoff Cooke. Even in his deadpan, blazer-buttoned way, just like the sombre knight of Ipswich he is not averse to pre-match boasts. Like this time: 'I don't see how we can lose.' Then, victory achieved, he eschews all vaulting lunar elevations and cloaks his obvious excitement with the flat-vowelled moderation of a rather bored coroner. 'By heck, boys,' you wanted Cooke to explode on Saturday night, 'we ruddy stuffed those cocky Reds good and proper. We could have put 50 past them if we'd bothered, too.'

This is how it came out, low-key as he softly fingered the knot on his regulation tie: 'We had some satisfying passages of play, but we are still making too many mistakes, indeed missed a number of good chances which we failed to nail down with a try. On a number of occasions we ripped Wales apart, then allowed them to get tacklers back when we got a little too excited.' Ah well, that presumably is Twickspeak for delirious exultation. And the truth is that England could have posted the half-century, easy.

What wailing in Wales this week. The captain of the ruined band, little Robert Jones, most chivalrously gave best to the foe, then fingered the graze on his flattened warrior's nose, closed his eyes and shook his head. 'It still hasn't sunk in yet,' he said, 'except that it'll be talked about for a long, long time.'

Raising hwyl to the roof at Twickenham
England 6 Wales 9
6 February 1978

It's becoming awfully tedious. 'Feed Me Till I Want No More' is a nice enough song to sing, but, damn it, allowing England but one victory in the past 15 games is bordering on gluttony. As one gloating Taff warned in the bar afterwards, 'I'm afraid, boy, we will now have to consider seriously dropping the fixture.'

At half-time I thought, 'Stone me, the homesters were actually going to pull it off at last.' The eight stout yeomen whose limbs were made in England gathered in a steamy huddle around their leader, Beaumont. They were now eight chocolate soldiers: they looked a different side to their backs who, for lack of opportunity, were still in pristine white, like male nurses who had just clocked on. Not that Young and Hignell especially had not been playing marvellously well. Any road, the banner 'JPR Doctors Englishmen' was looking pretty limp up in the south terrace as half-time was called.

In the little scarlet bunch, Bennett was talking and gesturing passionately. Gareth and Gerald chipped in. In a way, they knew they were lucky to be only three points adrift. I wonder what was said, for almost at once it was a different tale. Experience told, sure, but also nothing less than nationhood. The blood had been summoned up at last and the brave English had no hope of matching it.

I was reminded of the yarn a few years back about Clive 'Top Cat' Rowlands whose pep talks before the Welsh ran out were really something special. 'You're going out there to win for WALES!' he would scream, punching the air while building to a crescendo of *hwyl*. 'You're going out there to win for your country, for your fathers, for your mothers, for your village, for your school, for your mine, for your firm, for your wives, for your girlfriends, for your Auntie Gwladys.' Thus, out they would clatter, determined to scatter a team of bulldozers for Wales. Once a new cap stopped on getting out to the pitch and said:'Hey, wait a tick – I haven't got an Aunty Gwladys!'

Soon after half-time on Saturday, England's fly-half, Horton (who had wretched luck to be baptised on such a day) sold himself a dummy when he went to link before he had caught. In a trice Gareth had raked an advantage of 60 yards. A minute later Gareth did it again, this time far away to the other touchline. And at once the amazing fellow put another to the very corner flag. England were on the ropes, and everyone knew (certainly themselves) that they would never again get away – and at that precise moment a whole little country burst into song ... 'Feed Me Till I Want No More.'

And in the evening there was yet another marvellously enjoyable *Parkinson* show. 'That Gareth,' said Cliff Morgan, 'is the greatest thing that God ever created.''Surely not the greatest?' tut-tutted our host whom Emu bemused. 'Oh yes,' said Cliff, 'saving your presence of course, sir.'

Morgan told of meeting Gareth's wife just before the kick-off in the queue at a Twickenham tea store, rain bucketing down, hair soaking wet, waiting to have a cup of tea and a sandwich. What's this, he asked her, why wasn't she up in the dining room with all the other players' wives? 'Because I am with four friends from home,' she said, 'and I cannot leave them.'

'Now that to me,' said Morgan, 'is what this Welshness of ours is all about – it's all to do with togetherness isn't it?' And that's also one very good reason why they are awfully hard to beat at rugby football.

Line to line in 17 seconds
England 21 France 19
18 March 1991

Four momentous tries gilded Saturday's climax, with the first possibly the most opulent since old men with memories were themselves at their grandfather's knee. That takes in all the rich history of the Five Nations championship.

The very context sharpened the grandeur of its daring, dotty conception and the nerveless joy of its execution. For the challenge, in bold relief, matched England's substance, nous and penalty power against France's airy elan, spontaneity and dextrous tricks and treats. At once the two philosophies collided. England missed a long penalty and all eyes and senses, certainly those of the England XV for a moment, relaxed and prepared for a 22 drop-out.

Suddenly all hell broke loose or, rather, the incomparable Blanco, dusky warrior-captain of France, did. '*Moi, moi,*' he shouted to Saint-André. Blanco has always put his trust in gods who favour the foolhardy. He was now across his line but still by only 10 yards. In a trice the ball was with Lafond outside him and the wing's left hip took out Andrew, first to spot the danger, and an instantaneous finger-tip pass allowed Sella, at speed, to round his own despairing white marker.

Sella was over the 22 and momentarily clear as England regrouped and frantically funnelled back. The stalwart Probyn had tanked across to confront him on the 10-metre line. Sella feinted to knife inside him and, as he did so, he turned in a dummy-scissors loop and fed on the outside again, the delicate Camberabero. The pit-a-pat fly half could now snipe across the halfway mark.

Then, with dainty exactness, he slippered the ball over the head of the retreating Hodgkinson, caught it in full-pelt stride and was now up to England's 22-metre flag. Though England's bold general Carling had remarkably made it across the field he could only fling himself at Camberabero a split second after the Frenchman had dapped the most perfect cross-kick to within five metres of the posts.

This took out the corner-flagging Hill and left Saint-André to compose, collect and triumphantly launch himself at the line as Guscott's all-in, last-gasp dive lassoed his ankles. The palpitating thing was done.

From line to line it took 17.25 seconds, four more than the previous collective marvel of the age, for the Barbarians at Cardiff on 27 January 1973, when the dancing Bennett dared, and set in train that breathtaking passage down another touchline. For Dawes's phoney dummy there, read Sella's phoney scissors here; for Quinnell's genius slip-catch from David, here was Camberabero's chip-and-catch.

But that Barbarians epic was done with licence to cavort. Saturday's audacious try was inspired by all the vivid intensity of the grandeur of the Slam.

Memories of another inspired collective score, touched by angels, came to mind when the cockles calmed themselves: in 1980, high on the veldt of Northern Transvaal in May, the Lions were losing 16-19 with minutes to go. With defiant courage Quinnell (again), Patterson, Richards, Renwick, Woodward, Hay and nine others poured themselves in desperate tides at the opposition line through five rucks, 33 pairs of hands and a minute and three-quarters of optimism until Slemen plunged in the killing thrust under the posts.

But that was no Grand Slammer and those who were there that day agreed this weekend that the palm was now for France, the grandest of the grand. As the Barbarians' score in 1973 will always be 'Bennett's try', so will Saturday's be 'Blanco's try'. What a way to go.

Two hours after he had showered, and easily into his 10th cigarette, he was shruggingly explaining the sweet 17 seconds. He was in his *'je ne parle pas Anglais'* mood but the translation is roughly this.

'The try? It is communion. No one man scores a try, the whole team scores it. The communion made this try, because all of us opened our minds to score it. No one man has the vision, the whole team has the vision, 15 as one man.'

Had he seen the English momentarily drop their guard?

'Non. Il est instantané, il est spontané, instinctif. C'est le rugby. Finis.' His dark eyes glistened. He smiled and lit another cigarette from the glowing stub of the previous one.

Along the corridor the heroic, relieved English were rightly celebrating. All they had wanted was to win something tangible, they had insisted, and they dedicated their victory to their grandchildren.

'Is it true, grandpa, that you were in the Grand Slam final way back in '91?'

'Yes, my child, I was.'

'Tell me, grandpa, was Blanco's try as good as the history books say?'

'Argghhh!'

Why skimp on the gateau?
4 February 1995

From mid-morning yesterday there was a sense and buzz of occasion in the Eurostar salon at the Gare du Nord in Paris and, by midday, a fair jostle of French rugby men – jaunty berets accentuating cauliflower ears – chorused a rounding *'Bonne chance et Allez France!'* as the first major international sporting team set off for a match by way of the Channel Tunnel.

All things considered, it would have ben easier to fly as usual, but when the idea was mooted, the French Rugby Federation, with typical panache, went the whole hog and simply hired a special train for their first XV and hundreds of attendant alickadoos. There was not a seat to be had in first class. The mood was touched with the adventure of it and much jollity. To begin with, that is.

'Sûrement, pas d'problème,' the French captain Philippe Saint-André said when asked to say how confident he was for Twickenham today – but first he said he needed a couple of glasses of *rouge* by way of aperitif before lunch was served. Ah, yes, lunch. First things first. *Vive la France.* We edged softly out of Paris and the team tucked their white napkins into their oversized, already straining collars – then tucked in themselves.

For starters, *Assiette Gourmande* – a stacked platter of bits and bobs from smoked salmon to caviar tart. Then a choice of fillet steak, or (probably chosen in the circumstances to make a nice Gallic political point to the Brits) *Mignon de Veau aux Morilles* – veal with morel mushrooms – and *haricots verts* and *carottes,* no cauliflower. Then trays of cheeses, gateau, fruit, washed down with either or both of a 1990 Bergerac Château Plaisance or a Sauvignon 1993 Côte de Duras. Hey, steady you guys, you're playing England tomorrow.

The charming captain and his two immediate predecessors, the clothes-prop Roumat and the legendary Sella, sat together, each fingering their designer stubble or their fashionable carelessly spiky Tintin hair, styled like it had been barbered with blunt scissors. They joshed each other, smiled at private in-jokes.

Suddenly, just like that, the meal was finished – at least they turned away Armagnac or any digestif – and simultaneously almost to the minute our 186mph flyer ducked with a whoosh into the darkness of the tunnel and the steward announced watches to be put back an hour.

At that stroke, the frivolity of the Paris farewell and the enjoyment of the meal was switched off. The hum of conversation died, the team became silent, focused, staring in their now solemn reverie at their own reflections in the windows and thinking of going over the top in less than 24 hours when England would be first teasing and then tearing into them at Twick. 'It's like playing 15 Cantonas,' the England vice-captain, Brian Moore, had said.

And no, *excusez-moi*, Saint-André after all did not want to say anything about the morrow. At other extremities of the 18-carriage train, the wines were having a different effect on the supporters – and the Marseillaise was sung slurringly as soon as, with a sense of occasion, we had burst out of the blackness under *la Manche* and into the slatey-bright afternoon light of Kent.

Of course, history keeps repeating itself. Well, in different ways. Almost 40 years ago, schoolboys of a certain age might remember Leslie Mitchell's golly-gosh tones of utter amazement on the Movietone newsreel reporting, wonder of wonders, that the England XV of 1956 were pioneers by actually flying to the match in Paris.

There they all were in grainy monochrome grinning sheepishly and standing in front of the stepladders alongside a tiny BEA twin-propeller aircraft with the couple of Nissen huts which then comprised Heathrow airport – Eric Evans in his first year as captain, Peter Robbins, Sandy Sanders and all, plus a lanky London Society referee who was to be touch judge the following afternoon in the old Paris stadium at Colombes, one Denis Thatcher.

Yesterday was, in its minor way, an equally historic trip. Also an evocatively pointed one. The first rugby club ever to be formed in France was in 1872 when an Englishman called Longstaffe founded Le Havre RFC. Mr Longstaffe was the agent at the Channel port for Southern Railway ferries and boat trains. Not till 35 years later, in January 1907, did a French team first make the ferry journey to Dover for their first match on English soil – beaten 41-18 at Richmond Athletic Ground. They had boarded the train at the Gare du Nord after taking Friday off work.

Not all that different from yesterday really. Except that we did not arrive at Victoria station. Was there more of a resonant betting man's tip in the fact that for today's match the French arrived at Waterloo?

France duly met their Waterloo, 31-10, and England went on to win the Grand Slam.

Going to Blazers
8 May 1995

Old Farts. Nice one, Will. Not the least of Master Carling's achievements in being forced out of the England captaincy has been to bestow an almost scholarly imprimatur on an expressive phrase. From now on, it has found its precise definition – a sporting collective noun, meaning blazered buffers' bumbledom – I bet it will make the next edition of the *OED*, between 'old country' and 'old guard'.

Not before time does 'old farts' supersede the previous rugby word 'alickadoo' – denoting the clubhouse freemasonry of club-tied, blazer-badged administrators and hangers-on who were involved in the game without playing it – which has been in use since the twenties.

This time Twickenham's alickadooing old farts have even outdone their city cousins up in the feudal fields of Lord's. In 1986, Lord's officially did no more than smile through gritted teeth when Ian Botham was quoted (by a radio reporter who had smuggled himself into a private lunch) as saying the England cricket selectors were 'just a load of gin-swilling old dodderers'.

But just as Lord's 'got' Botham in the end for past indiscretions, so Carling should have realised that a number of committeemen at Twickenham have been biding their time to get him for years. The most relevant exchange of this weekend was the Friday night phone call to the captain from England's manager, Jack Rowell – 'Hello!' 'Will, you're a total prat!' 'I know, Jack.'

Meanwhile, the nation can again revel in the fun of another English comedy of manners and class, of strut and stubbornness and donkeys' dignity. It is a cultural collision which has enlivened just about every English sport down the centuries since Gents invented, and administered, them and Players began seriously playing. But a cataclysmic rugby issue it ain't. Not for England's team. OK, they leave for the World Cup in South Africa next week, but this little malarkey could well serve to raise the team's danders – 'We were playing for Will out there.' They will certainly need this if (for all their talking-a-good-game swagger) they are to make even the semi-finals.

The fact is that any one of the XV let out of the cage for England's first match against Argentina at Durban on 27 May could be named captain and it would not make a ha'porth of difference who carried the ball out and tossed for ends or kick off. Performing those chores, reciting a couple of unlistened-to lines of King Harry before Harfleur in the changing-room, uttering a few cosy clubhouse meanderings at the post-match banquet for the farts to punctuate with 'hear, hear' over the brandies and, er ... that's about it.

The duties of the captain of the England rugby team cannot remotely be compared with those of the cricket captain who commands the whole five-day strategy. The difference between Carling's tactical and schematic appreciation of a match campaign and Michael Atherton's is the difference between Captain Mainwaring's and General Eisenhower's view of World War Two. England's record at rugby under Carling's captaincy – it has been the best half-dozen years in their history – would have been equally as good whoever was captain, although the team's general continuity of selection (and captaincy) has helped hugely – in the six years before Carling, England fielded 10 captains.

But this is where the perceived old farts come in. Carling's tenure as leader has coincided exactly with an enormously higher worldwide profile for the game itself, dating probably from the first World Cup which was held, with a great deal of establishment hesitation, only in 1987. Simplistically, the big union guns in the southern hemisphere – Australia and New Zealand and, after their exile, South Africa – have been shameless about turning their game into a semi-professional one, mostly to allay the threat from the dreaded rivals of rugby league. Players in those three countries are awash with dosh and perks. Carling and his fellow players feel they should get a slice of the action. The men in blazers, who love the game they knew as boys and its amateur Saturday-night ethos, don't see it that way at all. So Bryan McAllister's cartoon in Saturday's *Guardian* was a gem. A blazer was confronting Carling: 'Old Farts, indeed! Old Fartonians, if you please.'

The man who admitted yesterday that he drove the dagger into Carling's back the deepest was RFU president for the year, Dennis Easby, a 70-year-old Reading solicitor, who had captained the Old Redingensians in the 50s, became a Berkshire Society referee and touch-judged England's match at Twickenham against New Zealand in 1964, and worked through various committees with solid conscientiousness to take his 1995 Buggins' turn at the top.

Taking notes at the meeting was the RFU's paid secretary, Dudley Wood, a man with a genial but put-upon air who is 65 and so retiring this year back to his Suffolk acres, to the ducks, geese, and self-bred golden retrievers. In an earlier career, Wood was an ICI high-flier, marketing new products around Europe. He seems to enjoy, with a weary twinkle and shrug, being spokesman for King Canute's court.

When Wood joined the RFU just over 10 years ago, the Twickenham phone number was ex-directory. Under his olde worlde stewardship, Twickenham has been transformed physically in quick time – with a new state-of-the-art stadium and a 50 per cent increase in marketing. But he has been as publicly ruthless as any of the game's administrative dinosaurs in his defence of the game's 'recreational amateurism', which has so disenchanted the leading players. These players, including Carling, have realised that they have been the young workers responsible for Twickenham's gross of £1.5 million for each of England's home matches – and yet not until this season have they even been allowed to bring their wives to the official post-match banquet in a snazzy West End hotel, while the wives of committeemen and sponsors are welcome at the trough.

When England last May sent an expedition to South Africa to reconnoitre this month's challenging tournament, the team was accompanied by a delegation of blazers from Twickenham, plus wives. And why not? All those hours in smoke-filled committee rooms deserve some fresh-air perks, don't they?

But the players, back from arduous practice and lolling just for an hour or two beside the hotel pool, cast narrow eyes at them from the sunbeds. As did the vast ego which is organising the World Cup for South Africa, the one-man committee and roughshod-rider Louis Luyt. He said then: 'Look at them, true amateurs the real world has passed by. I was there for the World Cup they organised in England three years ago. They spent their time fighting over who could wear the special World Cup blazer when they met the Queen. Or who would sit next to her in the grandstand at the opening ceremony. Or who qualified to go to the dinners. And who would be at the top table. And whose wife wanted to sit next to which wife, or not as the case may be. Amateurs? You bet your life they're amateurs. But MY World Cup will be professionally run.' On that tour, Luyt accused Carling of 'professionalism'. Had the awful South African television shown that grimly twee ad of Carling and his missus endorsing some microwave dish? I think so. The 'old farts' of England have never challenged Carling about the ad – he presumes that they presume he does it for nothing.

As Beer has said: 'England players moan about wanting money, but they have no idea that out of the RFU's £9m income last year, £7m went to youth development, coaching and tours, promotion, publicity, and rebuilding Twickenham. Yet if every administrator claimed all their legitimate expenses for phone calls and petrol, which they ignore, the game would be finished by midnight.'

It may be finished, for sure, by the end of the century. Certainly the game which countless devoted old farts have played, refereed, known and cherished with so fierce a passion may have only a few years left. The present and fulminating rugby league turmoil brought about in Australia by the television moguls Kerry Packer and Rupert Murdoch – and already spreading with eruptive consequences to England – has to take only one step more to drag in rugby union. If multi-millions continue to be thrown about in rugby league, in no time the rugby union boys will want some of it (or rather, lots of it) and it will be denuded of all its stars.

Of course, if they put on a 15-a-side match between monkeys at Twickenham the place would be packed out for a while yet. But soon the standards of play would be so abysmal that even the corporate hospitality hordes would rumble that something was amiss with their day out. If rugby league has so readily, and even swooningly, fallen into the arms of television, then rugby union could do the same. Then it would be a players' revolt – not one by greedy club chairmen – which would take them into the world of the greenbacks.

And, with a merciful sigh, England's old farts would return whence they came, back to the Saturday night clubhouses of the shires, polish their blazer buttons at the cuff, fill to the foaming brim their personal pewter mugs hanging on the clubhouse wall and – wives washing up at the back – break into their songs of old, as if the bad dream had never happened in the naughty nineties ...

Mandela helps usher in a brave new world
25 May 1995

CAPE TOWN: The momentous kick-off this afternoon resoundingly and very genuinely transcends the routine major international sporting tournament. The start of the third rugby union World Cup is a historic occasion for sure.

It may only be a rugger match but the World Cup's beginning at Newlands also represents certain, and even voluptuous, confirmation that the long-time pariah South Africa is being heartily welcomed back not only into the brotherhood of sport and general good fellowship but into the whole global scheme of human activity. South Africa has never held an event such as this. Businessmen have done business, but they have their own, secret, freemasons' code of things. Let them get on with it. But succeeding generations here had presumed that sport would never get back to normal.

In the President's Box today, as the furious intensity of the opening fixture swirls below on the field, will be sitting that serene colossus Nelson Mandela, totem and unbitter icon of this whole testament of human grandeur.

Had even he considered that such an event could really happen in his lifetime? He was released from prison after 27 years in February 1990, when Mike Gatting was playing a preposterous rebel cricket tour. Four years later, in April 1994, all South Africans – all – voted in general elections. In May 1995 rugby union's World Cup kicks off.

And this afternoon this battered, benighted and now suddenly so bonnily brave country – still head-shakingly amazed with itself – will come to a stop. South Africa is hoping against hope it might have a team to win the tournament. The pressure of expectation on its 15 young men may be too immense.

Today's kick-off is a crucial symbol as well as a signpost for rugby union itself. It is only the third World Cup ever held.

Through the century the game's ruling body has shrunk with horror and outrage at the very idea. Damn it, some aspects of such an event would have to be run by professionals.

In the end it gave in, and eight years ago the first World Cup was held thanks to pressure by Australia and New Zealand – but anyone who attended that tournament and is here today will compare the two as the difference between a folksy Tom Forrest Ambridge garden-produce fete and the Chelsea Flower Show. And it is (literally) a pound to a penny that this will also be the last World Cup played by young officially amateur sportsmen – solicitors, soldiers and the like – enjoying a spot of rugger for fun and where the only greenbacks are on Irish shirts.

Or as Twickenham's official laws begin: 'The game is only amateur. No one is allowed to seek or receive payment or other material reward for taking part.' The world has long known that to be utter claptrap. Certainly the 30 players who will open the revels this afternoon laugh in your face when you quote that. By the next World Cup in 1999, players will be paid for taking part, no doubt about it.

And if what the referee begins today with his whistle is the last peep of rugby union's shamateurism, on a much more heroic level it is grand that in front of President Mandela himself it also signals a triumph for all those, pilloried and discredited by the establishment, who shouted for a world sporting ban of the apartheid state.

Cricket's D'Oliveira scandal of 1968 and Peter Hain's campaign of 1969 most handsomely and happily come home to roost today. It will be good for you back home that the ITV commentator is John Taylor, the first leading player to opt out against apartheid's Springboks. Time was when three of the teams here this month, Western Samoa, Tonga and the Ivory Coast, could not have stayed in the hotels they are in, let alone played against white men. It was a happy and poignant day all round yesterday as Mandela visited his all-white Springbok team to

133

wish them luck. 'You will help bind our country into a single unit,' he said.

No matter that they were all white men. Mandela has no bitterness. Across from the Springboks' hotel, Cape Town's Holiday Inn, grim and grisly lies Robben Island, where the man was incarcerated for the length of some mature men's lives. 'Oh yes,' he told his team. 'When I was there I used to wish the Springboks to lose. Not any more, oh no. You fellows now represent our whole country.'

Parisian hearts broken by Paddy's weekend
France 25 Ireland 27
20 March 2000

PARIS: What's auld Gaelic for *incroyable*? This result will leave a winking asterisk in emerald neon in history books all down the new century. Ireland's victory was as deserved as it was dramatic. Any old Irish rugby man who missed it will curse he was not there. And after that he will have been gleefully seeking out the nearest pub wherever he was in the world.

The fearless and now forever famed Irish general Keith Wood was born on 27 January 1972, the very week, can you believe, that Ireland last won in Paris, at the Stade Colombes. His father, the late Gordon, also an Irish front-row Lion, was not in Limerick for the birth of his son that day. He was on his way to Colombes as an official and doubly celebrated in the boulevards after the match. Gordon would have been looking down last night with that same emerald gleam in his eye.

Immediately at the final whistle yesterday the touchline PA announcer thrust a microphone at Wood. All the bald blighter could come up with was some sort of Gaelic exclamation which sounded something like, and certainly meant, 'Yippee!' If generally the stadium was stunned by the result – as well as the breathtaking switchback of a contest – the travelling Irish portion in the crowd also fully deserved to acclaim themselves.

The resplendence of the victory was crowned by the theatre of its curtain-call finish, but all through the wonderful show had been garlanded by the unceasing glories of young Brian O'Driscoll in the centre. In this March weekend's tale of two cities, the freckled 21-year-old from Blackrock upstaged England's hat-trick man of the day before, Austin Healey. O'Driscoll is that rarest of talents: an old-fashioned centre of dash and daring with a jink and a shimmy and wings on his heels, let alone in his hair. In an age of played-for midfield collisions, and narrow-eyed and relentlessly grinding body charges by over-muscled half-robots, O'Driscoll shines out like the full-beam Fastnet light does off the Cork coast.

Though Ireland survived France's early onslaught, it looked all over soon after half-time when France led 19-7. But, as Ireland continued to ignore their own mistakes and even upped their gallop, there began to grow an unmistakable feel of history on the cards.

The green surges rolled on, lots of butter fingers but more of self-belief. And, as France began to stumble and panic at being trussed up and knocked down, the whole enthralling spectacular became reality with O'Driscoll's wondrous second and third thrusts, as each time he left the cover standing and was off to the line like a startled hare to a hedge.

In *Boys' Own* the young match winner used to be cheered off in his dreams on the shoulders of his grizzled confrères. Yesterday at the Stade de France it happened in real life – and Paris settled down for a two-day-late St Patrick's Day parade and night-long party. *Incroyable.*

The strain of being the people's friend
3 May 1979

I'll tell you one thing: Mike Yarwood can't do Eddie Waring half as well as Eddie does himself. I heard him coming a mile off as I waited for him the other day in the bar of his beloved Queen's

Hotel at Leeds, greeting every Tom, Dick and gatepost in a flurry of 'Ey Oop!' optional aitches and jettisoned gees. Eddie Waring makes use of his vowels as expansively as Magnus Pyke makes use of his hands. A musician might call the resulting sing-song dissonance a quaver of Yorkie bars. But it has the desired effect. As I say, you know Eddie's coming.

If John Arlott's is the voice of passive, pastoral summer and cool drinks in the lolling shade, then Eddie Waring's is the voice of murky, muddy winter and crumpets by the fire. This Saturday at Wembley he is, of course, hosting the nation for the big one. While a whopping majority of the land cannot name the teams involved in this year's rugby league cup final – let alone one of the 26 players – everyone knows the voice on the BBC don't they? Too reet an'all.

First impressions of Eddie in the flesh are exactly what I had expected. Except he left his famous trilby with the hall porter. Everything else, by gum, was larger than life. But as we enjoyably talked through our roast beef and Yorkshire, what happened? He relaxes and lets slip the mask of bluff bonhomie. It turns out he is really quite a dour one is our Eddie. Long before the pudding I sensed that it was perhaps becoming an awful strain getting out of his early morning bath each morning and having to don the redcoat gusto of an Uncle Ed that has revived and made worth watching many a dull game from *It's a Knockout* to *It's an Up and Under*!

Like many journalists, he is very suspicious of his own trade. It takes one to smell one. When I had written this piece, he insisted, could I telephone through any direct quotes I planned to use. He said he had checked up on my 'credentials' with the BBC before agreeing to meet me. The public figure is a private man. He did not want to talk about his family at all. He was coy about his age; he said it was nobody else's business, though a friend yesterday confided that he's nearer 70 than 60, which is staggering both in terms of the all-round verve of his performances and amount of hours he crams into a day. Certainly I was not to mention the hotel he is staying at in London: everyone will bother him for tickets. The real Eddie Waring is writing a book and finding it very hard going: the TV Eddie I thought I knew would surely have dictated the whole thing into a tape at one sitting.

Twice when I chided him about his privacy he did perk up for a split second and exclaim: 'That's Eddie!' as though momentarily he was talking about someone else. I'm afraid I was reminded of that cracking piece about Mrs Thatcher in the *Observer* on Sunday when Conor Cruise O'Brien said that both Dag Hammarskjold and Mrs T 'had a humourless twinkle in their eyes'. On admittedly short acquaintance I must honestly report that I had the same feeling about Eddie, the people's friend. First Dag, then Mag and now, surprisingly, the nation's favourite wag.

It may be that he is still suspiciously on guard against the long-time criticism of his broadcasting approach to RL by the game's establishment, who say his commentaries turn a noble pastime into burlesque. He knows that the BBC have been officially asked to drop him. He knows that a prim petition with an alleged 10,000 signatures was once delivered to the Head of Sport 'deploring the manner in which the BBC abuse, exploit and misrepresent the game'. Rightly the BBC answered with two words and one exclamation mark.

A couple of thousand people understand and enjoy rugby league every weekend. Ten million people understand and enjoy rugby league with Eddie every weekend. 'Why, Mr Waring,' demanded a parochial Northerner once, 'do you always tell 'em down there that it's two points for a goal? Let 'em find out for th'selves.'

Eddie was born and schooled at Dewsbury and joined the local rag as a sports reporter. He played both codes of rugby and once had a soccer trial for Nottingham Forest. Surprisingly he cannot remember (that's Eddie!) the first time he saw a RL final at Wembley. It was a 15/6d day return in the late 1930s and all he recalled is that later that evening he fell asleep in the Palladium.

By the end of the war – during which time he was manager of Dewsbury when they won the cup – he was correspondent for the *Sunday Mirror*. He paid his own way – £11 11/3d single fare on the aircraft carrier HMS Indomitable – to Australia to cover the 1946 British tour.

In 1948 he was one of three journalists asked by the BBC to comment on the final at Wembley. The seed was sown. After the 1950 tour of Australia he returned via Hollywood and he says Bob Hope and Jimmy Garner both urged him that television was the thing to get into. Next winter in England he went to a rugby union international at Twickenham and got a seat as near as he could to the TV commentator. To get the drift, to see the drill.

By the late 50s he was on his way – the warm, friendly voice eeing and aahing for the world's good books, for a local minority's bad books ... and for the top of the bill on the *Mike Yarwood Show*. Simply, the rugby league cup final without him to the huge majority would be like *Desert Island Discs* without Plomley – no, more; without the seagulls squawking.

A code worth cracking
Wigan 28 Hull 24
6 May 1985

The comparison was chilling: after enduring in recent winters a string of tawdry, inept and sullen rugby union internationals, in which the standard of play and of chivalry had scarcely done justice to either the occasion or its anticipation, one's faith in rugby football as one of modern man's finest minor inventions was fully restored on Saturday.

It has become worthless to bang on about the rugby union's patronising attitude to its brothers in the league. Surely every sane man agrees on that outside the blinds of south-west London's suburban bunker – but I must say you could twig after Saturday's salutary show why the rugby leaguers were dismissive in the autumn about Mark Ella, the Wallaby tourist who so inspired the state of the Union. He would not get a game for his country if he changed codes, said the RL boys.

Saturday's opposing half backs happened to be blood brothers. If Brett Kenny of Wigan deserved to be man of the match, his compatriot, Peter Sterling of Hull, was president of the day. From the same Sydney club, they rose to fame together with the 1982 Kangaroos; both came over to play this winter, culminating in this confrontation.

Kenny, at out half, can sell a dummy with the twitch of an eyebrow. He stands on the periphery, uninterested, fingering his top lip, wondering what's on the television ... then, of a sudden, he can double-declutch about six times in four strides as he sweeps away from defenders.

Sterling was everything I have been told and more: low-slung, straw-mopped; a workaday scurrier, you think, just perkily on the look-out for the odd quick single like a Clive Radley, and then outrageously he is drawing in two, three, even five great thundering tanks into the tackle, and at the very moment he is clattered, pops out the perfect pass, short, long or under-arm, and his man is in the clear.

The wingmen were set off on more fliers than a Biggin Hill bank holiday. If their Union counterparts in England like Underwood, Smith or Trick – who honestly tell you they go whole weekends without a pass – were watching on television, surely their applications will be in the post to somewhere up north with a first-class stamp.

Gill, on one Wigan wing, riddled the spine every time he got going and, on the other, the Aborigine, Ferguson, kept going off like an arrow. Like Basil D'Oliveira, Ferguson is a leading sportsman late to the big time. Like Basil, who stayed 34 for years and years until Bill Frindall, ever meticulous, blew the gaffe on his birth certificate, John is happy to remain 30. Some say he is coming up to his 10th 30th birthday. That obviously offends the Australian national selectors, who have yet to give him a cap, though he has long been in everyone's World XIII – with 99,801 more voters on Saturday.

Whistle stop for still-hungry Lindop
30 April 1988

As soon as the hooter goes for full-time at Wembley this afternoon, Fred Lindop will be on the cadge. For something 'a ruddy sight more substantial' than the pot of tea and dainty, southern, cucumber sandwich square with no crusts that will be waiting for him in the referee's dungeon.

'The pangs of hunger will be something rotten,' he says. 'I won't have had a bite all day, I get that nervous.' At his last rugby league Challenge Cup final in 1982 – this is his fourth – his famous beady eye softened as it settled on a matey Wembley waitress at the official lunch beforehand and, bless her, she saved Lindop a right Northern slap-up of roast beef, Yorkshire and all the trimmings for afterwards.

He'll be looking for the same today. He'll scoff it greedily, but sadly. He won't be reflecting on his part in the previous tumultuous 80 minutes, but on the past 22 years, for the game's shrill finale will be, too, his own poignant last post. The full-time hooter cruelly pensions him off. Lindop is 50 in July, which means automatic redundancy from the Senior Referees' panel on which he has been a striking fixture and an institution right back to 1966.

A few have carped this week that it was wrong to award Lindop this last and most illuminated stage of all for his farewell performance. Whinges the Wigan coach, Graham Lowe: 'It is crazy to appoint the cup final referee on sentimental grounds. He should simply be the best there is; it shouldn't serve as a 50-year-old's birthday treat.'

Lindop says: 'Yes, such stuff is hurtful. But sentiment hasn't come into it. Refs are marked each week, and I've finished top man again this season. It's as simple as that, and I'm sure it's nothing to do with a farewell present to send the old bull out to pasture. I work at my game as I always have: at least 20 miles a week, rain, shine or snow.'

In what you might call civvy life – without, that is, a whistle or threatening notebook at the ready – the engaging, chummy Wakefield print rep is not at all bluff and gruff Yorkie-fierce. Lindop has dismissed with finality many more dangerous and dissenting heckles than the likes of those from Lowe this week, since the faraway day he peeped for kick-off for the very first time: 'Barrow vs Rochdale, 1966. In they went, boomph, trying to test out this young sprog in black, see. Within three minutes I had to send off old Bill Payne. It was him or me. Took too big a gamble, he did, so I had to respond with a gamble. I was scared stiff. "Off!" I said – and off he ambled, and I was into my stride.'

A season later Lindop, astonishingly, got the first of his many Test matches. '21 October 1967, the Aussies at Headingley, and I remember those shivers up my spine for evermore. You know that phrase "His hair stood on end"? Well, walking out there that day, mine really did, all spiked up, it did and that's a fact, so electric was the atmosphere that afternoon.' He reffed all three Tests of that epic Australian series.

You mention matches, men and moments in which Lindop has been both tetchy and tactful conductor (for just £37 a game, plus paltry exes), and he punctuates your flow with delicious, unobtrusive, matter-of-fact murmurs – 'Aye, great player, him', or 'Mischievous blighter, he was', or 'Had him off sharpish that day I did, oh aye.'

To me, Fred Lindop seems the very model of the modern magisterial, his sweeping command of gesture keeping both tempo and tempers smooth and unruffled. But very much the boss; like this afternoon, when 90,000 souls will know as one exactly the severity of the crime simply by the time his little wooden whistle trills as it tra-laas through the whole register from friendly chirrups to short sharp shepherd's demands or shrill sternness, right up to his long, emphatic, doom-laden judicial summons that has even the dressing-room attendant quaking as he leans forward to turn on the bath taps.

If Lindop is the best in rugby league, then he is very, very good by definition. His game is played by uncomplicated sportsmen who seldom moan, for they know their sport demands muscle and commitment keen and sharp enough to split an oak. The league reffing has, I fancy, almost always been of a higher standard than that of the union, who specialise in weak, white-kneed officials scared to get tough with toughs, or soccer where both ditherers and Hitlers proliferate and petulant mass protests are tolerated 10 times a match, and the whistler is oblivious to exactly how many yards make 10.

'Not that discipline is what it was in league,' says Lindop. 'Respect for authority is an outmoded idea right through the country, I suppose. Aye, I've seen it creep up right down the years. I've gone through the generations, like. Guys I sent off are middle-aged blokes now, and I'm keeping their sons in order.' And the famous piercing eyes, that have turned hulking props to jelly, mist over, and you grin and keep mum as you let the old bull spool back in flickering sepia his afternoons calming the breathless, super-charged hurry:

'Oh aye, most of them knew when they had to go. Most of them know when the long walk beckons. Even in French. Oh yes, sure I speak French. You need to over there. They're tough, but I think people here exaggerate their toughness. I love it over there. But devious isn't in it: once, under the Pyrenees, I was in charge at Saint Paul, and had to send the same bloke off four times. Four ruddy times he went – and four times he came back in a different numbered shirt. 'C'mon lad,' I said to him each time. '*Quittez le jeu. Allez, tout de suite!*'

7

OOH! I SAY!

Tips from the great Tilden
9 July 1979

We've all heard the story of how Mr Borg made his eight-year-old son his first wooden tennis racket. It has been told more times than Roscoe Tanner has been called 'the man from Lookout Mountain, Tennessee' how Mrs Borg asked if her nine-year-old son could enter the neighbouring village tournament's women's doubles to give him more match practice.

Ad tedium has the yarn been repeated of how the spoiled 11-year-old prodigy crowned an umpire in a tantrum and was told he would never be champion of the world if he ever again so let his concentration waver – so he never did.

Often I have heard how Björn Borg, just a tiny 12, heard on the wireless in July 1967 that the brand-new Wimbledon champion John Newcombe had said that he had originally learned to play the game by reading a 50-year old instructional book *Match Play and Spin of the Ball* by the one and only Bill Tilden – and that Mr Borg had scoured Sweden's bookshops for a translation so that his boy could stay up nights reading and learning by heart Tilden's '13 Points for Young Players to Remember.'

But nobody seems to have actually chronicled this list the little boy had learned over his cocoa before snuggling down with his racket for the night. I paraphrase a champion's baker's dozen that so inspired another:

1. Get the ball back.
2. The main object is to break up the other man's game.

3. Tennis should be played defensively with an offensive attitude.
4. Play to your opponent's strength but exploit his weakness at crucial points.
5. Double faults are inexcusable so develop a second serve as difficult as your first.
6. Returning is just as important as serving because 50 per cent of all points begin that way.
7. Never ever blow an easy shot.
8. Realise a champion will miss as many shots as a non-champion – but he will never miss them at critical moments.
9. Play hardest of all at 30-15 or 15-30.
10. Start a match with one alternative strategy up your sleeve – but never change a winning game.
11. Decide where your opponent might return the ball and head there pronto. Anticipation is just a fancy word for guessing right.
12. Results are more important than form. Vary pace or spin if your opponent thinks he is in a winning groove.
13. Have a killer instinct but also be a sportsman.

Between games, Ashe might meditate and Connors reads notes from his long-dead granny ... could it conceivably be that this successor to Bill Tilden as the most devastating player of tennis the world has known silently chants this 13-point catechism which he learned in 1967 as he so determinedly re-drives his arms and racket grip under the sign of the Robinsons Barley Water?

I may have seemed as excited as those around me through Saturday's fifth set in the final against Tanner. But there was not really a glimmer of doubt who would win, was there? Especially if you had, that morning, read the same passage that one of the players down there had discovered when he was at a very impressionable age. Wrote Tilden:

'When two players start a match, remember it is always a battle to see who will dominate and who will be pushed around. One or other will ultimately impress tennis personality upon the other. The one who does will win, because by doing so he forces the recognition of impending defeat upon his opponent. One of the surest ways to achieve this state of affairs is to set your own tempo and hold it at all costs. Do it courteously with all due regard for your opponent's right, but do it.'

And so did Tilden, a golden jubilee away, sum up a midsummer Saturday in 1979. When Muhammad Ali beat Frazier we knew he was great: when he beat Foreman we knew he was truly the greatest. Long before Saturday we know Björn Borg was great: now as he fell to his knees to mark his fourth Wimbledon title and the world got to its feet to raise the roof, we knew he was truly the greatest.

Our boomerang
5 July 1980

Everybody's sunshine girl kissed the grail – and only then did it start to rain again. The new-found sentiment for her opponent round the cabbagey-green old Wimbledon pile has done everyone a world of good, but for a long-time Gooly lover there was only one girl in it. Evonne Goolagong-Cawley, mother of three-year-old Kelly, beat Chris Evert-Lloyd 6-1 7-6.

Nine years is a long time between championships. So is the 66 years since a mum held up the gilt gingerbread. Mrs Dorothea Douglas Lambert Chambers did it in 1914 and quite horrified the remnants of the muscular Edwardian chauvinists at what sort of modern hussy they had let out of the bag.

Earlier this week Evonne admitted that in 1971 she was not half the player she has become. 'It wasn't a fluke exactly. But I didn't realise what was happening.' Wimbledon was then just another tournament for the lass with the liquid backhand, the heavenly stride and the shoulders overwhelmed by the protective avuncular, hairy right arm of Vic Edwards. At about that time too, all the other girls started their grunting. Not Evonne.

At her first starchy Wimbledon function in the secretary's tent before 1971's opening round, an elderly cockney waitress had got to chatting to the bewildered sprite. 'I do 'ope you do well, luv,' she said. 'If I do,' said Evonne, 'I promise I'll come and see you immediately afterwards.' It was a joke. But she did. She finished her press conference with the world and went to see the old lady with the grey hair and the black dress and white pinny and gave her a kiss. 'Like I promised.'

Glory be! Our enchanting faun has done it again – that very female tomboy whose first game was to chase pigeons at dusty Barrellan, up in the barren-baked, sunbright bush of New South Wales, chasing across the narrow, perilous planks of the tiny town's grain elevator. Wheat from chaff!

Cricketing in Australia in February we suddenly came across a signpost to Barellan. It was nearby – give or take a couple of hundred miles. 'I insist we go there,' I said to the driver, 'Evonne was born there.' He talked me out of it. 'She's dead and gone. Her legs all shook up.' He got it wrong.

Dan, Dan, for 60 years the Wimbledon man
28 June 1984

Dan Maskell, loved and listened to every midsummer by a worldwide audience measured in many millions as the voice of Wimbledon, has been part of the All England Championships for far longer than the BBC.

The first final he ever saw was at the age of 16 in 1924, when Kitty McKane beat Helen Wills. That was three years before the BBC even tried a wireless transmission, Cochet beating Borotra through the crackle of the crystal set. They were allowed to broadcast that day only on condition that the commentator,

Teddy Wakelam, whispered, and that the Corporation first agreed to pay for a pane of frosted glass to hide their hut from a view of the players' lavatory.

The first television transmission was in 1937, a 25-minute part of a Bunny Austin match – and the next morning the *Daily Telegraph* reporter said: 'People could observe from some miles away every movement of the players. Even the passage of the marks of the lawnmower were distinctly visible in the grass. There were also scenes of spectators in the stands and some of the faces could be seen quite clearly.'

Long before that, Dan Maskell was a fixture: the players' friend, adviser and coach. Three years earlier, for instance, on the morning of the epic final between Crawford and Vines, he had worked out with them before they took the court. Vines wanted Dan to slice backhand after backhand as heavily as he could – and 20 minutes later Crawford demanded that he should be fed on fast, flat forehands. In the event the forehand prevailed – as Dan had suspected.

Half a century ago the baby from Fulham had already come a long way. The Everington Street Elementary School was almost exactly equidistant between Craven Cottage, home of the people's game, and the Queen's Club, home of the rich men with rackets. The youngster was taken to the soccer on Saturdays by his father. After school on summer evenings the ragged-trousered philanthropist-to-be and his urchin mates earned pence as ball boys at Queen's.

He might have won a scholarship but things were tight in the family. 'A friend of my father's was a coach at Queen's and he told him: "For a ball boy your Dan always seems to be listening intently whenever I am coaching a member on court."' So he became a professional ball boy and in time a coaching assistant. And so began the reciprocal love affair with the game. Since 1929 he has not missed a single day's play at Wimbledon. That's nearly 600 days: an awful lot of 'New balls, please!' In 1951, Dan took over from Freddie Grisewood as the BBC's commentator. Grisewood's voice was as mellow and evocative to that generation as Arlott's and Dimbleby's – and Maskell's – would become to the next.

Before play next Monday, Maskell himself will present on court the centenary pageant of women's champions. The still strikingly handsome, square-faced old cove is overwhelmed by such honour to a one-time ball boy. The spaniel's eyes will sparkle and the laugh lines grow deeper, and they will be moist as royalty makes its entrance.

And he will be sure to make a point, as he always does, of focusing on that particular place: 'the third row back, seats four and five, where another ball boy, my friend Ernest, sat with me that first midsummer afternoon in 1924 ... Oh, my goodness me, little did I know then ...' Seventeen of the surviving women's champions will parade on Monday. 'I played with 12 of them, y' know.' Not a bad boast.

But in the evening, as he ever does, he will have raced back home in time to watch the television highlights – his sheet of notes and hieroglyphics on his knee, checking and rechecking his facts, that he has not talked too much, nor left in too many of his favourite phrases: 'Ooh! I say, what a shot! Well played indeed, sir!'

Ooh, I say, what a lovely fellow! Well played, indeed sir.

Ace for freebies, second service for the faithful
30 June 1989

Wimbledon's poignant moments repeat themselves each year – and I don't necessarily mean John Lloyd's moist-eyed impersonation of Kim Hughes as he handed in his badges after yet another first-round calamity, or even Annabel Croft's ditto departure.

The poor lamb said afterwards she'd had a rotten headache all through the match, but her new agent from Mark McCormack's IMG was undaunted. 'It should be easy to find lots of sponsors for her because she is so attractive,' he said. Wimbledon is a sponsors' beanfeast now. If Wimbledon didn't exist, no sponsor could have dared invent it, but seeing it's there, they are working on it. Oh boy, do they keep in the poignancy!

Though it easily could be arranged to sell a number of season tickets on a first-come-first-served basis to the general public for the fortnight, they do not do so because nothing is more poignant each day than to have the privileged corporate guests helicoptered and limousined past the bleary, blanketed, tennis-loving hoi polloi who have camped outside the gates all night. This is one hippie army the establishment does not move on, for this lot proves the very point of their privilege.

That 12 o'clock rush by the dawn queue for any left-over standing room on the centre court used to be a touching thrill to be in on. Now it seems as seedy and forlorn as it was always unfair. For just across the way, out of sight, the smoked salmon and champagne is being guzzled by captains of industry, who can't tell a backhand pass from a tennis elbow, and their clients, who can tell even less.

The grandest parade at Wimbledon these days takes place long after play has begun, when the captains and their clients, cigars chomping at one hand, and a parasoled Poll at the other, hold sway. Every day this week they have stepped, blinking and briefly, into the real world of unshaded sunlight, sweaty armpits and concourse crush to make their way as quickly as possible to the reserved exclusive reservation of the centre court seating.

Wimbledon – quite simply the finest laager in the world, now a corporate outing. A freebie for BP, ICI, BAT and all that lot, and the talk is not of sport but of deals and dollars. Of course, Wimbledon and its oligarchic All England Club (membership less than 400, with three free tickets each day) was ripe for the plucking from the moment, some years back, when old Bagenal Harvey, the same London agent who persuaded Denis Compton to smarm his hair in Brylcreem, suggested that Wimbledon charge a little more for Robinsons Barley Water to put their product under the umpire's chair.

Now it is Coca-Cola, of course. You might not have actually seen any player this week with tell-tale brown stains smudging his lips after quaffing the revolting American fizz, but as long as the paper cup has Coke printed on it, that's good enough for the marketing men. Business is business and business is booming.

They make strange bedfellows, but opposites attract. Big business does the deals while the All England keeps up appearances. At Wimbledon, sweets are called bon-bons. Alongside the centre court there are a series of temporary crush bars where you can wash down a £1.50 hot dog on a paper plate with a £22 bottle of non-vintage champagne. Or perhaps sir would like 10 soggy strawberries in a paper bowl at 10p per strawberry?

You stand with your paper plate on this acre of concrete surrounded by signs which read 'No glass may be removed from the Lawn – By Order of the Committee.' Lawn? What lawn? The committee bangs on: 'Spectators are requested NOT to take crockery or cutlery away from the catering area.' Crockery? Cutlery? What age are they living in?

The clock of St Mary's church strikes four – and the Royal Box rises at once and goes in for tea. If a match stood at two sets all, 5-4 and 40-30, they'd still go in on the stroke of four. And that's where the real crockery clinks. Sarah Ferguson was there on Tuesday. She seemed to enjoy it. Martina was playing, but about 50 cameramen kept their lenses trained on Sarah throughout. The bon-bons passed round the Royal Box like at a pantomime matinee. Sarah had more than most.

A couple of years ago, John McEnroe's father asked if he could meet, at his convenience, the Wimbledon boss, Air Chief Marshal Sir Brian Burnett, to clear up a couple of matters relating to his son, the champion. 'Impossible,' came back the withering message via a minion, 'Sir Brian is far too busy entertaining royalty.' What a heck of a two-week job for the old boy.

Mind you, this week has been a bad one for the club. Stares are blank and upper lips twitch when you ask a member about the essays their former Supremo, Major David Mills, has been contributing to the *People*. In his three-page spread last week the Major, 16 years the club's secretary, unaccountably and luridly filled in the space under such headlines as 'Sex Scandal of the Women's Stars', 'Wimbledon's Sodom and Gomorrah', 'Perils of the Women's Locker Room' and 'The Day I Nearly Spanked The Brat'. This was the man who for so long called royalty in for tea at 4pm precisely. If he had stayed longer perhaps he would have flogged the royal teatime to the highest bidder.

An epic joust lives up to the occasion
10 July 2001

More than two hours later a couple of hundred Croats were waiting on the Wimbledon concourse to acclaim him. This would be nothing, said the winner as he was mobbed, compared with the 150,000 'who will welcome me back to Split tomorrow'.

The first wild-card winner is something for Wimbledon history. But in the whole legend of comparatively recent sport, this comeback of Goran Ivanisevic, this restoration of a career which seemed doomed, must rank along with Muhammad Ali's jungle rumble back from oblivion against George Foreman, or the ageing Jack Nicklaus's last fling in the Masters, or possibly Don Bradman's century on the resumption of his career in 1946 after eight years away.

The roof on the old stadium's stands could seldom have been raised with such a tempestuous clamour. It was always on the cards somehow that the match-up between the two veterans, Ivanisevic and Pat Rafter, would ignite into something wondrous and, to be sure, as the script unfolded its epic passages, the two men took turns to light red-hot bonfires all over the small but famous field.

It was puncher vs boxer, the classic confrontation: the Croat man-mountain with a raging temperament and an axeman's swipe, against the cool-hand all-action Australian crowd-pleaser with the slippered tread and more deft, cunning and calculated touch. There was the whiff of grandeur about the occasion as well, a whiff of the medieval jousts of honour and chivalry. When last, if ever, did two bearded knights play out this midsummer festival's grandest of grand slam finales? As the match ran its pulsating course, the twists and turns of the plot, the exits and entrances of each new riveting scene, piled in on one another, acclaimed by the two vociferously opposing choruses decked in green and yellow and the chequered blood-red of Croatia.

One was convinced that the utterly heroic Rafter as good as had his hands on the favours of legend when Ivanisevic was footfaulted at that crucial moment in the fourth, followed at once by what the fuming Croatian presumed a bum call by a centre-line judge (it wasn't). Ivanisevic flipped, hurling his racket to the grass and so wild he seemed in two minds whether to kick it away or jump on it to make it kindling wood. Instead, he executed a dervish dance and you feared for him throwing the whole match away in his anger. And, knowing him, you would have bet on it nine times out of 10. To his immense credit he pulled himself together: 'I got a little crazy, you know. But this is the final, I say to myself, and I am calm already. I say, this is your last chance, you are going to win it, just keep cool. You cannot afford to go crazy in Wimbledon final.'

From then on you fancied he was ready to sail – if not serenely – to his destiny. Then once more he steamed up like a boiling kettle with a rattling lid as he lost the fourth 6-2. This meant Rafter would serve the first game of the final set and so, presumably, be ahead throughout with Goran having to play catch-up on his every serve. But once again the lid stayed on.

'I was scared. I say, he is going to serve first and maybe I will lose now,' Ivanisevic recalled. 'But I kept my head and kept catching him up. At 5-5 I say, if I win this game I going on to win match.' But he didn't. It ran on to 7-7, and then the deed was as good as done. Wonderful winner, wonderful loser, wonderful crowd, and wonderful Wimbledon.

8

THE THRILL OF THE CHASE

A day of dog-collars
17 March 1977

I've borrowed my dad's brown trilby and been to Cheltenham races. I knew it was cracked up to be something, but never anything quite like this. St Patrick's Day gone mad. The festival starts at Paddington, where first class, non-stop morning specials leave on the half-hour full of the buffeting champagne and cigar gentry, every man-Jonathan of them smirkingly knowing a thing or three.

I caught the orthodox second class. More Irish. They know a thing or two of that as well. So they tell you. Our buffets were more scruffy. Brown ales and scarce a Wills Whiff to be seen. Everyone deep into the *Sporting Life*. All wide-eyed expectation as a cover for furtive, blotchy-faced despair. And, quietly, in corners, sheepishly studying *Timeform* as if a breviary, a host of Irish clergy.

And once at Cheltenham station, in the long queue for buses and taxis you can't finish your count of the dog-collars. Sunday clergies with the glint of midweek sport in their eye. And, I'd bet on it, twice as many again in civvy collar and tie and having told their abbots and bishops that they're off for their annual retreat on the mainland at some unsuspecting convent school or whatever. Certainly Cheltenham's racecard could be printed in Latin and half the fancy could read it.

Mark you, Cheltenham races and the Catholic Church have long been hand in glove. A lively settlement of Romans was established there by refugees from the French Revolution. And when the merry Captain Berkeley founded the race meeting below Cleeve Hill in the early part of last century, the Irish brought over their nags to join in the fun. Many stayed there and then. Indeed, a hundred years ago Cheltenham had to build itself a new cemetery, for as the old refrain went: 'The churchyard's so small and the Irish so many; they ought to be pickled and sent to Kilkenny.' To the Bible-thumper Dean Close the horse-racing Irish of Cheltenham were the pet hate ahead even of drink. 'Papists, gambling and profligacy,' he ranted in 1835, 'are essential concomitants of horse racing.' But he failed to wipe even a smile from their face and he stomped off to Carlisle.

Cobbett failed too. 'Cheltenham on race day is the resort of the lame and lazy, the gourmandising and guzzling, the bilious and nervous.' Now that's the sort of thing I would have been thinking of if I'd caught the first class.

Hey ho, but what a lovely jig the Irish give to the prim place. Not that the residents stir to wake out of their doze, unless they're hoteliers or traffic wardens or shopkeepers. One daft local grocer, for years now, has made a tradition of presenting a posy of jasmine and a packet of Polos to the Queen Mother as she's chauffeured past his shop on her way up to the course. The Queen Mother has a horse called Isle of Man. 'Good luck to the Isle of Wight,' said the grocer in his blushing confusion. But the Queen Mother seemed beamingly oblivious as she accepted the gift.

Yesterday, bewildered but rubbing shoulders with the clergy, with shady cockneys and nobs from the shires, I chanced across our film critic, Mr Malcolm, looking knowing like everyone else, even more so he in his porridgy oatmeal coat. With flamboyant confidence he gave me Checkov 'for classical reasons' to win the first race. It lost. He was certain about Flitgrove for the second. Not a flicker. Well, Birds Nest for the third. Nowhere.

I console him with the posy I'd bought specially in case I met the Queen Mother. But he won on the fourth when I didn't bet. So I gave him the packet of Polos in celebration. To the uninitiated

Cheltenham is no place to find the winner. But, now, if you are looking to be converted to the one true faith...

The grey horse that won the blue riband
17 March 1989

The more resplendently silver the lining, so often the more wretchedly gloomy the dark cloud. At the moment Desert Orchid was heroically gathering himself at the third from last to make his emperor's entrance into Cheltenham's frenziedly welcoming amphitheatre another game innocent had the gun to his brain. Literally.

As Desert Orchid was hurray-ed home with – truly – a demented swirl of frisbeeing trilbies, men were beginning to erect a screen round Ten Plus and a sombre-faced vet was loading a gun. It was the fifth shot to ring out at the meeting. So one of the most purple passages in the history of sport was garlanded in black crêpe.

One thing the tragic death of Ten Plus did was set in bolder relief the pre-race dilemma of Desert Orchid's devoted owner. The vile weather overnight had turned the greenest turf into a wickedly treacherously skidpan. What should they do? Risk their priceless grey for a paltry £50,000 and the overwhelming insistence of what seemed to be the whole British nation? They chose to run and quite spectacularly, indeed, inevitably, public demand had its day of days and the bookies were skinned alive. Corals alone admitted to coughing up half a million yesterday. Some bookmakers said it was a pleasure to lose their dough to such a horse. Oh yeah ...

It was a huge thrill to be there, barged hither and yon and speared by umbrellas. Feet wet through inside the wellies – but mouth as dry as tinder as the multitude willed the gallant grey into not so much the winners' but the immortals' enclosure. I never thought Jonjo's epic cavalry charge on Dawn Run could be topped when it came to stirring the cockles. It was. Or Arkle's dramatics. And old men were even admitting that yesterday's buzz matched Gordon Miller's fifth in 1936, the win which they say finally and indelibly lodged National Hunt racing in the nation's noddle. I cannot remember a press room anywhere in such a froth of excitement. Look at that, the Queen Mum's wearing an orchid buttonhole. No, it's a huge posh diamond broach.

The owner, Richard Burridge, is a tall, tweedy man, craggily handsome and as highly strung yesterday as his nag was not. Still, a cascade of tears of joy were colliding in rivulets down his kestrel's nose. And his hands were still shaking. 'Today was as rewarding and satisfying a day as to last us the rest of our lives,' he said. He had parked his car at 9.45 and just sat there mesmerised by the windscreen wipers and his rotten luck. 'I just couldn't believe what the weather had turned up for us.' His inclination was to pull the horse out.

'Shall we, shan't we run?' His hands had started shaking then, but for different reasons. But once I'd spoken seriously to David Elsworth, the trainer, the serious doubts began to evaporate. 'David was for running; he told me, "If you've got the best horse in the field, it is up to us to prove it; what if he gets a little strain next week, and we'll never know if he could win the Cup." That was good enough for me. It was too, wasn't it? Once over the last I knew he'd never give up. Though I must say I wasn't seeing all that clearly by then, my glasses were too steamed up.' So, long before then, were everybody else's.

Follow that? Extremely difficult. Surely Desert Orchid should bow out now. The fourth Cheltenham immortal. One man who was there when each of the three others did their stuff was Fulke Walwyn. He is now 78 and rode Royal Mail second to Golden Miller's fifth win in 1936. Yesterday morning Walwyn unveiled a statue on the concourse to his one-time rival, The Miller, and spoke with wonder of the horse. The tragic irony was that within a couple of hours the bluff old man, Walwyn, was himself stricken as his own Ten Plus was lying on the turf as grievously immobile as a statue. In many ways it is a rotten, heartless pastime in the name of sport.

Racing dynasty falls under the hammer
1 June 1989

Poignant stuff in the noonday sun. Fred Winter's blissful, rose-pink Queen Anne farmhouse at Uplands under the Berkshire Downs at Lambourn stands imposing four-square sentry over one of National Hunt racing's most legendary training yards. Yesterday, sadly and almost eerily, the front door remained solemnly closed.

Swirling around it, out in the yard, was all the hubble and bubble of barter like an upmarket car-boot sale of tack and blankets, snaffles and saddles. Inside in their gloom, the ailing 'Guvnor' and his wife Di were not once seen even peeking through a curtain. Just one window was open, so they must have heard the businesslike young auctioneer's trilling staccato as it dispersed the memories and minor trappings of one of horse racing's most celebrated quarters of a century.

Two years ago, irony of ironies, the man who was four-times champion jockey and who had bounced up with a toothy grin from umpteen frightening falls at fences, fell down the stairs at home to set in train a run of grievous bad health that, to all intents, ended with his official retirement marked by yesterday's sad dispersal sale of 'racing and general stable equipment'. Winter's former assistant, the youthful Charlie Brooks, now takes over. He will move into the house when the Winters find another home. There was sadness in the air yesterday. Tinged with relief at the businesslike handover, and also, yes, a sense of celebration at the end of the resplendent career of the heroic old champion jockey and trainer.

'We're not here to dwell, we're here to sell,' announced the brisk young auctioneer, Andrew Coney – and he was off and away, knocking down with his farmer's knobkerrie the 460 lots from '19 pair broom and muck forks' to 'French racing snaffle complete with Irish martingale'.

Of the 200 or so mix of bidders and gawpers, nobody seemed determined on any romance. Lot 343, for instance, fetched a routine £25, similar to the dozens of saddles around it. But Lot 343, dark, teaky and as leather-brown and crinkly weatherbeaten as the old hero's famous face, just happened to be Fred Winter's own saddle. Had he won his two Grand Nationals, his two Gold Cups, his three Champion Hurdles on that very same little age-shrined throne? What a snip at £25.

They sold the saddles in the stable next to that in which Jay Trump had lived before his famous Aintree win in 1965. In the very box that Anglo had left for Liverpool the year after, they auctioned off Fred's daughter's eventing tack. Those two Grand National wins – in his first three years as a trainer – had set up the 'Guvnor'. When he had climbed down from the saddle in 1964, his friends had misgivings about him training. He started off at Uplands with just three horses, two of them sent to him by Sir Michael Sobell, the TV magnate. Suddenly he was only the second man in history to ride and train a National winner. Through the 1970s he was champion trainer seven times out of eight. His last championship came 18 months before his debilitating fall.

Yesterday, between Lots 295 (five nylon head collars) and 301 (an osteopulse kit, complete) came 'a number of bridles and bits'. I wondered if in that little lot ('Will someone start at £20? OK, what am I bid? £15?') might have been the bridle that broke on Fred when he was on little Mandarin in Le Grand Steeplechase de Paris? It snapped in the first mile: the game nag broke down three from home; but Winter, riding like a Wild West Indian brave, got up to win. It was, of all of them, probably his most legendary ride. £15? Dearie me.

But they can't really sell off the memories. Can they? Just in case, to keep them in, the front door stayed closed all day.

Memoirs of a fox-hunting hypocrite
22 December 1990

Last week, in Hereford's High Town, I went out of my way to bung a tenner into the young man's hat. He was collecting for the League Against Cruel Sports. Yet only last Boxing Day I happily forked out a fiver when the cap came round at the local meet for the hunt servants' Christmas Box.

Perhaps the invitation to put my X last month in support of all the National Trust resolutions to ban hunting concentrated the mind and forced me to admit at last a mature-ish middle-age, and so officially renounce all Satan's mounted satin-hats and all their pomps and preens. Not to mention their wives and their daughters, sisters, cousins and aunts.

Footslogging Francis. Although a farmer's son, only on one solitary occasion did I actually sit on a horse at a meet of hounds. And then only for a couple of minutes. Near Nailsworth when I was on the *Stroud News*. Borrowed my Uncle John's bright fox-brown sports jacket, and scrambled tremulously up into the saddle of a docile thing just to pose for a Your Intrepid Reporter Was There pic, as well as impress whichever Minchinhampton Moll, Sheepscombe Shirl, or Brimscombe bint was currently taking my fancy. The wretched four-footer bent down to nibble a daisy or something, and I somersaulted straight over its ruddy neck as sweetly as Olga Korbut on another sort of horse.

Down the years, I've followed on foot – sat snog-snug or snowbound in Land Rovers, or hung around hedges with hipflasks – such diverse packs as the Surrey Union, on those blissfully snooty downs around Dorking; the fanciable, eye-catching West Kent; the grand Garth & South Berks; the North Hereford, on its honeyed hillocks speckled by spinneys; the Ledbury, the Cotswold, the Berkeley, the Heythrop and, once, the Beaufort, one of the grandest 'olde money' hunts of them all, where one mounted grande dame looked across with almost a shudder at the aspiring equestrian, Michael Heseltine, in full, new-tailored rigout, and whispered to her companion with a sniff, 'My deah, obviously the sort who had to buy his own furniture.'

That was the day they sent me down to interview Prince Charles on something or other, long forgotten. It was a stupendous morning: springly-tingly, chap-lipped, white-bright wintery and invigorating, with the Severn glinting like a precious-stone necklace far below the ridge. When, at last, his retainer ran off to run his bath, and the young Prince dismounted, he said breathlessly, 'Golly, one can scarcely recall one having had such a tremendously exhilarating day, what?'

I believed him – and caught the buffet-car back to Padders from Temple Meads arguing successfully against my pallid liberal conscience that gruff old AG Street had been dead right when asked to defend hunting years before on *Any Questions?*. 'Defend huntin', he growled, 'I would no more defend huntin', than ploughin', sowin', reapin', lambin', muck-spreadin', or any other totally necessary event in the country calendar.'

I suppose in this new conversion to the footpaths of righteousness I'll have to give up *Horse & Hound* and the *Field*. In the latter, many years ago, its editor decreed: 'The dropping of the final g, as in huntin', is often done. There is no law against it. Yet it causes anger among persons who are themselves not free of idiosyncrasies in diction. To drop the final g is no worse, and certainly no better, than speaking with a regional accent, the shock effect of which went out with the suffragette movement.' And, he added for good effect, 'Hunting traditionalists refrain from saying "Good Morning" on Non-Hunting days, the approved salutation being "Good Day". But when hounds are out, "Good Morning" comes into its own because there is no such thing as afternoon to hunting people.'

I'll for sure miss *Horse & Hound* and its timeless, unchanging format. It must be the last serenely confident weekly magazine which can have changed barely an iota since my boyhood; or,

I dare say, since it was founded 106 years ago. It is the much-loved log of the suddenly beleaguered, almost surrounded, clan; hunting is at bay, but *H&H* fights its corner tooth and claw.

I gave up my sub in the week of the National Trust vote. My last *H&H* carried a piece about hunting horns in warfare. Splendidly typical. 'Foxhunters should be proud,' it said, citing such as Colonel John Campbell, Coldstream Guards, who rallied his men with his horn at the Somme, to such frenzied effect that 'they stormed the German trenches and he gained a VC'. Likewise, a war later, an MC for Major Ted Worrall, West Somerset, 'for a similar incident in Sicily at the Battle of Primosole Bridge'. And so on – all leading up to the topical exhortation, citing Montgomery's launching of his attack on Alamein by wishing his Eighth Army 'Good Hunting of the Desert Fox'. Urged *H&H*: 'Those Desert Rats' successors are now embarking for the Gulf to deal with a quarry not worthy of the name of Fox, but rather more akin to a Hyena. May we wish them "Good Hunting" and suggest a hunting horn might be a useful bit of kit which does not take up too much room.'

My pile of back numbers makes for a touching read, especially hot on handy hints. Except, mind, how to cadge with absolute certainty a decent supper after the day's exertions: that, I've found, is always up to the form of the individual con-artist. But usually okay once you twig that the game is very democratic in fact, and hunt followers on foot are almost as welcome to join the evening jollity. (It helped in my youth, I suppose, being on the local rag: even the dear old *Slough Observer* would encourage you to infiltrate Hunt Suppers.) As long as you didn't wipe your nose on the sleeve of your houndstooth.

Hunting folk are very generous. Well, up to a point: some would rather lend their wife (or husband) than their favourite nag.

Once in, the menus haven't changed all century: for breakfast, strong tea, tot of brandy, cold game, porridge; for supper, roast anything, three veg; 'schoolroom' pudding, like spotted dick, apple pie, or brown-bread-and-butter soaked in navy rum and blended with clotted cream, strawberry preserve and three eggs. Proper Cheddar, real Stilton, or Blue Shropshire – 'certainly no cheese remotely south of Dover'. Always, warned *H&H*'s etiquette column at Christmas 1975, 'Remember Hunt Master does not want a roast immersed in a lake of pureed apricots; nor will he appreciate conversation being drowned by the munching and chomping of raw vegetables.' And the wine, sir? Claret, lashings of.

Followed by, perhaps, another piping hot soak in that deep, long, country-house bath tub. Not for the mud this time, but for the scented suds. Don't wallow too long in it: one of those nostril-flaring, winning and whinnying women might be just along the corridor; she who got up that morning (probably with somebody else) and dressed to kill, now undresses, intent on doing near enough likewise. Someone said the other day that hunting itself was very much like adultery anyway – endless hanging about; false starts; great expectations; moments of sublime thrills and passion; lots of hurt; extremely expensive, and morally indefensible.

But not, unlike adultery, for very much longer, methinks. Perhaps I'm getting out while the going's good. Full confession and firm purpose of amendment. The closeness of the National Trust vote on hunting on its land has determined the Trust on a serious, two-year, non-fob-off study before, I warrant, it gives a conclusive, unceremonious, thumbs down to the huntsmen: two years is an awful long time for committed lobbyists.

The fox and deer certainly have the most active on their side; hunters seem to have accepted the inevitable. Then there is Brussels: they will be getting their oar in for sure by 1992. By which time, I fervently trust, the Labour Party will have gained power in Britain. That would put the kibosh on the redcoats. Labour's recent policy document on the environment determined, without equivocation, immediately to allow a free vote on hunting, and if it favoured abolition, which it surely would, to allow parliamentary time to introduce the necessary legislation.

Last Boxing Day we had an incredible choice of eight morning meets within a radius of less than 30 miles – the Golden Valley at Hay-on-Wye, the Monmouthshire at Abergavenny, the Ludlow at the Castle itself, the North Hereford at Ledbury, the Teme Valley at Knighton, the Radnor & West at Kington. We took in two others, for God speed, hail and farewell to the horses, the horsemen and their crisp-laundered crumpet; plus a few large, warming toddies at each. The Ross Harriers met at Harewood End, the South Hereford at the Grafton Inn. Nothing snooty in the least. Mostly farmers.

Mornin' Jack ... Mornin' Mabel ... Alright then, Squire? ... Mornin' Major ... Compliments of, Colonel ... Farmer Giles, Master Sprog, and the Misses Thelwell by the darling dozen ... a butcher, a baker, and, honestly, a couple of Postman Pats ... a classless, comradely gathering of the countryside tribe, showing off at Christmas and pretty harmless, if truth was told, even to wily friend Reynard. From what I've seen they hardly catch a thing from one week to the next: usually you catch a glimpse of the fox amiably going thisaway, grinning, and the huntsmen frantically going thataway, hollering and scanning the wrong horizon.

Last year a brave huddle of good and bejeaned, mostly wispy-bearded, Antis stood at a distance on the main road kerb. A banner said, 'When Blood Flows, Clots Form'.

To those Boxing Day meets I'd taken my old Mum, in her mid-80s now and still full of the joys and an ever more radical leftie with each passing day: both those Hunts had galumphingly galloped over Dad's land at Little Birch in the 1930s. 'Quite a nice scene, I suppose; but stupid, conceited things really, aren't they?' she said. My kids will soon be old enough to enjoy the Boxing Day meet. They won't be going – nor will they want to; they know better than their Dad that animals have rights: certainly rights to live.

Last year had been a final splurge, although I hadn't realised it at the time. I'd just got home, on Christmas Eve, from Exmoor.

I'd been following the Devon & Somerset Staghounds on foot and Ford Escort. Lorna Doone's barren, beautiful, forbidding territory. Diana Scott, joint-master (and, I might add, beautiful, forbidding, and just 40-ish) invited me back for tea, crumpets, and a claret.

She had been up and out since dawn. The stag had outwitted them. Now, back (and bathed) and bonnily committed to the cause – 'We cull, we love nature' – we were taking tea and admiring her oils and watercolours in front of the yuley fire.

I had walked down the drive and through the farmyard as the marvellously muffling film director's mists rolled in off Exmoor and then bounced down the plump Brendon Hills. In the evocative, shrouded gloaming you could just make out the horses' heads in their stabled half-doorways. Old retainers, ostlers, and farmboys passed with the mellow-soft clunk of wooden buckets; farm dogs sniffed at your crotch. You felt you were Fielding H, or Cobbett W, at least.

Inside, snugsville. 'I understand you totally,' said smashing Mrs Scott. 'To sell newspapers you have to say we're just savages with a bloodlust.' At which, with the marvellously rolling-eyed venom of an aforesaid Fielding squire, burst in the other joint-master of the Devon & Somerset – Mrs Scott's husband, Maurice. He had followed the later scent. He kicked off his mud-splattered, blood-spotted boots.

'Did you kill?' asked his wife, matter of fact. 'Yes, about 2.30, down at the deep combe near Exford.' 'Oh, jolly good, well done, ol' boy,' said his wife.

Mea culpa, I thought. For all the fun, the cry must be Up The Antis!

Hunting with dogs was made sort-of illegal in 2004. With minor adjustments to their routines, the hunts still meet, eat, drink, chase and occasionally kill.

Tracking down Tullamore
3 February 1978

It is not even on the main road. If you drove due west from Dublin to see the sun go down on Galway Bay you would have to turn off after about 70 miles and meander across the low green sodden carpet of County Offaly towards the Grand Canal and Port Laoise prison.

Tullamore (pop. 7,000) is one long high street. There are, naturally, a number of bars, but only one poshish hotel. Willie John McBride made the place slightly famous round the world, for when the mood took him he liked to order Tullamore Mist, a sensitive, delicate brew, wondrously evil, which combines the warming, heart-good aroma of smouldering turf of Tommy Keirnan on form.

Tullamore is a typical, drowsy small town/big village. Like anywhere else in the green and pleasant there are a lot of black-and-white mongrels about – folk are of the mind that they make for a cheaper dog licence – and like everywhere else they have their donkeys, their tinkers and lots of girls with green eyes. Nothing but the Mist factory and the aforementioned Hayes Hotel makes Tullamore any different from the thousand other market towns.

Until this week, that is. Tullamore today stands proud in the world of sport. And I kid you not. I do mean the world. International big business is still catching its breath. For on Wednesday tiny Tullamore Harriers (membership 325, best athlete, the under-14 cross-country runner Johnny Wrafter) ceremoniously cut the first sod in a field near the town before building a full-sized eight-lane tartan running track – 'Sure boy, exactly the very same thing the fellows ran on at the Mexican and Montreal Olympics.'

Tartan, a subsidiary of the giant 3M company, have laid 306 tracks around the world but never ever had even one inquiry from an amateur athletic club. No wonder, even in America or

Japan or Germany, only sponsored institutions can remotely afford them, for you get scarcely any change out of £1 million. Peanuts, said Tullamore. If that French geezer made a fortune out of writing *Clochemerle*, what in heaven's name might he do with the yarn of Tullamore's Tartan track?

Tullamore Harriers were founded just before Christmas 1853. Their first year's balance sheet read – Income £92 1s 6d. Expenditure £92 2s 9d. Loss 1s 3d. They were not long in the red. Plonked (and I choose the word) in the very middle of a very thirsty land, they were ideally placed to cater to men's needs in that direction.

The little band of athletes did their thing too – for instance Noel Gowran won the Irish cross-country title in 1957, though I could not substantiate yesterday that Tullamore's tug-of-war team were once disqualified in the national championships – for pushing! Anyway, by the start of the 1970s the Harriers had 300 athletic members aged from six to 60 – and over 12,000 social or drinking members – nearly twice the whole population of the town.

In 1971 they opened a spanking new clubhouse to fit in an extra few miles of bar. I've heard of wall bars in a sports pavilion but this was ridiculous. They also bought two adjoining fields, one on which to build some houses, the other set aside for Paddy Larkin's dream – an eight-lane Tartan track just like they have in the Olympic Games. It will be ready for running in August. And sure, if the local Gardai need a few white lines to use at closing time, there'll be plenty of them.

When the pin-striped executive whizzkids at massive 3M first received Paddy Larkin's little letter asking for a Tartan track on 23 July 1975, they did not even bother to reply. Who could blame them? He wrote again, pained, on 21 September 1976. This time 3M at least sent some bumf. They are mortified now at their lack of response.

Then, last year, a clipping arrived from the *Irish Independent*. 'Tartan Track for Tullamore,' it trumpeted, adding that the

Harriers were still awaiting a visit from 3M's representatives. Tony Ward, the charming London bigwig, thought he had better put in an appearance at least. Paddy Larkin, the Harriers' secretary, a soft spoken broth of a boy of 45, met him in the Hayes Hotel in his Sunday suit. He showed Tony the derelict field 'with a hump in the middle' and bought him a drink in one of the gigantic bars.

It will be a wonderful thing if Tullamore can produce some Olympic champions because of our track, Paddy told me yesterday. So, his dream a reality, would he now be settling back to his own work in the building trade? 'Not a bit of it,' he said, 'We are working on this new plan now to spend £1.5 million on a new indoor sports complex. It'll be off the drawing board by December and if the weather holds we might make a start before Christmas ...'

And his voice got misty. Irish misty. And, to be sure, it was only the furious clink of glasses and the contended sounds of swallowing in the background that made me realise that to drinking men in Tullamore all things are possible. If you want to dream, do drink. You know it makes sense.

The track and the Harriers still flourish in 2014, and there really is a gym and 'magnificent changing facilities' – the 200 active members getting the benefit of 3,000 drinking members. An Olympic champion is still awaited.

Skinny army is ready
8 May 1982

We had a debate in the office this week about whether the London Marathon should be covered on these pages. Well, is it sport? Or is it just fun? If it's not real competition, should it be on some sort of Leisure Page? Or tucked under the Ramblers' Association Notes?

I wouldn't be surprised, forecast one bright spark, that come Monday morning the whole thing will be pretty big on the obits page. He may have a point there: it is mighty hard to screen medically 17,906 people, especially a collective of 17,906 wild-eyed, obessionist *Sunday Times* readers – fitness freaks and knobbly-kneed exhibitionists whose telly spectacular has come at last. Perhaps tomorrow morning they will all be issued with singlets bearing the legend 'Hello, Mum!' Or in some cases, like our pessimist said, 'Goodbye, Mum!'

It cannot be remotely considered competitive. Last year the two 'winners' jogged through the tape hand in hand. Anyway, even real marathoners seem uncompetitive. Some time after he had won the Munich 26-miler, I remember Frank Shorter saying: 'No, there is no rivalry between us as you sportswriters know it. At the end there's just thankfulness. No thought of vanquishing. We just look at each other with love and say "Hey, dammit, we made it!"' Thus mountaineering isn't on the sports pages. Or walking the Ridgeway.

Ah, the loneliness of a long distance runner. Lonely, my foot! They're a great skinny army on a collective high. 'Look, Mum, it's me, your little solitary hero!' Jogs there a jogger on his jog who does not see himself smugly as the world's last intrepid maverick, spiritual and soulful heir to St Brendan of Ireland, to St Brendan of Gateshead, to Jack Hawkins on the bridge of his Elstree frigate, to ... yea, verily, to Christopher Brasher himself?

Four years ago, Brasher, a glinting, wild-eyed obsessionist if ever there was one, set about his vision. Last spring, with 7,000 plimsolled disciples, he saw it come to pass: both spiritually and economically the triumph must have surprised even him. This time, at 17,906, he has more than doubled the capacity for spirituality – as well as, presumably, for profits.

Perhaps the event should be on the Financial pages, come to think of it. Sponsors have been fighting mad to clamber aboard the accompanying fleet of ambulances. At a similar bunioned beanfeast in Boston a few weeks ago an electrolyte health drink company was refused permission to supply their specially treated water along the route because they wouldn't pay enough for the privilege. At the end, the winner, Salazar, collapsed, surrounded by doctors and had to be given five pints of a saline solution intravenously. It was an hour before he could even get to his feet. He said he would have been okay if the electrolyte water had been available.

Brasher's committee, pronto, have done a deal with a sports drink company. For potty good measure, the kitty has also been primed by Heineken lager – whose bumf adds 'there will be a team of 20 Heineken girls to egg on contestants when the going gets tough'.

Perhaps we should start a weekly Sponsorship Page? Indeed, by next year what could also come to pass is the prophecy made to me 10 years ago by the US marathoner, Dave Bronson – 'one day I will come across them, a pair of shoes that will make running on streets seem like running bare foot across bosoms of maidens.' Brasher's probably working on that. He is (I presume everyone knows) director of a running pump company.

And yet ... and yet near 18,000 nutters plus Jimmy Savile will see tomorrow as their ultimate challenge.

The London Marathon is believed to be still going strong in 2014, its reputation sky-high. The same emphatically cannot be said of Jimmy Savile.

Grand prix grand master
11 July 1987

The welcome is so affable, so cheery, the face so animated, the brain (as you are about to discover) so keen-sharp, that you totally forget yourself and stick out a mitt for a matey handshake.

He grimaces and endeavours, wincingly and uselessly, to hoist his elbow or bend a wrist to crank himself up to offer at least a flicker of his hand in greeting. Frank Williams cannot shake hands. He was paralysed from the shoulders down 16 months ago when he drove his car off a minor road in southern France. It is an understatement to say he is lucky to be alive. But he doesn't mention the fact.

Today and tomorrow, his wheelchair will be gently eased into place on the pit wall at Silverstone and a microphone placed at his lips and earphones clamped to his head, and he will be in direct, dramatic contact with his two drivers, Nigel Mansell and Nelson Piquet, as they fume and vroom around the British grand prix circuit in Northamptonshire. When they cacklingly call Williams from their cockpits, he will be ready to tell them the score.

Radio reception is perfect. The pitmen only speak if spoken to: 'There's no way we call up to say "Hi, Nigel, you've left your rear offside winker on!"' Mansell is far more talkative than Piquet. What sort of stuff?

'Well, about lap 10 last week in France, Nigel comes on to say he's picked up a bit of debris from another car and it was affecting his handling he reckoned, "I'm coming in, I'm coming in!" he radioed. We told him "Stay out there" because I could see his lap times were dropping only by a quarter of a second each lap.

'So then he asked "Can you change the front wing when I stop for tyres?" Again more discussion and he was given a definite "No – too much time and it could mean a gigantic cock-up." A new wing or nose can take 60 seconds – And then only if you get it spot on. It would have cost him the race. So a good decision, right?' Right.

Really and truly, a fairly phenomenal fellow. The Williams-Honda hurtler already leads the grand prix constructor's championship by a mile. It is becoming a habit. Not bad for a paralysed second-hand car dealer.

His schoolboy ambition was to race. As a tearaway in the early 1960s he drove an Austin A40 in official saloon car rallies before gypsying around Europe, cadging drives in Formula 3. Then he set up a stall as dealer in wheels and deals for clapped-out Coopers and Brabhams. Wanna banger? Go see Frank.

By then he was sharing a flat in Harrow with the fast set which included Piers Courage, his first driver. Together they took to the circuit with panache. Piers won Formula Two and was immediately a Formula One cracker in 1969. In 1970 Piers was killed at speed. Frank Williams mourned and kept going in his memory. Williams is now the most famous and successful non-driver on the whole narrow-eyed, bread-and-circus, jet-set merry-go-round. Life, however limp your body, must go on.

Ten days ago, bound for the French Grand Prix, Williams revisited the spot where he almost killed himself. 'Just curiosity, I suppose.' Now he has to have somebody feed him 'like a baby' – and two men carry him into cars and on and off aeroplanes. Sixteen months ago, light-hearted as he ever was, he had been in a rush to get from the Ricard circuit, east of Marseilles, to Nice airport after a test session for the 1986 season. He careered off the little, shortcut B road at Moulinon. Now he returned there. He was shown the exact spot. 'Totally my fault. I just cocked up, didn't I?'

He knew he should have died. He survived. He has been to a lot of other people's funerals. His all-time fast-favourite Jochen Rindt killed himself in 1970 at Monza. Courage, dashing charmer and flat-mate, went away the same year at Zandfoort in a black-orange plume. Suddenly for Williams, it was no longer public schoolboy fun, but business.

'It was a major setback emotionally. And, racing-wise, it was pretty debilitating as well. But you have to carry on, don't you? ... I've buried a lot ... I've been to a lot of funerals. But fewer and fewer. They're petering out almost, touch wood.' He makes to touch his wooden topped desk, but the hands can't feel a thing.

'I admit, I always had this passion to be a driver. If I'd taken out a racing licence and did what I did that day in France on the track instead, I'd probably have saved myself a lot of aggravation in the past 12 months.

'I had a go in the early 60s but I never had enough money and, anyway, was always too erratic, always flying off the track, literally. When I gave up it was only because I hadn't enough money. I always meant to return. Never did.'

Driven round the bend by Nigel
15 July 1989

Take it from me: with instantaneous death only split seconds away a multitude of trivialities and absurdities cascade through the tatters of your brain – plus a few absolute, God-fearing, confessional certainties.

There I was, hurtling uncontrollably for this brick wall in a convulsive spiral of bounding acceleration in Northamptonshire the other morning – and I found myself thinking, oh well, pity that I'll be dead and gone before I get to hear the lunchtime Test score. Blanched with fear and numbly quivering with terror, I then got to worrying if I was going to bring up my breakfast. Messy that, for the ambulance blokes from the Brackley morgue.

It was the total certainties of my past life that struck me as I was catapulted down Hangar Straight at 180mph. This was a flaming set-up and I was going to die because I'd fallen for it so gormlessly. Sheer, gloating revenge, and I'd been hook, line and sinkered. Single to Valhalla, please. Well, I suppose that is where all these hare-brained heroes of motor sport end up.

Yes, sheer revenge, and I had strolled, unconcerned and unsuspecting, into cunning little Nigel bloody Mansell's well-set trap. Revenge on Fleet Street and I was carrying the empty can as this chortling prat strapped beside me in the blood-red kamikaze capsule was cruelly corkscrewing us up this crazy corridor to the very doors of death. I have never been so petrified in all my life.

I could see it all so clearly now – the revenge, I mean. I had last met Master Mansell in Mexico City airport two years ago, only a few hours after he had failed to clinch the world drivers' championship by neglecting to engage first gear on the starting grid, just like you or me in our Escorts when amber turns to green.

I had rather sarkily remarked on this in these pages – also the fact that our Nige that evening was carrying the most tourist-trapped souvenir sombrero of green and silver bobbles and tassles which he had docked like a garish toy spaceship on the chair beside him before ordering up a steak, 'without no mish-mash Mexican stuff on, just a bottle of ketchup and an extra dollop of chips, please, ta.' Endearing, but not quite world-champ class, I had remarked in print.

Then, only a few weeks ago, *Punch* had rung me up to ask me what I thought of a piece on Mansell being 'the most boring Brit sportsman', and, though I said, 'No way, I'd have to do one on Nick Faldo or Steve Davis first', the mag still ran it and I suppose I was stuck with the blame. Hence this stupefying, petrifying revenge.

I had not smelled a rat nor had a penny dropped – imminent, horrifying death curdles the metaphor as well as the brain – when the editor of the racy glossy, *Autocar & Motor*, chummily rang and said he had fixed me a spin round Silverstone with Mansell in the incredible new 202mph Ferrari F40, a millionaire's plaything of which only two hundred are being made, the nearest any non-racer could get to simulating a Formula One grand prix drive.

Sure, I said. A pootling tootle with good ol' Nige round Silvers, what? Nothing to it. I presumed he would just go slowly, pointing out the corners on the way. 202mph. I had never been more than 102mph in my life, other than with my eyes shut and rosary out at Heathrow.

I started the violent shakes when they gave me the crash helmet on the pit apron. Before they crammed me, quivering, into the terrifying tube of a coffin, mechanics, machine-hands and general motoring buffs had shaken my hand, wished me luck and said how tremendously envious they were. I thought of making a run for it.

Too late. Mansell, with a diabolic grin, prefaced the torture with the question: 'Do you like doughnuts?' I had no time to mutter any sort of incomprehension, when I found out: with an excruciating howl of revs, a bellowing retch of burning rubber and an acrid, angry, purple-grey plume of smoke, the car was suddenly prancing on its back wheels in a pirouetting spin of quite incredible danger.

The world seemed to be caving in. Mansell just chortled at my petrifaction. And then, with a terrifying bound, we were released as if from a rocket launcher into this crazy corridor of fear. For the next three minutes I did not swallow, or breathe, I'm sure. My senses were stampeded, my heart not beating.

At least my tape-recorder, microphone pinned to Mansell's overall, spooled on, unconcerned, through the devilish din. Even when I played the tape back to write this article, I was in a cold sweat again. This is the gist, including my despairing, last-gasp, gulping expletives:

Wa-hey! Enjoy that, did you? Doughnuts are a balance of clutch and power, so called because the 360-degree turns leave tyre marks with the hole in the middle ... that was Copse that was ... now, on Sunday, through fifth and sixth and flat out for the slingshot through Maggotts ... and like crazy for Becketts, up to 180, then brake hard and down to third ... just drift through it, 120-plus ... easy through Chapel and then let her rip down Hangar, looking for 200 here. Wa-hey!

Stowe can be a blighter, fast and dangerous, a dab on the brake and through it in fifth, 150-odd ... and let fly for Club, another incredible corner, hang on here, the track's a bit greasy, down to fifth for a bit more grip ... now grab sixth and have a run at Abbey, take it flat, bumpy here, hold on, 160 ... and, quicker than Hangar this, as we're looking for Woodcote ... brake, right down to second, we're going to skid here, wa-hey! then left-right and accelerate like crazy out of it, third, fourth, fifth and sixth ... into Copse again, 160 down to 130, take it steady ... and let fly for Maggotts ...

Please. No more. The pits went by, other cars glinting like tracer bullets lighting up the night sky. Bullets that were earmarked for me unless I kept my head down and eyes closed. Which I now did. It was all a grotesque nightmare, surely it was. Please let me wake up in my lovely little *Guardian*-issue blue Ford Escort.

Mansell babbles on – cruel, cold, calm executioner. Don't worry, open your eyes, he knows this track like the back of his hand.

Best day here was 1987, showing Piquet what-for at Stowe. Two laps to go. Right up his arse. Feint left, then right, then left again. Flat out, 200, he is convinced I am taking him outside, and I duck in and dive through his inside, missing his gearbox by millimetres.

Best day of all for me here, that. Better even than testing in 1980, when Lotus gave me a trial and their engineer, Nigel Stroud, said he would not even bolt on any aerodynamics 'cos there was no way I'd lap under 1min 15sec. So I put my foot down and give it a go, and then come in all depressed, thinking I've blown my chance, and Stroud comes up and says, 'I suppose you think you're bloody clever, Mansell?', and I look at the time and it's 1min 12sec, the fastest lap ever recorded by Lotus at Silverstone. Yeah, that was a big break.

Talking of which, here was the biggest break of my little life: for we were actually slowing down. This speeding sadist beside me was actually sliding this suicide cylinder of mine smoothly down the pit lane and, Jesus, Mary and Joseph, merciful trio, we were actually stopping.

Kindly, good-egg Nigel clapped a hand to my knee and said: 'All right, you can open your eyes now.' But why, old son, he asked, had I not asked him any questions during our spin? I opened the lockjawed slit of my mouth but no words came out. I wanted to ask how it was remotely possible that 25 other raving idiots would on Sunday be competing at 200mph on this tiny ribbon of track? Mansell sensed the question. 'The knack,' he said, 'is to win as slowly as possible.'

And then they were gathering round, and helping squeeze me out of my coffin, and slapping me on the back, and I was still quivering and now my legs had turned to rope. 'Was that the most fantastic experience you've ever had?' asked someone, happy for me but his face glistening with envy.

Fantastic, I said. Nothing to it, a doddle, thanks to good ol' Nige. Now, I wonder if anyone's heard the Test score ...

9

THE BEST-LOVED GAME

Tycoon Tony has it taped
24 January 1980

SYDNEY: What, asked the secretary, do you actually want to talk about? Nothing in particular, I said, I just want to report back to England how their former cricket captain is getting on. Has he grown any taller, for instance?

He is just the same. Before we went to lunch Tony Greig had one or two things to do at the new insurance company just across the bridge at Sydney. Just for my benefit, I fancied, he bawled out a minion: 'I want figures man, I don't want your thinks or thoughts. I don't want pie in the sky. I'm back from lunch in two hours and I don't want waffle. I want the real figures, man.'

In the lifts going down we were accompanied by a perky little widow in her seventies who had been up in the skyscraper sorting out her life insurance. 'Did they look after you?' asked our beanpole Dale Carnegie. 'Thank you, Tony,' she said. He signed her an autograph for her grandson, held the door open for her and she trotted off like a preening sparrow.

The managing director is alive and well and doing very nicely, thank you. Who wants to be a millionaire? He does and he's well on the way. When he set aside the England captaincy, joined Kerry Packer's flying circus and everything hit the fan he insisted on a contract that set him up for life when it was all over. So his friend, the hammerhead shark who bit cricket's establishment off at the knees, set him up as a managing director. A year ago he bought eight big leather books to teach himself all about insurance.

'I planned to learn them word for word,' he says. 'I went to Canberra, to a fellow at university who knows more about insurance than anyone. He told me "throw away those books, just be Tony Greig, and you'll be able to sell more insurance than you've ever thought of."'

He drove me away in his plush big car with reclining seats and a back window which could be opened by electric power. He pushed in his cassette of 'Songs From the Shows' and in his own head he turned on the cassette to spew out what he thought was what I wanted to hear. 'Kerry and I ... totally vindicated ... More people watching cricket than ever before ... county cricketers have doubled their pay ... He always preached compromise ... I have no regrets ...'

C'mon, Tony. For all your smart, blue suits and cold, blue eyes there must be some regrets. He switched off the recorder and admitted: 'Yes, well, on Sunday at Melbourne with England needing 25 to win and Brearley went in, I thought that could have been me. I wanted to pick up a bat and just go out there. Knotty and I would have got those runs, you know.'

Not that this pillow talk meant anything against Brearley. 'I have a high regard for Mike. He's a bloody good bloke, and a bloody good captain. Name me the last five captains of Sussex,' he asked. After each name, from Mike Griffith to Jim Parks, he said: 'Sawn off at the knees!' then I had to name the last five captains of England before him – Denness, Illy, Cowdrey ... 'Sawn off at the knees,' he said after each name.

'I did not want to end up at 35 doing radio commentaries like Fred Trueman or writing like Denis Compton. Kerry approached me and it was all very businesslike. I was businesslike back then. Inside two years I knew there would be a compromise. I insisted on a contract that gave me some sort of job for life, some new challenge. The first day I played for England I promised Donna I was not going to be all washed up, an ex-sportsman with nothing to do at 35.'

His house in Sydney's swishest suburb overlooks the bay. In the summer his swimming pool is full of the Martini set, in the winters the parquet floor of his ballroom creaks to the footsteps of the very important people. He says he always intended to come to Australia anyway. He was surprised I wanted to talk about cricket proper rather than cricket politics. He remains the only England player to have scored 3,000 runs and taken 100 wickets: he's proud of that. Only Hammond and Cowdrey have taken more catches for England: he's proud of that too. He remembers practising fielding as a lonely boy in South Africa, practising, practising, practising.

He remembers putting a ball in a sock and hanging it from the branch of a tree and hitting it for hours. To his grave, he says, he will take the memory and pride of his 110 for England at Brisbane in 1974. It was the first time England came up against Lillee and Thomson. EW Swanton said: 'No innings was calculated to do more for English morale since Dexter took Hall and Griffith apart on that memorable day at Lord's in the early 1960s.'

Lillee, says Greig, is the best bowler he has ever seen. Of the batsmen he cannot decide on the two Richardses for genius. After them come Geoffrey Boycott – 'a phenomenally dedicated player. The Richardses pretend they don't care, but they do. The afternoon before last year's Supertest at Perth, Barry asked me to bowl to him in the nets. For three hours I bowled at his off-stump. He just wanted to practise playing straight. Every time the ball went backward of square on either side, he would drop his bat and do 50 press-ups in the crease. Fifty! In that three hours he must have done 600 press-ups. Next day he went out to bat pretending to everyone he hadn't had a net in weeks. He scored the most fantastic century I have ever witnessed.'

It was hard to drag this sort of stuff out of him. He only wants to talk about his friend Kerry Packer, or what he thinks he has done for every ordinary English country pro, or suggest you might like to comment on his latest and blandly boring TV ad for motor cars or breakfast food or insurance. He admits that in the end the criticism he received in England hurt badly. 'The only difference now is that I know there are real friends.'

He shakes his head at the memory. 'Do you know that one established cricket writer in England wrote a pompous and hurtful piece headlined "The immorality of Tony Greig".' The guy honestly thought I was immoral for simply changing my job for four times more money.'

He dropped me at the hotel and revved off to play tennis with Kerry. After that he was due at a board meeting. He would doubtless be rude to a few minions on the way. Of the 50-odd men who have captained England at cricket I bet Tony Greig will be the first to become a self-made millionaire. He looks down at you and laughs at that. A real chortle – but there is not much twinkle in those cold blue eyes.

In the winter of 1981–2 there was a hiatus between Guardian *cricket correspondents. Frank, having been on the previous winter's tour of West Indies as book writer and gadfly columnist, was then asked to go to India and Sri Lanka on his own, responsible for full daily coverage. Objectively, the Test series was one of the most tedious of all time. In his hands, it somehow sounded riveting.*

England to stroll it – and that's exclusive
9 December 1981

BANGALORE: England's bowlers are going to win the second Test match, which started today in Bangalore. No problem. Take it as read – and remember you read it here first.

I can also reveal exclusively that England will win the third Test in Delhi, lose in Calcutta, draw in Madras and emphatically win the decider in Kanpur. A little bird told me so yesterday.

I booked a consultation with Dolores Perira, a restless brown sparrow in her mid-60s with a beaky nose constantly pecking away at you as she talks 19 to the dozen through a pinched, pursed little mouth smeared with lipstick. Her neck is hung with bangles and beads and her sari is gaudy and flowered. She advertised herself as India's most celebrated soothsayer and claims to be by appointment to the Prime Minister – 'I keep dear Indira on the straight and narrow, I'm telling you. Why only the other day she said to me "Dolores, my dear, what should I do about ... ?"'

You have to pay the receptionist downstairs in the stately marble old colonial house. You are given a pink docket and go up the polished, creaking stairs. The fans swirl lazily above. The curtains are drawn. She sits at a low table on which she is eddying and shifting a face-down pack of playing cards. I shuffle and cut whenever she orders and the card that I turn up is a signal for her to start spouting. She presumed I wanted a personal service and got straight in. She did not know me, I'm sure, from Adam Faith but she told me my date of birth to the very week. And on my mother's was only two days out.

She said I was a Catholic (true) and must stop killing fellow Christians in Ireland. She said I would love a girl whose birthday was either 19 or 20 February but should strongly resist. Because she saw money piling up on my doorstep I should advertise in England for an heiress, a duchess or something like that, whose birthday was as near to mine on 4 October as possible. Knowing that would be very nice to be going on with, I said I was in India for the cricket and what gives with the Test match?

'How amazing you should ask that,' she said at once. 'I myself was only thinking of the cricket this morning. Oh my goodness, how well the English bowlers will bowl. The batsmen of India will have no chance nor in the next Test either, for their confidence will be in shreds.

'England is Aries, India is Capricorn: the ram against the goat. Everything is content for the match: the grass is good but always the ram rules the mountain goat. England will always rule

India, always in the long run. The bowlers will rule the match for England, no problem.'

I kept cutting the cards. What about individual performances? 'You have two champions,' she said. 'One is old and one is young.' I nodded, thinking of Boycott and Botham. She went on: 'The old one will do very very good but he must take care of himself. I see him having trouble with his neck, always with his neck and sometimes with his wrists. You must tell him to put oils on his neck and wrists tomorrow. Don't forget that he is worried about something at home. Is not he very worried?' (Yorkshire, I nodded again.) 'But tell him not to worry because he is going to get married and live a long, long life in a white man's country.

'And the young English champion is very good but very lazy. He likes to be famous but mostly he likes to be lying under a tree asleep. Tell him he's got to rouse himself up and concentrate but he will do very good in Bangalore for certain. In a year or so all his hair is going to fall out. Tell him that. Tell him to write to me if his hair has not all fallen out in five years' time.'

I made an excuse and left. She called me back and asked for the pink receipt the receptionist had given me. 'Just to make sure that they pay me my money,' she said. 'A lot has been going missing lately around this place.' She suddenly looked a very fierce little sparrow and I didn't dare to ask whether Gatting would play.

He could have demanded a refund. India having won the First Test, the remaining five were boring draws. One practice match did, however, come briefly and blazingly to life.

Botham's bit of humpety
23 January 1982

INDORE: A stupendous, power-crazed innings by Botham electrified this patch of India yesterday. Indeed his 122 lit up the whole legend. It took 55 balls and 55 minutes. It included 16 fours, seven sixes, three twos, 10 singles and only 19 dot balls off which he failed to score – and 11 of those were in the first three overs when he was playing himself in.

The central zone fielders were reduced to shambles. He went from 50 to his century in 19 balls, and, before he was caught, at deep mid-wicket, the previous four deliveries had gone 6-6-4-4. Gatting turned the knife with a sparkling century of his own.

Botham arrived at the wicket at 87 for three to join Gatting, who had not scored and had managed three when Botham reached his century. England had made heavy weather of things and in fact there was a whiff of fury in the air. Geoff Cook had been given out to a questionable catch and Fletcher, having angrily joined in the resulting kerfuffle, was immediately caught at mid-wicket, obviously still seething at the decision against Cook.

The Somerset celebrant of swipe strode in looking none too pleased. He'd had supper the night before with Cook, one of his particular buddies and one who, as everyone knew, was playing for his place here. For once, I noticed, Botham didn't cheerily swing his arms as he bristled in, his now curly long, gingery locks twining round the edges of his floppy white sunhat. He doesn't trust Indian barbers and isn't going to cut it till home.

He played himself in with narrow-eyed and untypically heavy menace. The night before, in a throwaway forecast, he had promised 'a bit of humpety in the morning'. Cook's dismissal determined him on it. This was an hour great-grandchildren will gape over – Botham at Indore. It has the same ring already as Jessop at Hastings and Harrogate, Fender at Northampton or Gimblett at Frome.

You name it, Botham hit it. Like WG, his blocks were going for four. He tried two of his patented reverse sweeps. Four, both times – for the last man a captain wants for Botham is a third man. In all the glorious, galumphing mayhem, as always with Botham, there were one or two quite mesmerisingly wondrous strokes; this time, the ball after celebrating his 50 (34 minutes,

28 balls), with a forearm heave over midwicket, he stepped inside a delivery curving in on leg stump and bludgeoned it in a soaring arc high over the long-off boundary.

You feel even Hammond wouldn't have attempted that shot in a first-class match. Then, after scoring his first two to take him to 61, he predetermined a sweep but, as he genuflected, the ball dropped shorter than he expected and still on one knee, he adjusted to send the battered red apple soaring high over the mid-wicket line. The century came with a genuine sweep for four (50 minutes, 48 balls, 14 fours, five sixes).

When, five minutes later, he walked in to tumult from the disappointingly small crowd of 10,000, he received cherry garlands of oranges. Grinning again, he met those too full on the meat of the bat. Gatting had given all possible strikes to his marauding friend. Of the 55 balls Botham had needed, the stand of 137 only needed 75. Once Botham had departed, Gatting himself cut loose, and there was no end to the merrymaking until the shadows lengthened and the umpires called a halt, with England 367 for five, Gatting on 108.

Years later, Frank would tell the story of the previous night's merrymaking, when he and Botham stayed alone in the bar till cockcrow and the barman fell asleep on the floor. The mystery is not only how Botham managed to bat like that but also how Keating managed to file. The same day's paper also included the following piece (presumably sent earlier), which for me is perhaps the most exquisite of all his profiles.

A Yorkshireman to go into the jungle with
23 January 1982

The Yorkshireman was promenading along the beach in Antigua, the blissful Caribbean island that Nelson developed for his fleet and which England introduced to cricket, so that Antigua itself could ultimately produce Vivian Richards, handsomest god of them all.

The man from the West Riding presented a squat, stocky figure under the midday sun. The fierce hawk eyes under the steel-grey scrubbing brush of his NCO's hairstyle were flaring at sunbathers wasting their day. He wore black plimsolls of the post-war variety, short yellow nylon socks, an incongruously gaudy beach shirt and elastic-waisted shorts which looked as though they'd been cut by a blind tailor with a blunt pair of nail scissors. His pink arms and legs were splattered with angry red bites from angry black mosquitoes. He had been scratching them. Under his arm he carried a shabby old shopping bag which doubtless held a tape recorder, a travelling Scrabble set and a pile of well-read airmail letters. Don Mosey, of the British Broadcasting Corporation, was taking his constitutional.

From the shade of a beach hut we watched him stencilling his Man Friday footsteps across the glistening sand. His friend and mine, Terry Brindle, of the *Yorkshire Post*, remarked: 'Y'know, it's hard to understand isn't it, how a nation of Moseys colonised and ruled for over two centuries a nation of Viv Richardses.' The thought has struck me more than once now we are in India and I'm making my second tour with Don. He still sports his eccentric uniform, his beady eyes are always on the lookout for a phone box that works. He still carries his always increasing bundle of airmail letters. He's a character is Don, and proud to be. He pretends he is always a crotchety old cuss, but that's just his way. He is actually what you'd call a 'good tourist'. Certainly he is a man to go into the jungle with. He'd even smell out a phone box near the mouth of the Orinoco.

He did once. It was this time last year, the day before we were thrown out of Guyana over the Jackman rumpus. There was a match upcountry in Berbice, the ground cleared out of the jungle. Don found a hut. In it was a cobwebbed telephone. He picked it up. It worked. He got through to Broadcasting House in London. The newsroom seemed to be out to lunch except one secretary. 'Who are you?' she repeated. And 'Where are you?' 'I am Don Mosey,' he seethed, 'and I'm standing on the banks of a shark-infested river in the middle of South America ...'

'Oh,' said the girl, 'do you want to give any news?'

'No,' rasped our exasperated hero drawing himself up to his full pomp before slamming the phone down, 'I want to give a pint of blood.'

There have been one or two similar, if not quite so graphic, adventures on this trip, now word has seeped back that there has been some angry correspondence in the *Guardian* about his 'offensive and gratuitous remarks on India and Indians' during his broadcasts. He cannot understand it. He spent the last months of the war here, and a year after it.

'Since then, I have always nursed not only a great affection for the place, but also the determination to return one day. For 30 years I'd recalled the mellow pleasure of India at sundown, the last rays of the sun on the hibiscus and bougainvillaea ... All those years I've cherished this affection for India, for its birds and butterflies and mountains. I've had this great nostalgic urge to come back, and I haven't been disappointed.'

The people, and their sense of humour and concern for their guests – 'their endearing, caring kindness' – he can get quite misty about. Nevertheless, he says, to paint a proper picture he has to mention in his broadcasts 'the dust and dirt, the communications chaos, the unfamiliar sanitary arrangements and the fine disregard for time-keeping'. For Mosey is first and foremost a journalist.

He is a Libran, born in 1924, the eldest of three boys 'of kind and loving parents who never had a penny to spare in their lives – and never expected to have.' His father worked three days a week in t'mill for 30 shillings, supplementing that with 'anything he could find' like debt-collecting, or tending the local cricket pitch at Eastburn, a village between Skipton and Keighley. Don first played league cricket at the age of 11, and was later to become a demon bowler in the Airedale and Wharfedale League. The three boys all won through to Keighley Grammar School, which was more expense.

He started 'in newspapers' at a tender age with a paper round on his bike before school. When he was 16 his mother – 'the driving force' – presented herself at the local rag in Skipton and asked for a job for her eldest. The men had gone to war. There remained an editor, and young Mosey became the editorial staff of one. When he was of age, the boy himself went to war. He does not like to talk about it now, but he was in RAF aircrew and ended up in the Iraqi desert teaching English to Indians. He travelled a lot, and learned to play bridge – 'a great social asset'.

It was also when stationed in India that he came upon another determination. 'I thought the time had come to start improving my speech. I was pure bush West Riding, "Ee, ba gum" and all that stuff. Not that I had any visions of a posh accent – I was proud of being North Country – but I thought socially it could help me have a better life, just as bridge could. I thought if I could tighten up the discipline of my speech and enunciate better, it might get me somewhere in life.'

It did. But not for some time. He was an ace newspaper reporter in Nottingham, where he sent the odd bits and pieces to the BBC Midlands Radio, encouraged by the deputy news editor, Peter Hardiman-Scott. Then he was, successively, a reporter on the *Yorkshire Evening Post*, the *Daily Express* and the *Daily Mail*, in their Northern newsrooms. One day in Manchester, he deputised for a colleague and made a broadcast. The producer, Jack Harrison, said: 'You've done this before, haven't you?' Mosey, by then, had transferred from news to sport for the *Mail*, mostly covering cricket, and doing an increasing amount of broadcasting for Harrison. In 1964, he resigned from the *Mail* and became a freelance. One day, Jack Harrison suggested Mosey put in for his job as an outside broadcast radio producer. 'What, a Yorkshire hobbledehoy like me?' said Mosey. He got the job and three years later he was to be senior producer for the next 14 years.

In 1973 Cliff Morgan, then head of all radio sport, asked him to join *Test Match Special* – and so 'The Alderman', as Brian Johnston calls him so aptly when his friend gets a touch too pompous, became part of the team that became part of the folklore of British sporting broadcasting. And that's why he's in India, filling you in every morning, usually after a maniacal game of Scrabble the night before. Looking gruff of mien, he plods the old empire in his shorts, ever on the lookout for a functioning phone. And under his arm will be his battered old bag, and in it his bulging bundle of airmail letters from his sons, Ian the pro golfer and Alistair who is in Australia, but most of them from Jo, his wife. They write every single day to each other.

'She is the nicest, most placid, pleasant and easy-going wife a wandering journalist could find,' he says, 'especially for someone as mercurial and vacillating and moody as me.' And he looks defiantly ferocious again and you think how he'd have given them what for in the Raj. Unless you know that underneath, he's really an endearing, romantic, old softie.

Sad story of a select few
6 July 1988

England's latest cricketing debacle takes the crispiest cream cracker of the lot – even in a short summer which has already seen the humiliation of an outclassed national soccer team, a quite appallingly inept tennis squad, and thrashings Down Under for spineless British sides in both rugby union and league.

Only Master Frank Bruno's quite ludicrous tub-thumping threats towards the relentlessly cruel heavyweight boxer, Mike Tyson, have managed to invest English sport with even lip-service to any idea of challenge.

On the radio yesterday morning, as the last rites were intoned at Old Trafford, I found myself for the first time in years agreeing with the bluff, gruff Yorkie growler, Fred Trueman: 'I honestly don't know what's goin' on down there,' he mourned. 'It's a very, very sad state of affairs – and it's not even funny any more, it's dead, dead serious.' England have not won a Test match in their last 15 attempts. In the last two games they have not twitched into even a token effort. They have simply curled up and died.

In any other even semi-serious branch of public life the men responsible – in this case the Test selectors – would long ago have done the decent thing and resigned en bloc. There is no remote chance of that happening. The chairman of selectors, Peter May, is a self-perpetuating oligarch and his cronies at Lord's would consider even the suggestion of resignation as boat-rocking rashness.

In Alan Watkins' glorious description, May is a man who 'views life from behind his collar stud'. May is a City businessman and cannot afford much time to watch first-class cricket anyway, so I fancy he has probably less idea of who to put in the team than the average cricket-lover who turns up with devoted regularity with his son and Thermos round the midweek county grounds.

May says he 'takes soundings' from senior figures in the game, like managers, coaches, umpires and county captains. I have questioned many of these chaps during his disastrous six-year stewardship, and have yet to meet one manager, coach, umpire or captain who has received so much as a single phone call from the wintery-faced mandarin.

May has a fortnight to get his new show on the road. Wholesale sackings will be resisted. For one thing, they would be an admission of guilt which is not Lord's style at all. There cannot have been such a succession of appalling selectorial blunders as in the past few years – both practically and, you might say, spiritually, as witness the pusillanimous attitudes over Pakistan, Broad and Gatting. If, as May will plead, the present England team is the best there is, he should crucially address the question of the psychological buffeting his chosen group have been subjected to over the years, expecially against the West Indians. It is plain to see to everybody but May, surely, that his team has no relish for the fight any more. Even such an outstanding player as Graham Gooch looked fed up with the whole syndrome at Manchester.

If the same side turn up to Headingley on Thursday fortnight they will be as good as beaten before they start. The series cannot be won. This team of eager freshers should be summoned forthwith to Leeds – Roebuck, Barnett, Tavare (captain), Parker, Maynard, Ontong, Russell, Thomas, Agnew, Childs, Lawrence. They would at least give it a go. Certainly they could not do any worse than the present lot.

Exit Richards, with three parting shots for the mind's eye
12 August 1991

As he walked off a Test match field, dismissed for the final time, Vivian Richards stopped, turned for a moment, doffed his cap and raised his bat like a battle standard towards the public seats.

For the club-tied members and fat cats in the Oval pavilion's hospitality boxes ahead of him there was no smidgin of a farewell gesture. For them, the smouldering patrician pulled the peak of his cap even further down his forehead and tramped up the concrete stairs with a glance neither to right nor left. And then he was gone.

The writer Raymond Robertson-Glasgow said of one of Richards's predecessors, George Headley – the man whose singular and savage batting was a preview of what was to come in Richards – that as he walked down the pavilion steps 'you expected, in hope or fear'. So it was with Richards. His final entrance yesterday, as ever, was that of an emperor setting out on a crusade, swaggering only in the innate conviction of might and right and dominance.

Hammond was said to have sailed in like a galleon. Sobers, Graveney and Gower in their prime would come in as if on an elegant morning constitutional. Compton had a jaunty, schoolboy's stride to the wicket. Bradman, they say, took his time, probably a touch embarrassed at the serial murder of the poor bowlers on which he was intent. There was never an ounce of guilt about Richards's intention to slay.

Sir Leonard Hutton once observed how Richards 'goes on about being descended from slaves and cotton pickers, but he walks to the wicket as if he owns the plantation'. For all this certitude of domination, never can a century from the West Indies captain have seemed more on the cards than yesterday. For most of the 98 balls he needed to reach 50; he pored meticulously over the task, going walkabout in deep brown study between each and every ball.

In that time there was just one glowering shaft of venom, a whipcord-wristed, disdainful block for four off Lawrence of Gloucestershire. Dr Grace, old men say, used to block boundaries. Having reached his half-century with a single off his old friend and foe Botham, Richards seemed keen to announce that the second 50 would be a voluptuous and wholly memorable thing. He simultaneously gave the impression that Lawrence's huff and puff was beginning to get on the great man's wick.

First he leaned back and savagely square-cut a fast riser on off-stump which scorched a path to the cover-point boards. Next ball, deep mid-wicket was wringing his fingers as Richards leaned into his trademark stroke, the squarish on-drive, dismissively swatted with a roll of the wrists from outside off-stump. The scheming Lawrence galloped in again. Crack. The retort of a rifle shot. A sumptuously cruel, utterly perfect off-drive between mid-off and extra, what West Indian supporters call his 'not a man move' shot. Next ball he was caught at mid-on. Gone. For ever.

But there had been three farewell and flawless flourishes to savour, and one remembered a dozen years ago at Sydney watching the Australian macho tearaway Lennie Pascoe trying to intimidate Richards in his high pomp with three successive and furious bouncers, each accompanied with a grunting oath. Off the very hairs of his nose, Richards smashed the three fizzing things into the crowd over deep square-leg. Off the first, he answered Pascoe's sledging venom with a withering smile and a muttered 'Butter, Lennie'. Off the second, 'Marmalade, Lennie'. Off the third, Pascoe now beside himself with anger and humiliation, Richards said 'Nice breakfast, Lennie'.

In fact, it has been a memorable feast for 17 years.

Goodbye Dolly but only au revoir
19 August 1991

Once soccer had so rudely elbowed its way in again, one could put off no longer what was always going to be one of the doleful duties of the cricket season's end: a final hail and fond farewell to Basil D'Oliveira, who is retiring as county coach to Worcestershire. He may well be the most loved figure in the game – for what he is, for what he did and for what he was; and for how, with dignity, he changed the world.

D'Oliveira is officially 60 on 4 October, feast of Assisi's Francis, though he admits that severe questions about his real age 'would not be met by writs for slander'. It took time, of course, for a shy but determined Cape Coloured man first to escape South Africa's racism and then to build a glorious Test career in England.

Happily, he is not wholly departing the scene now. The umpire and former Glamorgan player Kevin Lyons is becoming the Worcestershire coach but, as the county is planning to launch an appeal for an indoor cricket school, only one man could possibly front it. So Dolly will continue to be as much a part of the landscape down by the silvery Severn as the mellow old Norman tower beyond deep long-on.

D'Oliveira first walked over the bridge and, tremulously, into the ground in 1964. The Worcestershire chairman, Sir George Dowty, had clinched the deal by offering him a house to rent for £2 10s a week. After a season Sir George said: 'Basil, I think you'll be with us for some time. Why don't you buy the house? You can have it for the same as I paid for it years ago.' That was £2,500. He bought it and the family is still in it.

On summer days he may be found somewhere else. The famous old bear sits in his famous old lair, a higgledy-piggledy little wooden boxroom above the public loos and alongside the scorers in Worcester's splintery, ageless and evocative scoreboard on the cathedral side of the ground. 'I aim to watch almost every ball from here,' he says. 'Outside, well you know I love being collared for a good chat by everyone and anyone. Here in peace and privacy is my hideout, where the players know they can always come and chew over things, although no one believes I haven't got a big bar and drinks cabinet hidden away up in the loft.' When he laughs that great rumbling laugh, the old scoreboard timbers shiver and the scorers next door affably shush for hush.

Out there, on a golden late summer's afternoon and to a packed holidaymakers' house, the pastoral scene is regularly being punctuated by 'howzats' from his Worcestershire boys, who are handsomely bowling out the title pretenders, the city slickers from Surrey. The old man's son, Damian, smartly pockets another slip catch. It is romantic that the father is leaving behind this talented chip off the block. 'The boy,' Dad allowably boasts, 'must be just about the best slip on the circuit. Ask anyone.' One does and he is.

Another sort of heir, this one as England's all-rounder, is taking Surrey's wickets with regularity. Ian Botham finishes with five. 'Ian's been a triumph here,' says D'Oliveira. 'Nobody thinks of him as "the ex-Somerset player", do they? He's fitted in beautifully: with the club, members, sponsors, the ordinary guy in the street and especially with the young players in the dressing room. He's been helping them from the moment he walked in. He can play a bit too, can't he?'

And in the evening a younger champion comes in to face a vengeful Surrey in the shape of the cruelly sharp Waqar Younis. Graeme Hick skilfully keeps him out, then begins to build the foundations for a sublime century, guiding him hither and tonking him yon. 'Graeme's had a rough summer,' admits his coach. 'But all he has to do is leave his talent alone. I keep telling him, "Don't alter anything, just trust in your talent." The same as I said when he first came here as a baby.

'His talent was immense; he just needed time and experience. It is the same now with his Test career. Look at the pressures he was under. All he wants now is experience at the top level and, cross fingers, things will come right sooner rather than later. Sure, Test bowlers will be firing in short stuff at him every time he walks out now. But with the innate talent he's been blessed with, the more they bounce him the more quickly he'll learn the facts of life and then start dealing with them all in devastating fashion. You wait.'

And the grand old man recalls his own palpitating nerves in his own first county innings out on this field in 1964. 'Against Essex. I hit a six which hit the bottom of this same scoreboard. I was about 90 not out. Trevor Bailey had just taken the second new ball. Thwack! I hit it and, as Trevor followed down the pitch, I'll never forget the furrowed, quizzical look on his face, as if to say, "What or who the heck's this guy?"' Why, hello Dolly.

Within a year of that sixer he was playing for England and, three years after that, changing the course of blinkered international sport. Guardedly he welcomes South Africa's re-admittance, although he reckons it is not yet the time to be dogmatic, for or against. 'Enough to say that perhaps I share Viv Richards's feelings, and fears, that everything's happening too hastily.

'I had an often painful first 30 years of my life, then a truly magnificent and so-surprising second 30. I wonder what the next 30 will bring.' One answer is even more affection and acclaim, and then some more.

10

FROM BAY TO BAIZE

Through a glass darkly
7 August 1976

I now know what a Cowes Eye view is. It's lying flat out in the bottom of a bobbing barque staring at the stars over the Solent and clutching an empty bottle to one's sou'wester. Cowes Week ends today, and your intrepid correspondent was sent along to suss out the sailors' scene and report back.

For Cowes Week, they said, pack a compass, some plimsolls and an anorak. And a biro. Nobody said anything about a spirit level. Each and every pub is open all day and every day. The word 'extension' doesn't tell the tale by a long chalk. After breakfast there is a gangplank queue in front of the Island Sailing Club of chaps who are actually racing. They are stowing away case after case of the hard stuff before the cannons boom. By lunch time the moored marina – those who watch in the safety of accent and anchorage – is noisy with the tinkle of tiny glasses. By the time the eye of the needle is piercing the redball of the farewell sun, everybody's still at it. In fact things are just beginning. Talk about pink gins in the sunset.

Later, one must admit it, the marquises mellow. By midnight they're bosom buddies with us oiks. But next morning it's pot luck on recognition. Cowes Reported is to do with the sports pages and the classes of Tempests and Solings and Dragons and Mermaids. Cowes Real is simply to do with class.

Even so, it was the wrong year to come. As a man who introduced himself as Surgeon-Captain Whatever (not Doctor or Captain, you understand but Surgeon-Captain) guffed: 'This year's a frightful awful Week: no fireworks to speak of, no Olympic chappies competing and no Royals.' Ah, ahoy for the old days, dear old days, of Philip and Freddie Fox, Uffa and Duffer.

Bob Fisher does some lovely reports for us. But he doesn't get the half of it. Cowes Week is more than sailing. Ask the grey-rinse widows and the PR secretaries. It seems mostly to do with having a change of brand-new old clothes. Ambre Solaire, possibly a compass and, as Jilly Cooper put it so well, the ability to play deck coitus against Captain Bligh.

A Henley rest-cure
6 July 1979

From sparking morn to balmy eventide (that's the only type of language which is appropriate) the whole ambience at Henley came as a refreshing relief from the demented, dusty sweat and toil of Wimbledon.

A day off! Aboard the breakfast stopper at Paddington, a change at Twyford for Wargrave and Shiplake – I felt as a Saturday morning miner must, coming up from the tunnel and into the showers.

Henley, I fancy, must be what Wimbledon was like in the days of old when Edward ruled and the Robinsons Barley Water was actually served by Old Heathers and not a booming senior executive from the Special Events Public Relations Department. Mind you, I cannot resist the actual sport, the 15-30 bit at Wimbledon, so it has to be admitted that I accepted the order for a trip back in the time capsule only on condition that I could follow the fortune of J Connors electronically on the suburban sward. I was assured I could. Not a hope, however.

'Is that a portable wireless receiver?' asked the spotty and boatered young boatman manning the stewards' gate. 'No, it's a transistor,' I replied. He examined it. 'This is a portable wireless receiver,' he said. 'Please leave it in that tent with those confiscated perambulators.' The pushchairs he indicated were apparently not allowed either, but I did see a number of senile gentlemen being wheeled around in wheelchairs. Wheelchairs at Henley are not perambulators.

You may think I am already finding it easier to be cynical, but not a bit of it. To be there yesterday on this little land's most blissful summer's day for three years was a privilege. John Rodda had primed me: 'In the summer that tennis and cricket have never been offered more gross amounts of sponsors' prizes it is worthwhile remembering that this other legendary event in the English summer is still modelled on the old idea of amateur sport. No Sports Council grant, no sponsor ... no brown envelopes with unsigned cheques for cash ... no promoters of golden regattas waiting on the bank.'

Yesterday those were one's feelings exactly as the Pimms were haughtily ordered and, high on the river banks, the breeze tickled the chestnut and larch trees to a contented deciduous chuckle. If Olde England has gone, it certainly was not forgotten here. The girls were quite sensational in the hats they had planned for months, and the chinless slack-lipped old buffers standing at the front of the judge's launches could each have been mistaken for Robert Morley.

'C'mon Jesus, for God's sake!' shouted an undergraduate. 'Pull your finger out, Clare!' hollered another. 'It's deeply gratifying,' someone else remarked, 'that the Canadian crew all have English names.'

All the while, with symmetrical rhythmic grace, the oarsmen streamed on, even while Americans came and went in expensively-cut Madison Avenue denim suits – 'Sorry sir, no jeans' – and old men in badged prep-school caps walked about like happy zombies straitjacketed into minuscule wet-bobs' blazers. Tom Crooks, one of Britain's finest ever international oarsmen, was asked why he was not rowing. 'Because I've retired,' he answered.

When was that announced? 'I've just decided to announce it,' he said. 'Come and have a drink on it.' That's Henley.

'How's Jimmy getting on?' I asked someone in the steward's bar. 'He's okey doke, old boy,' he said, indicating his buddy. 'But I dare say you could get him a large Plymouth Pink.'

Cloth of gold
30 April 1985

Jarndyce vs Jarndyce was never so drawn out nor dramatic a case as Taylor vs Davis. All this considered, I dare say Charles Dickens himself would have approved: he always reckoned he was a man of the people.

The third episode of BBC 2's classic serial *Bleak House* which swam mistily into view in the early hours of Monday morning – put off by the continuing saga of Dennis Taylor's unlikely snooker epic – will be repeated this evening at six o'clock, replacing *Laramie*.

It was well past midnight and the lights were still on all over England when Taylor, the tubby little Ulster outsider with the tubby, glinting, bright-moon spectacles, sank the fortnight's very final black to take the World Championship from the cool kid and knowing metropolitan, Steve Davis, the nonpareil. It was like Sergeant Bilko beating Ali over the full 15.

And it was more than just the stuff of sport. An unlikely winner had an even more unlikely army behind him, witness half a nation of sons and mums, nobs and nobodies, debs and plebs and proles in shoals who blearily set off for their differing Monday morning shifts with bloodshot eyelids rimmed with red – or rather, pink, blue, green … not forgetting the black.

An initial guess from the BBC yesterday did not quibble at my suggestion of a phenomenal past-midnight audience of over 12 million. Even Dickensian scholars must have stayed hooked.

Quite a few of these one-off live dramas of the TV age have involved not only giant steps for mankind but nice little sporting extravaganzas. The World Cup final in 1966, of course; snooker itself once or twice, certainly when the Hurricane blew into Sheffield a year or three back. I remember a provincial High Street crowd almost blocking the traffic around Multibroadcast when Botham was batting against Australia one Saturday afternoon – or even the mid-week morning when Willis was bowling in the same series. Or the Gillette semi-final at Old Trafford when Lancashire beat Gloucestershire and David Hughes's sixes just saved the nine o'clock news being put back.

This Sunday night drama was italicised for taking us so by surprise. For two weeks the moving wallpaper has been gently unrolling in everybody's sitting room – a softly clinking kaleidoscope of colours over there in the corner, accompanied by a crew of somnolent whispering Ovaltinie old-time hypnotists. You could take it or leave it, flicking back and forth when *Newsnight* got too schoolmasterly.

By Sunday lunchtime there seemed the certainty that the fortnight of watching green-baize grass grow had turned into a dreadfully sad anticlimax. Taylor was 0-7 down and the only interest was to watch the waistcoated executioner narrow his eyes and lay out the corpse. The Sunday papers were almost ripe with obituaries.

Slowly through the day – clink, clink, pot, pot, glint, glint – Taylor fiddled with his spectacles and eked his way back.

The climax, off the last ball of the last shot of the last gasp, was tumultuous in its almost dotty fulfilment of dramatic unities. Alan Clark, the director, has filmed a Trevor Preston script into a hugely anticipated musical – *Billy the Kid and the Green Baize Vampire* – and reckons nobody backing it would have believed his ending of a title determined on the final black of all.

I rang a friend in Belfast to offer him some sort of second-hand congratulations. He had been unable to watch the last frame and had locked himself in another room. Rather like boxing with McGuigan, snooker in Ulster has crossed the sectarian divide. It is the working class pastime. Higgins is from the Donegal Road,

Taylor from Coalisland, in Tyrone, hitherto best known as the scene of the first reverberating civil rights march in 1968.

Taylor's parents named their tubby Dennis with two Ns after Dennis Haughey, the SDLP politician whom mum thought 'a fine wee lad'. His mother died last year and he seriously thought of packing up the game. He had only won £16,000 last year and had Denise, Damian and Brendan to educate. He rang his father Tom in the middle of the wee hours on Monday and could hear the bands playing down the street.

Next week Taylor, who has since settled in Lancashire, returns to his beloved Province where for two nights in Antrim at the Riverside, he takes on the locals who have been battling for months to play him in the *Sunday News* competition. The cheers from the beleaguered old gap-toothed bleak houses next week will match those across the water well after midnight on Sunday. And the bloodshot eyes at work next day will be coloured the same.

Shirty words, dirty weather
20 August 1986

Sometimes these days you get the feeling that top international sports events are run for the benefit of T-shirt manufacturers. The cottage industry subculture particularly lends itself to rowing for the army of participants at the world championships are, to a man and woman, square-shouldered and barrel-chested – all the better to display across those ample, heaving bosoms such legends as 'Rowers Do It Backwards' and 'Rowers Pull More Oars'.

I have yet to see the classic 'I Row Therefore I Am' but it's doubtless heaving around somewhere on this delightful if windswept stretch of parkland outside Nottingham. This is real rowing. Henley it ain't. These are the World Championships and also the people's championships. Not for Pimm's people. The wooden quiff of hills over yonder is broken by the working city's skyline and eight modern cathedral spires, the arc light pylons that corner those industrial shrines of Nottingham Forest and County. The real champions of the world have come here to await the crews from Scotland's Commonwealth Games. The weather is still wretchedly Scottish but the guns from the East are booming and frighteningly loud.

At lunch was rowing's Mr Big, the Maxwell-massive Thomi Keller, president of FISA, the sport's world body. He is a millionaire Swiss watchmaker and expects to get his way. On Monday he complained about cyclists following the race on the far towpath. 'Get their names and get rid of them,' he said. The regatta controller, Mike Sweeney, said: 'What do you expect me to do? This is a public park.' Keller: 'Get a shotgun.' Sweeney: 'Okay, I'll apply to the chief constable for a gun licence.'

Rowing's language is French. The command at the start, after the *aligneur* has seen all are settled and straight, is '*Êtes-vous prêt? Partez!*' Experienced crews pull on '*prêt*', really experienced crews on '*êtes*'. In the second heat of the coxed fours the crews flew so beautifully from the gun that the *aligneur*, Michel Doutre, was moved to remark: 'Ah. *Bon départ*,' forgetting that his microphone played the comment straight to the ear of the starter, John Stevenson.

To the astonishment of the crowd, including Keller, Stevenson rang his bell for a false start. The boats turned round mystified, and a furious row broke out between Keller and his starter.

'Why did you stop the race?'

'Because the *aligneur* said "*faux départ*."'

The argument went on stridently. Later, Keller stripped out the elaborate high-tech starting system and said they should use old fashioned flags. Asked why he had even tried such high technology, Stevenson, the typically phlegmatic Brit, replied: 'Just because it was there.'

11

THE GAMES

Game, Seb and match
13 August 1984

LOS ANGELES: As the Brits were stiff and glowing and still throwing sunhats in the air, a mischievous friend cupped his hand to his mouth and bellowed above the din with heavy irony: 'I still think we should have picked Peter Elliott for the 1500!'

It was not so many weeks ago that some seemed to have decided on behalf of the nation that young Elliott should run the race for Britain. The selectors fiddled and fretted but finally, for once, were not fickle. Peter Elliott? Who, where and what is he?

There was another domestic confrontation, epic in prospect, that remains unjoined. At the very moment Sebastian uncorked the pent-up fizz in himself and all of us, brave and surely misguided Ovett was prostrate, gulping for breath and being bound and blanketed before again being milk-floated away. The overjoyed Coe's lap of honour had taken him past the concerned huddle of ambulance men around Ovett. By then neither British runner was in a fit state to notice what extremes of fate had been visited on the rivals.

On the line, Coe had turned into the smiling embrace of Cram. 'I honestly was thoroughly delighted for Seb,' said the generous, uncomplicated young Geordie. 'I'd run well myself and was simply beaten by one of the all-time greats – and you can't have any complaints about that, can you?'

For one split second, Cram thought he might win. 'Just off the top bend I was moving well – Seb had the inside position and just for a fraction, I said to myself "I can go past and win." No sooner had the thought struck me than Seb knew it – he spurted and I knew then I was dead unless his ankles tuned to jelly. What an athlete!'

Cram is growing up a fine man – articulate now, even though he still calls lunch 'dinner' and supper 'tea', and always gracious. It was the first time I remember Steve not extolling the virtues of Sunderland AFC to a bewildered bank of foreign pressmen. Sebastian, however, was not going to be denied his ritual mention of his beloved soccer team, Chelsea. He explained that his gesture at the finish of elaborately pointing his two index fingers towards the vast throng was by no means a digital expression of bad humour directed at either TV commentators or Fleet Street.

It was a jubilant signal meaning: 'There's the second gold I promised you' to a small group of Chelsea fans who spend their summers following Sebastian. Who is or what is this Chelsea? asked a worried American journalist. The Barons Court Bluesox, I told him, and he seemed a little clearer.

A thousand backslaps later and a million microphones satisfied, Sebastian and his little family entourage were in downtown LA. His mother Angela was holding the bouquet of flowers that came with the medal. His father and coach was looking more than usual as he does on these occasions – in a glinting daze, rather like an eccentric, forgetful professor who is not quite sure why he's there except that he has somehow discovered the secret of the universe.

Which in his own little way, he has. He was a London engineer who liked cycling and most sport. Eureka! Peter realised early that his frail, pale son had a gift. Once the boy realised it might be true, the Olympics was the aim. All Sebastian can remember about the Tokyo games of 20 years ago was the BBC signature tune. Four years later, when he was 11, he was electrified by David Hemery's sensational run in Mexico.

By then the family had moved to Sheffield and, lo and behold, the man who had won the bronze medal behind Hemery, the straight-backed, crewcut John Sherwood, lived in the city. Not only that, John's wife Sheila had been the long jump runner-up. They had been feted by the city fathers. Seb was hooked.

'It showed me clearly,' recalls Seb, 'that an Olympian was something out of the ordinary.' Sixteen years later on, it is by no means outrageous to say that of all the Olympians of modern history, Sebastian Coe could well be the most out of the ordinary.

Young, gifted and arthritic by 40
24 September 1988

SEOUL: Lights, camera, action. It must have made for magnificent television at home, but the top of the bill at Seoul's gymnastics hall stank out the joint.

Showbiz metaphors fit. So do military ones. This is nothing much to do with sport any more. The grudge match, they called it. Russia versus Romania. The bullets to be fired by whey-faced, hollow-eyed, waxwork little girls whose 'smiles' are just part of a work-worn day. Weapons to be primed by commandant-coaches frantic for their jobs. Strings to be manipulated from way behind the lines, by cynical civil servants who go by the name of neutral judges. Let the Games begin ...

In the women's all-round individual final yesterday, it all rested on the very last vault. Daniela Silivas of Romania had led all through, on floor, beam and bar – chased by Elena Chouchounova of the Soviet Union. A minuscule 0.05 marks between them. Now just the best of two vaults to go.

Hey, down there, hang on a tick. Well, would you credit it? All of a sudden the six judges under the old pommel horse for this once-and-for-all decider have no 'unbiased' American or Canadian among them – and certainly no Romanian. It may mean nothing but in this neck of the sporting woods the word coincidence is very seldom coy.

The Russian judge – another 'coincidence' – just happens to be Nelli Kim, half-Korean and once the darling of the Moscow bars (no, not that sort), but now, alas, a solemn and grumpy official in the Ministry of Sports Culture. Silivas springs down the runway. Boof! Up and over, and it looks well-nigh perfection to this untutored eye. Later, in the hesitant and squashed-mouse squeaky voice of a tot who has suddenly realised she is caught up in something much too big for her, Daniela is to say: 'As I landed, I thought "I am now champion."'

She scores three perfect 10s, two 9.9s and only 9.8 from the stone-faced Nelli Kim, which at this level is a sneering slap. Not that such a derisory mark actually counts – though it still makes its point with venom – for after so much cynical political marking over the years, the top and bottom marks are ignored. A competitor's total score is now computed from the middle four markers.

But it conjures up one final chance for the Russian. Out of the blue, Chouchounova can now score six perfect 10s for victory – and, as sure as eggs, she does it. By a fraction of a mark, 79.662 against 79.637, so was won the war.

The photographers whose job is not to care about such things, leave Daniela in a swarm and head for Elena. The smile is suddenly on full beam for one last time. Soviet delirium all round: forlorn, resigned, teeth-grinding subjugation from the Romanians. Nobody who has followed these matters even half closely was in the least bit put out. They had forecast that the Romanians would, somehow, be put in their place. Romania, remember, had brazenly defied Moscow and had not only entered but enchanted the Los Angeles Games.

Then, amid, huge publicity at the last world gymnastics championships in Rotterdam, the Romanians had beaten hell out of the Russian team. They would pay in Seoul. And it might not be wise to complain. The Romanian coach, Adrian Goreac, at least did his heroic best. His shattered little charge, Daniela, sat by him in a daze. He left a consoling arm on her shoulder. The straight and obvious question was asked – but before the Romanian could compose a reply, his rival Soviet coach, Viktor Gabrichenko, leapt in with a warning gabble of Russian.

Goreac icily let him finish, then said carefully: 'My own unofficial opinion is that when a sportsman or woman receives only 9.8 marks, then it is not difficult he takes it not very well. It is a mark that does not express the highest level at which we have obviously performed. A mark such as this expresses in no way possible the level at which we have performed.'

He squeezed the drooped shoulder of his elf alongside. Had he lifted his eyes slightly higher, the stare he was giving the Soviet counterpart would have frozen the sun. Had the new champion understood, I dare say she would still not have twigged the world she had been born into. Well, you don't at that age, do you? She had been programmed into her 'programme'. For over two-thirds of her life.

Chouchounova trains for between eight and 12 hours a day and has done since the age of six. Her father drives a van, her mother works in a hat factory – or they did, before Elena's potential suppleness and elasticity was discovered in tests at the Leningrad Sports Club. Once the smiles had no need to be fixed any more, and the arc lights had been dimmed, it was a different 17-year-old who was paraded before us.

Off the set, so to speak, and with the smile switched off with the lights and the purple eye make-up scrubbed-away, she gave the impression more of a beleaguered and bored housewife at the end of her tether after a very long day. 'Sure, during training in all my life,' her Russian interpreter translated for her, 'I have often wanted to quit, to throw it all up, to go back home.

'But I always know I have to pull myself together, go out for a long walk, and determine to return, heartened, to do even more training.' As she spoke she did not even raise a smile of amiable resignation, just stared into the microphones.

And Nelli Kim hobbled away. So did the 1984 winner, Mary Lou Retton, after her waffle for US television – and the free interviews to anyone who asked, as long as you gave a mention to her advertising biggie, Breakfast Wheaties. Retton is 20-odd but, arthritically, going on 50.

What are they? What is 'sport'? What are we doing to these children? Last year, a project sponsored by Great Ormond Street Hospital in London tested 520 little bodies off the bars – and considered that up to two thirds of them 'could develop permanent back injuries inside 10 years'. In a survey in Gothenberg, Dr Alf Nachenson singled out the theatrical end-move at the close of each 'show' – the lumbar throw – which he reckoned was particularly dangerous to the spine.

But sod that. By the time they reach 40 they might be walking funny, like Mary Lou and Nelli, but the telly tells no tales.

New era begins with a chilly dawn
28 September 1988

SEOUL: I don't know how many Olympic competitors say their prayers night and morning as a matter of course, but I bet a heck of a lot more than usual woke up to Seoul's chilly grey dawn yesterday and, with a shiver, offered thanks: 'There but for the grace of God go I.'

Ben Johnson is taking the rap for a pretty large army.

Even the most conservative pre-Games estimates admitted a substantial group of athletes were taking performance-enhancing drugs. The president of the International Olympic Committee medical commission guessed six per cent – that is over 500 of those who woke up in the Olympic Village here yesterday.

Last month, when presenting the official report of the committee of inquiry into drug abuse in British athletics – commissioned by the British Amateur Athletic Board and the Amateur Athletic Association – even the chairman, Peter Coni QC, had to concede, when asked about the prevalence of drug-taking among today's athletes, that 'it would be a brave man who said that one in 10 was not a possibility.'

So in a British team here of 96 athletes, officialdom reckons 10 of them may be doped up – and Coni's brief, of course, took in none of the other Olympic sports where this pathetic pill-popping is even more prevalent.

It is a special thrill to witness a world-record run – and particularly so in the breath-taking short sprint because, stripped of tactics or intellect, you have before you the very basic proof that no one in the history of mankind has run faster. Well, all right, if you must, since the stopwatch was invented last century. Even if your great-grandchildren prefer piano-playing to sports, they will be mightily impressed that grandpop actually witnessed a bloke being the very fastest man in the history of the universe.

In Johnson's case, twice in 13 months, for on Saturday in Seoul the Jamaican-born Canadian became the only man in history to break his own world record at the 100m dash. So, perhaps, we should have been suspicious – as indeed we were. But excitement of the moment readily files conjecture to the back of your mind and submerges cynical suspicion. But what do we tell our grandchildren now? Wide-eyed innocents on your knee should not have to ask why Stanozolol makes a man run faster.

Johnson now forfeits his new record – but his old one of 9.83, set in Rome last year, will stand, for he was not officially nabbed for any illegality then. So for how many years will the new kids to the sport be chasing a tainted record? Will they grow up to know only that to break sport's classic barrier you have to be abusing yourself?

Unless the authorities really have broken through with a new and highly sensitive testing kit – and unless Johnson, as he claims, was nobbled – then the now former champion or his advisers must have been astonishingly lax at not coming off the drug in time or not using a 'masking agent' to hide its use in the bloodstream.

Johnson's performances in the last couple of years have, after all, been as such to make him the rumour-mongers' prime suspect – especially those who knew him as a skinny medium-pacer of a few years back. Even the NBC commentator for the programme beamed to the US forces out here was a touch near the knuckle during Saturday's race: 'Wow. He had another gear there that we didn't even see in Rome when he broke the record. The man's incredible.'

And later, on NBC again, Johnson's fierce rival, the American Carl Lewis, who was second on Saturday, brazenly told his interviewer: 'I don't know how he did it. He must have been hypnotised or something, but he did something to stimulate himself in the final.' Lewis was also quivering with innuendo in Rome, after which he called a press conference to complain about drugs wrecking his sport.

He did not exactly name his great rival, but he was miffed to say the least, telling how Johnson had been an insignificant rival all through the early 1980s, running about 10.1 or 10.2 for the distance until 1985. Then Lewis had 1986 off for a knee operation, and when he returned, 'I saw old Ben suddenly running better than anyone else; he didn't look the same and he certainly didn't run the same.' Poor old fast-footed, slow-witted Ben, carrying the can for his greedy little cadre of 'advisers' – as well as for those cheats, who must be numbered in the tens of thousands, who call themselves athletes from all over the world, east and west.

But a sad and sorry day for the Olympic Games and for the sport? Not a bit of it. Just as the nippy milky-white dawn that lay over our village compound brightened up with a fierce sun, the story, too, got hotter., So with a bit of luck and even more vigilance might 27 September 1988 turn out to be a glistening day of hope for honest sport.

The day the young upstarts came of age
3 August 1992

BARCELONA: The Searle brothers' palpitating victory put a glistening gilt lid on the most illustrious weekend for British men's rowing in modern times. It truly was *Boys' Own* stuff.

The two Surrey students were still considered novices at the event in the spring. Yesterday they gave 10 years in age, as well as a handsome start, to Italy's hitherto invincible legends and overtook them right on the line with one final, almost mischievous, heave. It was youthful bravado; it was also utterly heroic.

The previous day Redgrave and Pinsent had overwhelmed their rivals in the coxless pairs by the relentless power of their oars as well as their massive reputation. Each of the other boats carried an inferiority complex in its hold. At the finish a man from each of the silver and bronze medal boats was hauled out, collapsed and in distress, by crews of the ambulance launch, such was the intensity of the British pair's domination. Redgrave and Pinsent displayed awesomely cruel rowing. What the Searles did was not so much rowing as racing. This was hats-in-the-air stuff. This was Piggott getting up on The Minstrel, Desert Orchid at Cheltenham or Chataway vs Kuts at White City. And what made it the grander was that it was Boys vs Men.

The Abbagnale brothers have been world champions seven times. Yesterday they set a serene and severe course for an unprecedented hat-trick of Olympic titles. Horny-handed, unsmiling assassins, they train in the choppy dawn sea each morning in the dark shadow of Vesuvius, after running the five miles to their boat from their home in Pompeii. They started this Olympic final even hotter favourites than Redgrave's boat had been the day before. Who were these kids to challenge them?

The trusted tactics, as sadistically followed down the years, would destroy the upstarts – jump out of the traps at a lick, burn off the other boats by halfway, or three-quarters at the latest, then relax, savour the cheers and collect the gold medals. But even stony-faced granite, we discovered, can be dynamited by youthful will, daring and stomach-wrenching guts. The two part-time oarsmen and full-time British students – one at law school, the other in estate management – knew it would be terminal if 'the Abbers' led by more than three lengths at halfway.

And they were duly three lengths down – but only three and not desperately hanging on by a thread. 'Did you see our bang at 1,250 metres?' said Jonny. 'We poured on the power just when they weren't expecting it, and it must have given them a psychological shock to think what we might have left.' Their cox, Garry Herbert, told the Searles he could see their faces and said, 'C'mon boys, they really know we're coming to get them now.' And so they did.

Greg, who returns to his books at South Bank University next week, said at the finish he had been momentarily overwhelmed by 'a sort of dead silence of ecstasy – while Jonny and Garry just leapt about out of control'. Greg said he looked across at the two Italians, vanquished at last, all-in and 'suddenly very old, and I felt a sudden pang of guilt for having done what we had, for they have been very, very great champions, and I could tell how devastated they were and utterly gutted. And they rowed over and said "well done" and "bravo". There was really nothing else they could say but I was very touched by their graciousness and chivalry.'

Greg said he didn't think he could row in a pair with anyone but his brother. 'There is no one I trust more. We'll go on, I suppose, mixing sport with our studies. If I became a full-time rower, I think I'd become a very boring person.'

Every heroic image was capped by something seedy
5 August 1996

ATLANTA: To us in the vast congregation of hangers-on who piled out of the caravans three weeks ago, the true heroine of the 1996 Games was not a tweetie-pie gymnast, a runner, a jumper, a standing-still long-legged length of pulchritude frozen in concentration as she prepared to defy gravity in the women's long jump ...

To us lot in the invading army which has marched across Georgia, cursing, the heroine was Mrs Dick Pound – wife of

Canada's IOC bigwig – who kneed an Atlanta policewoman in the groin last Wednesday. It goes without saying that the cop was over-officious and over-harassed and over-the-top.

Every one of them has been, male or female. They have not been able to cope. Security was one thing, the traffic, horrendously gridlocked, another. The army of foreign athletes and media mayhem was another altogether. They hated us, and it was mutual. They could not stand the world invading their narrow space, seethingly criticising the little town of which they had been so proud.

But then there was Johnson and Redgrave, and Bailey and Lewis and Morceli and Suleymanoglu, and Pinsent and, I suppose, Black and young Ainslie, and, to be sure, many more of similar and valorous resplendence. Yet you could never get away from the day-to-day Atlanta.

Why should you hear now of journalists' gripes? We should count ourselves lucky being here, the epicentre of a fortnight's sport and sportsmanship, of endeavour and competition and athleticism. But that could seldom allow itself to break through. At every heroic image, there were just a couple of minutes to savour it before it was capped by something seedy and cynical and much nearer the bone and the knuckle of real and unpleasant life. Mrs Pound's feat was to do what we had all been daring ourselves to do.

It had begun at the very beginning, this good glow at once being topped by something crass and uncomforting and geared to commerce. Take the opening ceremony. It was a stroke of genius to ambush the world with the surprise appearance of the Olympian and nonpareil Muhammad Ali to light the flame of goodness and expectation. Up travelled the sacred lick of flame by pulley to ignite the Olympic bowl on the topmost plinth. Hurrah – till we saw that the bowl was cast in the open-shell shape of a gigantic chip-wrapper for McDonald's french fries. The hamburger conglomerate was cashing in.

I suppose, till these Games were inexplicably given the nod six years ago, the two sentences most closely associated by the rest of the world with this tin-pot jumble of derelict used-car lots cowering below a score of skyscrapers was 'Frankly, my dear, I don't give a damn ...' and 'I have a dream ...' The first from the 1939 Hollywood Civil War epic *Gone with the Wind* and the second, of course, that boomingly resonant damnation of slavery and segregation by Martin Luther King.

Well, a decade ago the Atlanta businessman Billy Payne, who looks and talks like a cross between the former Texas billionaire Bunker Hunt and the Dallas soap opera anti-hero JR Ewing, had a dream all right. Señor Samaranch and his IOC cronies fell for it. And now, the dream fulfilled, the rest of the world decamps back to civilisation this morning with the majority saying, 'Atlanta? Frankly, my dear, I don't give a damn.'

Payne and Atlanta's mayor Bill Campbell remained impervious: 'You whining critics should be taken up to the skeet range,' said the latter, forgetting the order that the Georgia penal authorities had postponed all prison executions for the duration of the Games. But only till today.

A French photographer mate had two days in the slammer and a five-grand fine for arguing with a cop at the football stadium. I escaped lightly: only two hours of heavy and scary menace in the nick for hailing a downtown taxi where apparently I shouldn't have been hailing one. The police throughout the Games were quite beastly to the heroic, gauntlet-running taxi-drivers, who were trying to make a crust for themselves, not for conglomerate commerce.

Just before I was arrested, a friend had driven me in on the airport road. You could see the jagged skyscrapers, like bad teeth in the mouth of a crone, in the smog-hazed distance. 'Ah me,' I remarked with a sigh, 'the dreaming spires.' 'What sport are you down to cover tonight?' asked my pal, jumping to the blessed reverie of the theme, 'a spot of cricket in the Parks, what?'

No, this was a benighted corner of a foreign field all right. And on impulse, together we recited,

Now stands the SWATCH clock at ten-to-three,
And are there junk-burgers still for tea?

There were. Exorbitant as usual. Inedible as usual.

12

AH, YES…

As the years went by, Frank found the past ever more beguiling than the present. And he started young.

United I remember it well
4 October 1977

October the Fourth. Today is the 20th birthday of the first Sputnik. It would have been Buster Keaton's 82nd birthday and St Francis of Assisi's 751st. It is (he claims!) Basil D'Oliveira's 46th. And it is, irrevocably, my 40th.

Fortified as I am with my first slug of Phyllosan, I reckon it is a time for old tyme, time for stocktaking having reached this age of mellowness; a time to hark back while I still might fancy myself to be 'full of wise saws and modern instances' before I shift 'into the lean and slippered pantaloons, with pouch on the side', as reckoned Warwickshire and England's finest spinner of them all.

The trouble with a 40th birthday is that it creeps up from behind, and puts its hand on your shoulder just as you were quite confident you were still in the prime of your youth, and all joy and standards were still unburdened by comparison. 'Ah,' I saged only the other day to a younger colleague as he rabbited on about the dreaded Woolmer's cover drive, 'it's not a patch on Graveney's. He looked pitying. 'You know,' he said, 'that I am too young to have ever seen Graveney.'

Only at times like that do you realise you were actually there with Tizer bottle and that it's 30 years ago next summer that you saw the blushing lank get the very first of his 122 centuries – against the Combined Services at the Wagon Works and that he was nearly run out at 78. Not only that, but can it have been a year even before then that Raymond Glendenning screeched all the way from Wembley to Stroud that 'Duffy has scored, Duffy has scored ...' so even more so today as I lie abed will I be indulging in a touch of the Maurice Chevaliers. For I do remember it well, when I was young ...

John Arlott saying 'and Bradman plays it out towards the House of Commons ... it doesn't go as far as that, mind you, but just silly mid-off ... So it's Hollies again ... and he's bowled him' or Raymond again going nuts in May, this time 'Stamps has scored' ... or my distress at the early morning news that Baksi had broken the jaw of my beloved Bruce ...

The only man to refuse me an autograph was Billy Wright when he came to open a playing field at Stonehouse. I never forgave him and always would call him Ambrose to annoy him – till he brought champagne to my 30th birthday party. (See, name dropping improves with age too!) I made my debut on the terraces at Bristol City but never saw a thing – I did not overmuch mind, for some reason I had a thing about Roost of the Rovers – so the first match I ever witnessed was from the stand at Villa Park against Fulham. That, for some perverse reason, was the start of my enduring affair with Fulham – probably because of Joe Bacuzzi's hair style, or perhaps because Stan Lynn of Villa missed a penalty which I swear to this day hit the corner flag, though I can't possibly believe that it did.

A regular fix of rugby union, of course, was early injected into any Gloucestershire youngster. But visits to Kingsholm or Fromehall in Stroud became routine and familiar slogs. Not until I was taken to Stanley's match at Oxford and saw Jackie Kyle slice through the Blues on the burst did rugby first blow my mind. Then came the wintry day when I was first taken to Twickenham: England vs the All Blacks in 1954, and I was on the very touchline alongside which Ted Woodward, whopping white-shirted winger, actually carried on his back his marker Jardine for fully 20 yards it seemed. I remember, too, bald Bob Scott catching everything the English threw up, and then the final exhilaration as Regan and Co. opened out under their own posts in an uplifting attempt to snatch a win.

I remember crying in front of Father Dunstan, my housemaster (he was pretty far gone as well) after we had heard Eamonn on the wireless go into gory details of Dai Dower's drubbing by the Spaniard Young Martin. I cried in the Talbot Inn at Leominster a few years later, too, when I was told about the Babes and the accident in the runway slush at Munich. Pals then were mostly farmers who had no pull for football, but there was not a word above a whisper in that bar that night.

But later that year I watched Murphy's team in the cup final on television. Bobby Charlton became a hero then. My first television cup final, of course, had been the Matthews match of 1953 when we turned the sound off even then to check on Raymond's radio eyesight – 'Perry has scored! Perry has scored!' I can still hear him now. It was long years later that I went to Wembley in the flesh. (It was Bobby Moore's first international there.) And not until my middle 20s did I see the centre court (Bobby Wilson was beaten of course), and even later than that I went to the Derby (Sea Bird skated it though nobody told us at Tattenham Corner for hours). Ah yes, I remember it well ...

But one thing will be worrying me as I ruminate on my pillow this morning: is it just half-time? Will I go the full 15? What rotten cheese if I'm substituted before the full 90. Meanwhile, happy birthday Basil. And thank you, too, for all the memories.

United on a day in May
29 May 1988

29 May 1968. What a day, youth still so clear-eyed, fizzing, full to the brim and fancy-free that we took it all in our stride at the time.

Yet, inside a handful of hours, it was the best time of our lives – the day of Sir Matt and Sir Ivor, of Best and Guest and Lester.

It was a sweltering belter of a heatwave Derby Day up on the Downs, with the classic of Classics won by, till then, the horse and jockey of the century. And in the sultry, thunderous Wembley evening, Man United won the European Cup for their manager to dedicate to his heavenly Busby Babes.

By a fluke, this small-time loiterer on the fringes of the big-time had somehow nabbed himself an intimate view of the glorious day. I was a fancy-pants, pink-shirted producer of outside broadcasts of ITV, which had the exclusive Epsom rights. It would be different in the evening at Wembley, for though we were transmitting the match, the nation still tuned in, on principle as it were, to the gabby Wolstenholme waffle for soccer's state occasions.

First, early to the Downs alongside peak-capped chauffeur (ITV still had its loot-printing licence), washed and brushed up and very much Mossed and Brossed, for one of my jobs was to liaise with the steward of the Royal Box, just above the winner's enclosure.

His name was Bernard Marmaduke Fitzalan Howard, plus a few others besides, and he was premier earl of all England and earl marshal, i/c ceremonial, and he had very little sniffing time, I'm telling you, for a Moss Bros oik with cumbersome television cameras keen for prying shots of Royalty gambling. He had a rubicund, pug-doggy face and he had crossed garters with me on other events throughout the year. 'Get lost, sonny, and take those wires with you,' was the tenor of his growl as he essayed a scuff at our precious cables with his bespoke little feet. But even Marmaduke left us alone to cover the race itself. It was like an oven as the sun hammered down, and the knife-sharp anticipation rose up to meet it. Sir Ivor was surely going to slay the bookies.

We had crossed the water a few weeks earlier to film the favourite at work on Vincent O'Brien's blissful gallops at Ballydoyle, and not one of our crew had returned home without putting his house down on the dramatic, wild-eyed bay with the spectacular turn of foot. We were surer for Vincent telling us he was hoping Piggott had bagged the bridge for the up-coming biggie and more so when Sir Ivor's owner, Raymond Guest, who was US Ambassador in Dublin, told us that over a year before he had plonked down £550 at 100 to 1 with William Hill.

The engaging Guest was furious that he would miss Epsom on the 29th because he had to attend the Wexford unveiling of Ireland's Kennedy Memorial, but when the race got underway I thought it was as well he was absent because his horse was not showing at all. The field careened like a huge colourful float down the hill to Tattenham Corner with never a mention of Sir Ivor. Round the bend and the long climb for home and still nowhere to be seen. Piggott was boxed in with the rear bunch that were already up in their stirrups peering into the distance to see who would win it, when, all of a sudden, whoosh! I've never seen such acceleration before or since.

In chocolate and powder-blue colours resembling an old-style rugby strip, Piggott launched himself out of the scrum as the horse went for the line in a way that still defies description. It was truly stunning – Piggott still reckons Sir Ivor his most wondrous beast – and for the first and only time I threw my top hat in the air.

I had to retrieve it soon enough, for the day was only half over. Hotfoot to Wembley. No way, though, that United could eclipse Sir Ivor. Wanna bet? United's progress to the final – an English club's first – had captivated all football, for it was surely Busby's last throw, exactly a decade since his finest side was wiped out on the Munich runway. But, like earlier in the afternoon, the early signals were unpromising.

It was bitty, neurotic stuff, with United petrified of the onus on them and Benfica narrow-eyed and oblivious to romance – though not, I hasten to add, content with anything like the tedium their team in the same fixture 20 years on was to inflict on the viewing public.

The fouls went tit for tat. Eusebio did slap Stepney's crossbar with a screamer, but Best was being chopped off at the shins, Stiles was replying in kind and Charlton was frowning and fretting, despite scoring the opening goal. The attrition wore on, the vast throng almost accepting the inevitability of Benfica's equaliser and, as soon as it came, only Stepney's galumphing last-ditch flop when Eusebio was clear put the thing into extra time. That was my cue. And the game's. And the moon's, which now raged down above the floodlit beacons, and United began to play.

By now, still in my Epson topper and tails, I had conned my way round the touchline – no cop man enough to challenge my nobby outfit – so I was crouched immediately behind Stepney's net at the tunnel end. Extra time meant we could steal a march on the BBC and, at the final whistle, grab anyone to interview on the pitch and go live into *News at Ten*.

So the climactic faraway flurry of goals by the mesmeric Best, bounding Kidd and bald, brave, blubbing Bobby were only sensed from my end. But I saw in close-up how the prowling Stepney, edgy until the very end, was crying too, and then, with the tumult quite overpowering, we got our hand-held shots and interviews at final whistle as Bobby fell weeping onto old Matt's chest, the two survivors of Munich. And afterwards, we searched and searched for Bobby. The celebrations were in full swing and he was nowhere to be found. We discovered him at last, being consoled by Pat Crerand, sitting in the litter and jetsam under the grandstand itself, still in tears.

We crept away, for there was another party that my gear might gate-crash to top and tail this day of days. It was already in full swing at the Great Room in the Savoy. Raymond Guest had already flown in, bringing with him Teddy Kennedy and the Irish Prime Minister, Eamon de Valera, no less. What a hooley. Sir Ivor wasn't there, mind, nor was William Hill – but everyone else was. And as the early hours got later, the double celebration got wilder. Racing and football came together – and there drinking alone at a table was one Irishman I recognised. It was George Best, waiflike, winding down, and sadly sullen amid the crazy carnival.

He refused congratulations with a forced, dismissive smile. But he accepted a drink, and we left him to his moping. It was some 10 years later that he explained to me how that night had demonstrated to him that he was no longer part of his team's laughter or tears. 'I was there,' he said, 'but I knew I didn't belong.' All around him all evening had been men and women celebrating the achievement of their lifetime's work and determination. 'It should have been that for me, too. Instead, although I couldn't quite phrase it at the time, it was the beginning of the end for me.'

29 May 1968 was in a way, I suppose, the beginning of the end for a whole generation – and come to think of it, I bet old Bernard Marmaduke went to bed that night in Arundel quite pleased about that at least.

Belle Vue dies – not with a roar but a whimper
1 December 1987

Manchester's famous Belle Vue stadium is to be demolished. The venerable 60-year-old pile which held the world's first cheetah race and Britain's first kangaroo fight has been acknowledged worldwide as the traditional home of British speedway. But it looks certain that 1987's cup final between Belle Vue and Coventry four weeks ago will be the last time the old monument shudders and creaks to the screech of sporting motorcycles.

Different engines will now be heard, for the 32-acre site has been bought by British Car Auctions, whose chief executive, Tom Gibson, said yesterday: 'Sorry, sad and all that, but there is no remote chance of any more speedway or stock cars at Belle Vue. We are not in that line of business at all.'

Says the clerk of the course for 30 years, Allan Morrey: 'It is an utter tragedy. Belle Vue was the Mecca to speedway; it's what Lord's is to cricket, or Man U is to the world of football.'

Just another tale of our times. In London recently, two of the legendary centres of the sporting century's subculture – White City and Harringay, whose very names stretch old men's memories – have been terminally laid to waste by the ball-and-chain of progress wielded by the same sort of heralds of free enterprise that erected them in the first place so proudly a few generations ago. The profit motive spares no time for sports fans' panegyrics.

Manchester's not-inconsiderable speedway lobby did not surrender without a hastily assembled protest, but in spite of a gallantly passionate meeting on Thursday night there seems nothing else they can do. There is no hope of them careering up on the outside to snatch victory at the wire like Peter Collins used to do.

It will not only be those suburban mystiques of speedway and stock-car racing that will be laid to rest with the official death certificate from the planning office. Other ghosts of long-gone back-page headlines stalk the evocative, dingy and dusty old Manchester playground. When the moon is up and dangling fiercely bright above the splintered old scoreboards, they say you can hear still the urgent cries and muffled clatter on the boards of the breathless programme-selling Saturday-night schoolboys, or the hissing aces on the woodwork of Fred Perry who packed out the place in the early 30s, or the ugly roar of either lions in the zoo next door or the all-in wrestlers in the ring ...

Or the snort-snort of the sea lion or of such prize-fighters who loved the place as Nel Tarleton, or Len Harvey, the Rochdale Thunderer, or Jack London, bald and bandy and belching as he kept frantically out of the way of tigerish Freddie Mills for the full 15 in 1944. Jack's son, Brian – 'I'm only a prawn in this game' – was beaten here by Henry Cooper, and Terry Downes, too brave for his own good, took an ultimate pasting from Willie Pastrano in the last world-title fight at Belle Vue 23 years ago.

But always the friendly enough snarl of the speedway bikes or the galumphing dodgems of the stock-car mayhem sustained

Belle Vue's weekly fix in the name of sport. 'Speedway never even closed for the war,' says Morrey. He finds it hard to credit that the end came only four weekends ago. 'Just like that. Not even allowed a farewell meeting. They haven't even given us a chance to put up a fight.'

The Belle Vue captain, Chris Morton, is one of the sport's most respected leaders. He still doesn't know if – certainly where – he will be leading out a Belle Vue team next spring. 'No, of course, no other clubs have approached anyone about transfers yet. It's utterly tragic when there are still thousands devoted to the club and the sport in Manchester. It's such a marvellous track, the best in the world, so wide it's like a desert and you can ride five different types of races in one night if you want.'

As the front-page ad in the *Manchester Evening News* on the eve of Belle Vue's grand opening for speedway 60 springs ago in March said – 'Roll Up! Britain's speediest! Great Gathering of Stars, Spectacular broadsiding. Wonderful feats. Fast and furious. Hair-raising!' 'Ah yes, them were great days,' says Frank Varey, 80 next birthday. He was Belle Vue's first captain and one of the legends.

He rode in that opening meeting: 'Of course I remember it, I had a Scott Watercool two-stroke. Hundreds of people, thousands. Best track there ever was. Belle Vue's dying, is it? Sad.' John Rodda covered Belle Vue's last world-title fight. He remembers the woodeny sawdusty night and the cries from the nearby menagerie drowning the grunts and biffs in the ring, and Ena Sharples being introduced before Downes charged at Pastrano for round after round until he had nothing left to give.

Now they say Belle Vue has nothing left to give either; poor, good, old Belle Vue.

The old stadium is still a car auction site, but the speedway team survived: their fixtures take place down the road at the dog track.

Read all over no more: last days of Pinks and Greens
24 January 2006

A specific and cherished, not to say colourful, glory of English football's once tranquil subculture is being harshly dismantled. Victims are being picked off one by one. As the cull reaches pandemic proportions, this one lone piper at least summons breath for this heartfelt, lamenting eulogy. I am talking Saturday evenings. Saturday evenings when a cosy world was garlanded with sameness, routine and order. Well, what was pink and green and read all over? Right first time: you get the message.

Two Saturdays ago, the *Bristol Evening Post*'s treasured *Green 'Un* withered, folded, died. This Saturday, Newcastle United played their first Saturday Premiership home game of the new year – and what was conspicuously missing on the streets of Tyneside as the throng dispersed? The *Chronicle*'s beloved *Pink 'Un*, for the first time, barring world wars, in all of 111 winters. Put to death at the end of December to join others also consigned in 2005 to the bleak, ink-spattered newspaper morgue of memory – Liverpool's fabled *Saturday Echo*, Manchester's once bonny *Pink*, Coventry's pink *Telegraph*, and the singular buff of Leicester's *Mercury*. Brave survivors battle on, among them the gallant *Greens* of Sheffield and Portsmouth, the dauntless *Pinks* of Middlesbrough and Southampton and, in the city which founded the English feast with its trail-blazing *Saturday Night* in 1882, Birmingham's intrepid *Argus*.

Their defiance is edifying. But, surely, futile, unless Sky loses its control of the fixture list. Simply, Newcastle's *Pink 'Un* closed because, in 21 games up to Christmas, the Magpies had kicked off at three o'clock on a Saturday 10 times.

Once upon a time, *Pinks* and *Greens* speckled the land. Even in my boyhood's cuddly Cotswold village of the 1940s, us foot-stamping addicts would gather in the after-tea gloom at

Stonehouse post-office, expectant for the van with the *Citizen Pink*s from Gloucester; sometimes, for a double fix, we'd then leg it across to the LMS station where a quire of Bristol *Green*s would be slung from the passing train.

Once, under the one platform gaslight there, I saw a landgirl lustily snogging all over her impassive soldier chap as he studiedly read his *Green 'Un* over her passionately gyrating shoulders – a vivid remembrance touchingly reprised in that peerless urban history, *Barnsley*, by Ian Alistair and Andrew Ward (1981): 'On Saturday evenings, the streets became a sea of *Green 'Uns* with perhaps a meal at the bus-station café, or a visit to one of eight cinemas; or the dancehall, where occasionally a man could be seen reading the *Green 'Un* behind his partner's back as they waltzed.'

Within a decade that half a century ago, I was working myself on those Saturday specials in Gloucester and Bristol. Stress in the workplace? Writing for one was tension enough, phone clamped to your ear on a frostbitten touchline, scorers unseen through the mist – and trebly so the fierce fret, exasperation, and exhilarating adrenalin rush of subbing back at base. Kick-off, 2.30 with eight blank pages – all chock-full and on the streets before 5.30pm.

They were defiantly homesters' logs: locals writing about locals for locals. See David Lacey's line here last month of United once losing 7-2 at Newcastle – for the Manchester *Pink*'s sub-editor, a devout Red, to splash the headline: UNITED IN NINE-GOAL THRILLER.

After Birmingham's pioneer *Saturday Night*, a year later (1883) followed the same city's *Post and Mail*, then Blackburn's *Journal* (primrose coloured) and Bolton's *Telegram* (1884), each costing one penny. By 1890, 18 Saturday specials (four in Sheffield alone) were registered; by 1915, 48 towns from Weymouth to Sunderland published *Pink*s or *Green*s or *Buff*s or *Blue*s. By then linotype machines, web-fed rotary presses and telephones were plugged in instead of pigeons, telegraph or cyclist 'runners'.

One of my apprentice jobs at the *Citizen*, which always led page one, of course, with rugby, was to run relay at a breathless lick, sheet-by-sheet copy from Mike Dineen at Kingsholm back to the John Street office – and vast teams of copytaker-telephonists were hired for the afternoon's 90-minute mania. By 1905 in London (the last of its three Saturday specials closed in 1964), the *Star's Green'Un* was printing 6,000 a minute between 4.50 and 5.25pm. And all over England, rolling on for a century: Saturday Night Fever.

Fifty years ago, before my first shift on the *Citizen Pinks*, the Dickensian editor took me to the office roof to show me the crumbling remains of the pigeon-cote where, aeons before, match-day copy would arrive. Arnold Bennett lived, and that night I looked up his Five Towns tale, when the frantic *Sentinel* sub-editor unfastens the message from the bird's leg: 'Midland Fed: Axe Utd vs Macclesfield Tn. Fog. Match Abandoned 3.45.'

From Arnold Bennett to Rupert Murdoch. Everything being abandoned now.

Against the odds, a tiny handful of Saturday sports editions were still just about alive in 2013–14, including one in Portsmouth, which had closed and re-opened – even though the team was in danger of being relegated from the Football League.

Not so much a programme, more a way of life
24 October 2006

The reviews and promotional blurbs have been tantalising for what looks to be an evocatively vivid new book. I've not yet seen *Match Day: Football Programmes Postwar to Premiership* (£29.95), but I'm saving hard to buy it for what it says on the tin: a host of bespoke and colourful designer labels, primeval relics of period and place.

Spoiled, celeb-spoonfed young mods will doubtless sneer at devotion to the memory of such (literally in some cases) tuppenny-ha'penny throwaway artefacts, but aeons before football's overweening saturation coverage, the matchday programme was a must-have. For our then-secret freemasonry (of hundreds of thousands) the purchase for a few pence of a prog was as much part of the Saturday ritual as the melodic clank-click of rusted turnstile.

Hot news and secret codes – no wretchedly distracting touchline billboards then, just a hardboard strip at each end on which were hung seemingly mysterious alphabetical hieroglyphics which, at lemontime, were infilled with various noughts and numbers to copy into the blanks on the backpage of your prog – and discuss: 'Ooh, the R's are one down at the O's' ... 'The Grecians are trouncing the Quakers' ... 'The Rams are all square with the U's'.

This new book concentrates on the singular speciality and variety of cover designs. I was always more taken with the prose notes of the programme editor, Mr Anon. 'Good afternoon, everyone', most would start; in some cases 'Hello, chums'. Tub-thumping optimism would follow.

My friend, the writer John Moynihan, has a Chelsea programme from early in the 1945 season and a couple of weeks after the destruction of Hiroshima and Nagasaki, in which the editor begins: 'If any intrepid airman is brave enough to stand up to the blast of 60,000 throats when the Pensioners start goalwards this afternoon, he will see something which will make the atomic bomb look like an Xmas cracker.'

A younger writer I admire is DJ Taylor, who wrote this year that crisp, telling monograph on amateurism *On the Corinthian Spirit*. He said: 'Any social historian worth his salt who wanted to discover what English life was like in, say, the period 1966–79, that crucial World-Cup-to-Thatcher span, could do worse than assemble a couple of hundred football programmes.' I reckon the couple of decades before were even more enlightening.

In fact, it was in the mid-60s that it began to change for the dear old prog. *Match of the Day* (however grey and grainy) had begun, Fleet Street was waking up and, crucially, so were the club accountants. In 1950 an Arsenal programme cost 6d, and it still cost 6d in 1960. By 1970 it had gone up sixfold, with a syndicated, dire, glossy-ish *Football League Review* included. By 1970 Arsenal were adding £6,000 per match to their profits from programme sales alone. It was the beginning of the end, generality overtaking singularity, and now, of course, the matchday prog is a brick-heavy pop-star catchpenny, the tosh unreadable in purple on black or yellow on green.

Till I dipped last week into my mouldering pile hoarded from the late 50s and early 60s (mostly Fulham) I'd forgotten how we would chortle over the editor's excuses for the week before's away defeat. Almost half a century on I found myself giggling again. Three from 1958: QPR: 'Who would believe we could have 60% of the play, yet lose 6-0? It was simply because the Charlton boys were much bigger than us and could hit the ball out of their mud and we could not'; and two from Fulham: 'Only half the Roker Park lights were lit, so goalie Tony Macedo was completely dazzled and never even saw Sunderland's winner'; and 'Small wonder we lost 4-1. Don't blame our lads at Stoke, their pitch was so thickly coated in mud that a gaping great hole a foot deep suddenly appeared near the halfway line.' Excuses Arsène Wenger can only dream of.

Advertisements were unchanging. At Fulham, just local pubs, hardware and linoleum shops, and, always, Claude Rye's 'Largest Range in England of Scooters, Mopeds or Bubble Cars'; and only a single one in all my batch features a player – Johnny Haynes extolling 'Mettoy's Vinyl Football: Inflatable, Repairable. In red or white, 6s 9d. Packed Individually In Transparent Plastic Bags'.

Gosh, packaging. And the shape of things to come, alas. Packaging in all forms.

13

WESTERLY BREEZES

Wherever Frank went in the world, he was always at his happiest writing about the people and places closest to his roots, roughly in a triangle between Hereford, Taunton and Cheltenham. Especially 'Chelt'. Such articles are scattered through the book. Here are a few more.

Close thing at Taunton
15 July 1975

After the first day's washout, Somerset and Northamptonshire went through some sunny enough motions on a slow but gentle turner at Taunton yesterday. There don't seem to be many realistic possibilities for the match today when, one fancies, both sides will be looking to sharpen eye and claw for the Gillette Cup tomorrow, when Somerset are at home to Derbyshire and Northamptonshire travel to Old Trafford.

Yesterday at Taunton's amiable, old-fashioned sports centre, an endearingly quaint sort of prefabricated Gothic – where even the press box still has inkwell holders – Somerset's battling fledglings put up a goodish show to score 278 all out. And in the evening they took two wickets as Northamptonshire finished 224 behind. The sun shone and there was a holiday feeling, not least because Bill Alley was umpiring.

The crux of the matter was Brian Close's combat with Bishen Bedi. One had looked forward to the possibility of such a duel as the train sped down from Paddington and, sure enough, the two enduring southpaws stepped out into the centre of the ring for a truly beguiling hour or so after lunch. Match of the Day. The bald old chewing yeoman heavy-footed his way to the wicket with unhurried certainty; Rose and Denning had batted promisingly enough, but Somerset had lost four for nearly 100; the sun and wind were now full of drying steam; the whole thing was finely polished.

Bedi came on at once – unhurried certainty, too, but of a different culture; no chewing gum for concentration and with a swot's wire glasses now, to go with a Cambridge Blue patka. The mature student poring over his thesis. Every ball a question, experimental or imaginative or querying, every ball serenely perplexing, gently imprisoning.

For a bit the grizzly bear hung about, encouraged young Slocombe, of the shiny, prep-school face, how to play the Indian. Answering every ball watchfully on its merits, but taking a measured chance or two in order to shake up the lulling rhythms, to grate the grooves. Slocombe was responding well, one felt, just when the placid, painstaking mesmerist's gentle curve was followed hypnotically by the kid. A dolly to one of the short-leg scavengers: 143 for five.

Close cued himself in: he had already focused his sights by twice swatting Sarfraz off his nostrils and past backward square. Now he chassied out and twice drove Bedi straight for fours off the full red meat of his old bat. Then, flatfooted, he hoicked him over mid-on and used his toes and balance to clip him through mid-wicket. In between times he watchfully dropped a dead bat. Both men were relishing, revelling in, the differing challenge.

Towards tea-time, Willey came on. For just three relieving overs. Fourth-change off-breaks. Third ball, Close, relaxing, tried to prod him past mid-wicket; it was straight and he was castled. But Bedi, out of things at third man, clapped as his adversary munched his way back to the pavilion, deadpan but somehow noticeably cursing his lunacy. The proper battle therefore remained unfinished. A draw.

And in the evening more old friends: Virgin, poignantly leading his new soldiers back to the camp where he scored 15,000 runs, was given some cheery bird as he went out to start Northamptonshire's reply – and even more chucklingly so when he returned within an over, leg-before to Jones for a duck.

Thereafter Steele, wise and grey and unflinching, showed why he must at least be seriously recommended as England's No.3, before, off-guard, he was caught behind when the beautifully-named leftie, Breakwell, pushed through his quicker one. Breakwell continued to bowl nicely into the evening sun. There does not seem to be very much to get worked up about today. Unless the clouds of state that were skimming across the Quantocks at dusk have some evil intentions.

I was there with 'Glorse'
16 July 1977

Gloucestershire have been up for a cup at Lord's once before, I know. But it was not the same for me, picnicking in a corner of some foreign field with a rickety wretched transistor. Today, I shall be there in person when they play Kent in the Benson and Hedges final.

It was exactly 30 years ago, before the days of gold awards and silver-plated cups, that the county reached the old-time equivalent of a cup final – when the accidental arrangement of fixtures allowed the two front runners in the County Championship virtually to play off for the title. When 'Glorse' lost to Middlesex at Cheltenham at the end of 1947's golden summer it was winner-take-all. The frenzy of anticipation for that long-ago epic has not been matched even in the West this week. I know, because I was there. Aged nine.

Both days – it only lasted two – my uncle and I took the dawn bus over the top from Stroud to join the bleary queue of 15,000 that was to ring the College Ground. People still speak of the match today. You can meet men in pubs who recite Gloucestershire's last innings scorecard. They got 100, needing 169. Bill Edrich's 50 was top score of the match, and then Sims and Young bowled too well. Tom Goddard's 15 wickets were not enough.

The very highlight was a boundary catch by an occasional first 11 player called Clifford Monks who sprinted, memory says, some 50 yards to catch RWV Robins. Memory also reminds me that it would have hit me on the head had he not caught it. Still the finest catch anyone could ever see. When Monks died 27 years later the *Cheltenham Echo*'s headline was 'The Man Who Made The Catch'.

With respect to Procter, Zaheer, and Sadiq (those well-known natives of Dean and Dursley and Downend), what a lovely Western side that was: doughty Jack Crapp, twinkling George Emmett, the one and only Charlie Barnett, who smacked bumpers, thwack! as if he was smacking down plaice on the wet slab outside his fish shops in both 'Chelt' and 'Soiren'. Then there was farmer Neale from Grace country, and BO Allen. For some reason, I loved the bowlers best: George Lambert of the lovely action we all tried to copy, and his new ball mucker, great trier Scott. Goddard was my first idol. Huge tent of a shirt billowing out behind him. Huge hands, huge heart, he could wheel and deal for wickets all day long.

Goddard's appeal would reverberate round the ring from Cleeve to Birdlip. 'Eh Ta-am, whadabou' a bloke atop o' Leckhampton Hill then?' we would shout when he set his field. Once Basil Allen had to leave the field and put Goddard in charge. Over after over he bowled on, though it was not a day for spinners. Finally Goddard, completely whacked, complained to a fielding colleague, 'Why don't the bugger take me off?' He had quite forgotten he was skipper for the day.

Goddard has been dead a dozen years now. His partner in wiles and guiles 30 years ago was young Sam Cook, still with us as an umpire. Cook, an apprentice plumber, had arrived unannounced at the County Ground for the first net practice after the war. He asked which was Mr Hammond and said boldly: 'I'm Cook from Tetbury, slow left hand, sir.' The great WR threw him a ball, faced him for a few, then announced, 'You'll play for England one day.' And he did, almost within 12 months. He took nought for 127, conceding over seven runs an over, against South Africa, in 1947's first Test, was never remotely considered again, but touchingly continued to wear his brocaded international blazer to the day he retired 18 years later.

The wicketkeeper was Andy Wilson, tiny tot with a massive appeal in every sort of way. After all his years keeping to Goddard and Cook, he took bets that he would be the only batsman in the whole land to read Ramadhin's wrong'un when the West Indies came to Cheltenham in 1950. Both times Wilson shouldered arms first ball to the little long-sleeved mesmerist. Both times he was clean-bowled.

That was another match that closed the gates at the College. By then new horses were leading our parade. Another TW too: for in that match young Tom Graveney got top score, all blushing silkiness. And just before the start, the announcer said, 'TW Goddard is indisposed and his place will be taken by JB Mortimore.' 'JB Ooo?' we all asked. We soon knew.

By then too we had the Bomber. Can any county have ever loved a man as Glorse loved Bomber Wells? In his first match, against Sussex, this bumper bundle of fun arrived on the bus from Gloucester with his sandwiches and his pa-in-law's borrowed whites. First ball they put him at gully, James Langridge cut gently, the Bomber tubbily gave chase – and they ran five.

He was at once moved to short leg. At the moment Lambert was uncoiling his action the Bomber, showing he meant business, spat in his hands and smacked them loudly together. Langridge, put off, pulled away complaining. Bomber was moved to deepish mid-on and there he stayed for the rest of an enchanting career. When his turn came to bowl in that game he had the Reverend

Sheppard out at once. By tea he had taken six for 47, and when John Arlott looked for him in the pavilion to do a radio interview he was told that young Wells was having a picnic with his mum on the grass by the sightscreen.

And on and on ... Now the county's thunderous trio to lead them to Lord's today are from other parts but, because of their natures and the way they play, Gloucestershire looks on them now as its very own natives. No one, not even Hammond, can have been held in more affectionate awe than 'Proc'; the same mellow drives we thought our Graveney had patented are now sketched as smooth by 'Zed'; Sadiq sparkles as Emmett once did ... and anyway still the West is served by the sturdy likes of Stovold, the bucolic charm of Shepherd; young Graveney, the nephew of Tom; young Shackleton, son of 'Shack'; Hignell, following BO Allen's tread from Cambridge; Childs, from Devon; and Foat, who fields as only Randall can ... or rather, come to think of it, as Clifford Monks could long, so long ago ....

Gloucestershire beat Kent in the final, and the local boy Stovold was man of the match.

Trap-door slams on Hereford
Hereford United 1, Brighton and Hove Albion 1
5 May 1997

An hour afterwards some 3,000 jubilant supporters decked in blue and encircled in their pen by stone-faced riot police were still hysterically acclaiming Brighton's continued football league life.

From the remainder of this dinky battlefield, in ones and twos and faces as white as their famous bull mascot, the Hereford corps had tiptoed away to their silent city or back to their hillocks and hills, leaving in the broom-cupboard dressing room under the low-slung grandstand their players still weeping unashamed tears – to give the lie to a taunt last week that they were but carpetbaggers, footballing mercenaries with no necessary allegiance to this once perky little rural club.

The man with the rustic burr took to the Tannoy microphone for a final time. He may well have been in tears as well. He addressed the Brighton throng, which was now essaying a delirious celebration conga. 'Could we now have some hush, please. Brighton, why are you taunting us so? I ask you for silence, some peace to let us here in Hereford contemplate our grief. It so nearly happened to you, not to us, so can't you spare one thought for our misery?'

The roisterers in blue took not a scrap of notice. Why should they? You do not heed worldly words, however poignantly plaintive, when you have just witnessed a miracle of football resurrection: 12 points adrift and dead and buried at Christmas but now, hey presto, a conjuror's leap from the coffin and a continued football league life after a one-off match, unique in league history, of excruciating tension.

The draw ensured Brighton's survival. Hereford, who had to win, should have been three or four up and out of sight by half-time after coming out to play with a sprightly carefree courage which quite belied the occasion. It was Brighton, familiar with this tragedians' Saturday matinee script for months, who were wracked almost throughout with the tremors and quaking heebie-jeebies. Hereford attacked the passion-play at almost a dalliance, took the lead early enough, surrendered it gormlessly after an hour and then, for all the further chances, could not steady their aim to take but one. They played well enough to make it ludicrous that they were anywhere near this tumbril in the first place, let alone kneeling under the guillotine.

Anyway, cue tears. Half the side were weeping buckets before even they left the pitch, while yards away Brighton's remarkable manager, the eponymously indomitable Steve Gritt, turned cartwheels between giving joyously incomprehensible interviews. Down in the dungeon his opposite number, the decent and chivalrous Graham Turner, announced his 'Man's-Gotta-Do' resignation and said Hereford 'must stay full-time to bounce straight back just like Lincoln, Darlington and Colchester'.

His dark blue eyes welled with tears. Somebody gave him a tumblerful of red wine. He looked long at it, then left it and let one big tear roll down his cheek. Around his tiny office, as for a child's birthday, every shelf and cranny was lined with good-luck greetings cards. 'Most are from little clubs like ourselves, your Exeters, Hartlepools, Doncasters, Darlingtons. They knew we'd become martyrs for their cause, they all felt terribly for us, that "there but for the grace of God go us".' We made our excuses and slipped away.

Meanwhile Hereford's chairman Peter Hill, an estate agent and a genuine fan who first watched United at five, valiantly spoke of a meeting with the council and a property company on Wednesday 'to stabilise our creditors and build for the future'. He wants Turner to stay: 'He's been first-class, he just hasn't had the breaks this year.' Brighton had scored both these mercilessly relevant goals. An own-goal by Kerry Mayo would have ensured as historical a notoriety as 'And Smith Must Score' 14 years ago, until the sub Rob Reinelt clipped in the stray bobbler for a draw and, for Brighton, immortal fame.

At the meeting just up the road at the Racecourse they heard the extended delirium of Brighton's cheers. A few minutes later the 4.30 race was won, at 5 to 1, by a nag called Magical Blues. Quite enough said.

Hereford did not bounce straight back but survived, under Turner, to return to the league in 2006. However, by early 2014 they were not just back in the conference but fearful of further relegation. Brighton, meanwhile, were not that far off the Premier League. So it goes.

Raise a glass to the monarch of the counties
21 April 2009

David Foot is 80 on Friday. Yesterday in Bristol, some 50 of his pressbox confrères from a cross-section of the generations took the West Country wordsmith to a surprise slap-up birthday lunch. The occasion was definitely not sponsored by any temperance society.

Seasoned readers will know how, for summer after summer for four decades, and from his beloved Wessex shires between the Severn and the sea, Foot's compassionate and earthy day-by-day chronicles of county cricket have warmed and illuminated these pages. As well, there has been a fruitfully impressive output of books, scripts and evocative monographs and memoirs on cricketers, heroes and fellow writers.

Locally, Foot remains a cherished eminence as columnist and champion of causes. His deadlines, too, have been met spot-on as a sharp and perceptive Bristol theatre critic down the years and, on a thousand winter Saturdays, 600 words on the whistle from City, Rovers, or his hometown Yeovil, where it all began 64 summers ago in 1945 on the weekly *Western Gazette*. The trainee 25-shilling-a-week copy-boy, just 16, tremulously cycled in from the family's East Coker cottage in his new broadish-brimmed brown trilby hat and six-guinea brown pinstripe suit fresh-off-the-peg of Yeovil's high-class outfitters, Messrs Bone & Flagg.

It was, of course, the straw hat and the loose, light skimpy linen jacket of cricket-watching which was to become David's favourite business uniform. Especially in high summer when the pressbox was relocated to a marquee on the boundary edge decked with hanging baskets and festive bunting at Bath or Cheltenham, Weston or Gloucester or Bournemouth or Frome.

In those languid gossipy days, Footie held court and sway, the press tent his very hearth and home, his sanctum. And in them, as decade followed decade, East Coker's kindly wise-innocent – with his charm and generosity and smile which lit up the lived-in autumnal face – grew to be this freemasonry's soft and scrupulous monarch.

David and I first met half a century ago. In 1959 he was a star top-of-the-bill performer on the *Bristol Evening World* – as a senior reporter, acclaimed general feature writer, ace theatre critic, and No.1 *Pink 'Un* reporter from Ashton Gate. I was the greenest of greenhorn sub-editors. Unlike most newsroom bullies, Foot was the kindest of counsellors to a bewildered cub.

Many years later and once again working for the same newspaper – this one – our paths would seldom cross because we'd both be covering different matches during my own relished and relishable stint on the county circuit of summer two or three decades ago. When they did, however, the catch-up made for a most convivial bonus. Around the turn of the millennium, Foot wrote: 'The pressbox is kinship; I love the chirpy, companionable aura. Repartee is sharp, incestuous jokes are traded, legs pulled. Whatever the public's perceptions, we all have a great affection for the game. We drink and eat and talk cricket. We all know we're bloody privileged. I dare say most of us are, very loosely, frustrated novelists. We certainly all like words, don't we?'

Long ago David told me how, having filed his copy and driven home after a long summer's day, his good wife Anne would always greet him with the inquiry, not of who scored what or who took the wickets, but simply: 'Was it a good box today, dear?'

When the *Evening World* closed in 1961, big-time Fleet Street seriously wooed Foot. Name his price. He preferred to be a freelance, as he puts it, 'jobber' in his own happy state of contented rumpled rusticity. And as well as the unending joy of 'good boxes', so did the good books begin to flow.

Under a variety of hard covers there were telling psychological monographs on such one-offs as Cec Parkin and Charlie Parker, Carwyn James, Kid Berg and Alec Stock. In *Fragments of Idolatry*, Foot's portraits of the olde-tyme polymath journalists, Alan Gibson and Raymond Robertson-Glasgow – each utterly joyous at the job, wretchedly screwed-up in life – are masterpieces. Two full-length biogs are already imperishable classics in cricket's canon – *Harold Gimblett: Tormented Genius* and *Wally Hammond: The Reasons Why*.

Of those last four names, two committed suicide, the other two seriously contemplated it. Such choices of subject are not examples of an author's own melancholic paranoia, but of his innate and instinctive compassion – the quality which, as many of you know, has always blessed Foot's writing.

Resolute four-square compassion – and the heartiest of four-score congratulations.

14

IN LOVING MEMORY

Ageing journalists increasingly get asked to write obituaries – it is a hazard of longevity. And Frank was a natural for this melancholy yet often strangely satisfying task. Some of these pieces were formal obits, others not; his on-the-spot report on the death of Ken Barrington is a particularly stunning piece of writing in dramatic circumstances against the clock. His last published article so far is his obit of David Coleman, written some years earlier, which found its moment in December 2013, nearly a year after Frank's own death; a couple of others are believed to be lurking in the Guardian *computer system, awaiting their relevant moments. The first piece in this section, on the death of the Welsh racing driver Tom Pryce, is infinitely the saddest. In motor racing circles, it still causes tremors. A marshal trying to put out a fire in another car walked into Pryce's path. Pryce could not avoid him and when the collision came was himself struck by the marshal's heavy fire extinguisher. As Frank characteristically teased out, this was not just a sporting disaster but a tragedy for a sweet and loving family.*

So shy and sensitive
Tom Pryce
7 March 1977

Tom Pryce had asked me not to forget to give him a full report of the England vs Wales rugby international when he arrived back home today from the South African Grand Prix. But now he's not coming back. Just before the match started we were told that the young Welshman was dead.

He is now just another tear-stained wail in the tragic litany of lives and loves lost in the name of motor racing – Collins and Clark and Courage and Cevert; Schlesser, Spene, Siffert and Scarfiotti; Bandini, Birrel and Bonnier; Bruce McLaren; Rodriguez, Revson and Rindt. And now young Tom Pryce, sensitive and shy, who didn't like talking about even the possibility of death. 'I'm not saying I don't fear it. But would I feel it? But I am frightened of it for what it might do to those I leave behind.'

I spent a lot of happy time with Pryce the week before he went to South Africa. And with those who are now left behind: his still blushing bride of two years, Nella, a trained teacher who wanted to open a riding school in the heart of the south-east's Thelwell country. And his dad, a police sergeant in rural North Wales and as proud as you can imagine of his boy. And his anxious mum who always 'knew, deep down' that it would end like this. If ever they went to watch him drive she would creep into the team caravan to pretend to listen to the radio commentary. It wasn't quite as bad as watching.

His father told me last week: 'Crumbs, race days are terrible up here. Our little house at Ruthin gets really excited. We close ourselves in all day listening to the wireless for news of the boy. If I'm on duty Mrs Pryce telephones when anything comes through. But they don't give much gen, and the TV's damned 'opeless, isn't it?' What a hideous way for them to hear the last news of Tom on Saturday.

Not that they called him Tom. His real name was Maldwyn, which is Welsh, see, for Montgomery, where the family originally came from. Tom spoke Welsh. 'Yes, we were very sorry when they changed his name to Tom. Very sad. But I suppose "Tom" is more catchy-like. Maldwyn has always been reserved about publicity. I thought he should be much more forward. It is good for him. He keeps promising to be better. He always said he would once he became a Formula One driver. After that it was "once he'd won his first Grand Prix". I wish he'd get better, 'cos I know you boys expect it ...' No need now.

Sergeant Pryce doesn't have a clue what inspired Maldwyn to take up motor racing. 'Crumbs, it can't have been when we gave him that first trike, can it? His mam thinks it might have been the pedal car he had for his fourth birthday. And we used to have our fortnight's holiday on the Isle of Man, mind you. And for some reason it always seemed to be TT week. He would have been five I reckon when he saw his first TT – Geoff Duke won it, I think.'

Tom Pryce couldn't remember much about the Isle of Man. But when he was eight in 1957 his dad took him to Aintree where Stirling Moss won a famous dice with Fangio in the British Grand Prix. Something must have rubbed off, although Tom only remembered clutching perilously with his father onto an advertising hoarding to see the cars pass, that and 'the terrible terrible noise'.

In 1964, Pryce the police swopped his country copper's push bike ('I'm a country bobby – sheep stealing, none of this drug trafficking up here, boy') for a Morris Oxford. Tom dreamed to himself at the wheel when it was parked outside their house. By 14 the walls of his little bedroom were plastered with posters of Grand Prix cars and drivers.

He thought of being a farmer. But no money. He qualified to go to college as an agricultural engineer. There was nothing he didn't know about tractors. Certainly that they only went 10mph. On Saturday they say he hit that poor misguided steward at 160mph. In 1968 Tom bought a mini van. In 1969 he sold it to pay for lessons at Mallory Park. Sergeant Pryce went with him, bewildered but quite keen nevertheless. It was £12 for a test lesson, then £8 for each one thereafter.

Trevor Taylor, the instructor, told the policeman Tom was very good. 'The rich guys did their course, wham-bang, and had finished it in a month. It took me a year, I was working at a local garage to save up for lessons. I'm sure that gradualism paid off. I learned slowly, see', so a year later he won a school competition sponsored by the *Daily Express*.

245

In 1973 he won a Formula Three race at Monaco. The Formula One offers started to come in, his rise since has been sensational. So, in a sport where fast bucks sometimes seem faster than fast backs, has been his loyalty to the Shadow team.

Pryce's gentle shyness italicised his reputation as a bit of a loner on the circuit. But everyone accepted that he was easily among the dozen best drivers in the world. 'Of course, yes, Nella is marvellously good for me. So is Dad. But the thing about danger is that you must not talk too much to them about it. I know it is a factor but for them I only try and relate to anyone else at all in terms of fear.' He said he never had nightmares. But his fingernails were bitten down to the quick, almost to the very knuckle. They were as badly bitten as the late Jim Clark's.

His car was once badly hit up the backside when he was forced to stop at Monaco. He walked away without a scratch. In the 1975 German Grand Prix he finished standing up in his cockpit, bathed in petrol. It could have gone up any time, but didn't.

We had a long, laughing lunch together a couple of days before he and Nella left for South Africa. Just before he went off to continue his wickedly compelling, nail-biting blood-spattered sport he asked me to make sure I came with him to the British Grand Prix at Silverstone. 'There's no doubt about it, I'm going to win that one, and, come to that, I'll win at Monaco and Nurburgring too. I bet you. And don't forget to give me a full report on how Gareth and JPR lick the English at Arms Park ...'

The Sage of El Vino
Philip Hope-Wallace, music and drama critic
5 September 1979

It suited Philip's ever wry and world-weary despair when they spelt his name wrong on the little gold plaque that the management of El Vino's nailed to the wall of the cubicle that he occupied daily from 12 to 3 and 5 to 7.

'What can you expect these days?' he would sigh, and launch into a blazing, always hilarious tale of the latest woes that had befallen him and England. He was especially good on sub-editors, copytakers, the Arab invasion of London and buses that did not run on time.

He was the funniest raconteur I can ever hope to meet. And by far the most generous man who ever kept his loose change in a war-issue leather purse. You just had to say 'Princess Louise of Battenburg' or 'The Peru National Airline' or 'Hay-on-Wye' and it would trigger off the entrancing flow ...

I went to sit at his feet and always ended up rolling on the floor. He would sit with his back to the offending plaque so he could see the end of his world go by, and also shout a sharp 'Door!' whenever some tyro barrister forgot his manners. He especially enjoyed pompous men being flung out of the place because they had no tie. And women from the 'Miz' mob who regularly attempted to defy the management's loony rule about women standing at the bar.

I like to think he did not mind us acolytes dropping in to learn all about things when things really mattered. 'Ah Keating,' he would say, 'find yourself a chair. It's your day for a tie, is it? How is our awful old paper going on? The spelling's getting so tiresome that surely we must close soon? While the going's good why don't we resign together?'

But I knew he never would. Deep down he loved the *Guardian* as much as it loved him.

Sleep like a lark ...
Ken Barrington
16 March 1981

He had been so hale and full of beans. So dynamite-chuffed at the end of the West Indians' innings in the morning. His nose crowded out the already jammed pavilion long room bar. His smile illuminated it. If, batting first, a side did not make at least 300, in this place they could consider themselves well and truly stuffed – and he was beaming because his boys had just bowled out the unbeatables for 265.

Across the change-of-innings pavilion barge and bustle, I caught his eye. You could only grin back as he gave a thumbs up. The last time I saw him was a little later on the players' balcony during England's afternoon collapse – choked as he was, but always first up with a great big consoling arm round the incoming batsman and some perky get-stuck-in encouragement for the outgoing.

Then, late in the evening, somebody whispered me off the dance floor and told me the numbing news. It just could not be true. Why, he was so very happy that his wife had come out for a holiday only last week. No, you could not take it in – nor could the players after the team manager Smith had summoned them before breakfast to his room at the end of the pier that juts from the hotel into the Caribbean. The young men tiptoed back across the boards almost in single file, the tan drained from their faces and looking shell-shocked as if they'd heard their very best friend had died in the night. For many of them he had.

Only since knowing him these past two months did I realise how heartfelt, even desperate, had been the demand from the players and the press that he be added to this touring party as assistant manager. When it was named in the autumn he was missing from the list for the first time in England's last five tours. Lord's were cutting costs – but the genuine outcry was relentless enough to make them admit their mistake and change their minds.

He was the players' man, both spiritual and temporal. Each morning he gave them all their individual alarm calls. In the nets he bowled at them and followed through to cajole or advise with tiny hints on technique; always a smile; always relishing the day like mustard. Perhaps he knew that there wasn't all that much time. On match days he was ever lifting spirits and humping kits. In the evenings his boys would gather themselves and a few beers around him and listen to the tales of long ago when cricket tours might have been to other planets for all these new jet-aged players knew.

Ken Barrington had done it all. The first of his 20 foreign centuries for England had been here at Bridgetown. For a dozen years till a first warning heart attack in 1968 when the doctors ordered him to take off his pads, he had squared his shoulders, jutted his jaw and come back for more; he was England's rock-solid, often unconsidered, trellis around which the public's favourite fancy dans and flash Harrys entwined their colourful summer blooms.

He was invariably up the other end, grim and determined as he conscientiously swept the stage for the entrance of the Mays and Cowdreys and Dexters and Graveneys, the last great quartet of the golden line of legend. They would not have done even half as much without Barrington.

I will never forget that midsummer Monday in 1963 during that second Test match of unremitting tension at Lord's when in the last innings England, needing 233 to win, lost Stewart, Edrich and Dexter to the blazing fires of Griffith and Hall with only 31 scored. Barrington and Cowdrey dug in and ducked and battled it out on into the afternoon. They were on the point of swinging the match with an epic stand when a withering delivery from Hall broke Cowdrey's forearm. Crack! At once Barrington, in answering fury and in spontaneous hate, struck Hall for venomous one-bounce fours over mid-on.

The rage was on him in manic defence of his wounded officer – but then just as suddenly, he took a deep breath, calmed his soul to concentrate, and turned to stand again to see out the day in England's cause. They always called him the Colonel, as befitted a soldier's son. But he was more of a kindly sergeant-major without any bark or bite. Mind you, just a large beak and larger beam.

He first signed for Surrey as a leg-break bowler, but they soon realised that he had too much grit and guts to stay long messing about with the twiddly stuff. In the end, it was a grim business he had worried and worked himself into. But after his ticker first complained at the unrelenting life at the top, he emerged to everybody's astonishment and joy from behind the ropes with one of the loveliest, hail-fellow natures that could be imagined. He bought up a successful Surrey motor business then asked if he could be of any more help to cricket.

Now he was in his element, talking about the old days. When one of his youngsters complained a fortnight ago about some aspects of the hotel service in Guyana he said: 'I dunno. When I first came here in the 50s with Peter May we stayed down the road at the wooden place, and the cockroaches were so big that you'd tread on them as hard as you could and you'd lift your foot and they'd wave up at you, say "good morning", and potter off into the woodwork without a care in the world.'

When his boys moaned about tedious waiting in VIP airport lounges he'd grin: 'Blimey, we had 27 hours in a Pakistan train once with only a bucket as a latrine.' Or: 'You should have come out here with us, mates, in our banana boat. First six days through the Bay and all that time you wouldn't see another player except the dying geezer in the next bunk. We were all simply seasick.' Or a complaint that a Trinidad steak was a bit small: 'Crikey. I had five months in India and Pakistan once when my total diet, honest to God, was eggs and chips. Closey, my roommate, was so ill for days that all he could do was crawl from his bed to the loo on all fours every five minutes. He'd had a curry. I stuck to egg and chips. You can't muck around with eggs and you can't muck around with chips, can you?'

We would log his malapropisms; some pinched-lip types thought we were sending him up. He loved it, and laughed back at himself. 'Well, Frank, you all know what I bloody mean, don't you?' Sometimes they were quite ingeniously perfect. A batsman got out because he was 'caught in two man's land'. When that minor riot occurred last month in Port of Spain, it might have been worse than the one he had encountered in Bangalore. Because there, to mingle with the crowd, the police had sent in '200 plain-clothes protectives'.

Between their sobs yesterday his boys could only have faith that now he will 'sleep like a lark' in eternal peace.

A lilting tribute from Cymru
Carwyn James
13 January 1983

Llanelli deservedly and most appropriately beat Cardiff 16-15 at Stradey on Saturday afternoon. Somewhere up there Carwyn James would doubtless have chuckled his little chuckle, hummed a snatch of Dafydd Iwan, and drawn satisfyingly deep on one of his now unlimited supply of free fags at the exuberant performance of possibly his favourite Scarlet-vested old boy, Ray Gravell.

Other former pupils were in the stand. Barry and Gareth and Gerald and Delme, Phil Bennett, and Terry Davies and Derek Quinnell ...

An hour or two before, they had been up in the hills to genuflect formal farewell to Carwyn at a memorial service in the tabernacle at Ceifnethen. Police unravelled the traffic. An hour before the service the tiny building was crammed. Many more hundreds filled the neighbouring vestry. On a sharp bright white winter's morning, the whitewashed chapel gleamed. Sunday suits were of charcoal grey. All was monochrome, the only two splashes of colour – apart from the oratory – was a spray of early daffodils, and, appropriately again, a big scarlet fire extinguisher near the door.

A car park had been made exactly opposite the Tabernacle on the scanty patch of overgrown ground. The children's swings were rusty now. On one side of the bleak field was Carwyn's little home. In spirit, the whole of the rugby union world was present on Saturday morning. No, much more than that. Has modern, organised sport thrown up such a man as Carwyn? At one and the same time poet and pragmatist and preacher, practiser and philosopher, wise innocent and melancholic optimist.

Wales is too small a land to lose a Carwyn. Not a word of English was spoken at the service. From the pulpit, in richly melodic Welsh, came wave after wave of lilting tribute and fire-and-brimstone grief. The singing was simply so sensational that even up in Heaven residents would have had to turn the sound down.

Of course, with Carwyn, it was not only sport that grieved and gave thanks. Not by any means. Spellbinding oratory from the archdruid, who offered gratitude from the ancient Celts, and Gwynfor Evans from the dead man's passion, Plaid Cymru. Carwyn's own Mynydd Mawr male voice choir sublimely thundered out the responses.

The world may have been watching, but this was a private ceremony – the enclosed, exclusive Celtic village paying homage to a favourite villager. I was the interloper, for while the spirit was moved, I did not understand one word of the lingo. I would whisper to my neighbour for an English equivalent. They would crease their brow to help, before apologising 'all lost in the translation, boy'.

I had found myself coming to Ceifnethen, not along the flat southern motorway but, in pilgrimage, through Carwyn country. I was glad, somehow. I had a new washed scarlet Ford escort to switchback through the sheep-speckled, rounded, green-grey beacons of Brecon; through Llandovery where, at college with TP Williams, he first taught himself to teach; up and down through Llandeilo and Bethlehem and Carmel, before tumbling down through Tumble and Phil's Felinfoel down to where the pylons stand sentinel over the beloved Stradey, red painted and warm: incongruous, primary colour midst all the greys of industrial scrubland.

O yes, there was one, just one, sentence spoken in English on Saturday morning. That, too, would have suffered in translation even by the archdruid. It was: 'He will not grow old as those of us who are left grow old.'

Publisher extraordinaire
André Deutsch
12 April 2000

Dear André. Think of a mid-European leprechaun and you've got the picture. He was already well into his 50s when he published my first two books. They were about cricket, of which he knew nothing, but he read the *Guardian* and had heard of Ian Botham.

The paper would pay my hotel bills for daily reports on England's 1980–1 tour of the West Indies, and André would stump up all travel expenses for the main wheeze – a spoof, ghosted autobiography by an imagined 17th member of the England party called Desmond (i.e. me), who would spill the beans on the tour. The day before we left, André gave me my 'expenses' – in the form of copies of personal letters he had already sent to, among others, Eric Williams, Forbes Burnham and Michael Manley, former black-movement student-authors of his, now prime ministers of, respectively, Trinidad, Guyana, and Jamaica.

I feared the worst publisher's double-cross. Not a bit of it. From day one in Trinidad, chauffeured cars were at my disposal, and the odd private plane. In return, I was fast into my stride with *Another Bloody Day In Paradise* – till the tour began to fall apart with the team being thrown out of Guyana on the back of South African apartheid and the death of England's manager Ken Barrington. Back home, André panicked. 'Drop Desmond and play it straight,' he wired.

Twelve months later, with another England team, this time in India, a beaming André arrived with some 30-odd copies of *ABD in P* and arranged a 'launch' party at the pricey Taj Mahal in Bombay. When the time came to leave, a week or so later, all party charges had been referred to my bill – and dear old André was back in London.

But I loved him. I last saw him a couple of years ago, looking sad, hunched, lonely. 'We should really do that spoof tour book again,' he said – and his leprechaun's eyes were glistening with pleasure and anticipation once again.

Into the dark, cold night
Cowdrey and Statham
Wisden Cricketers' Almanack 2001

A radiant era, rich in recollection, seems in a sudden rush to pull down the blinds and shut out its sunlight. In 1997, cavalier nonpareil Compton; two years later, merry gallivant Evans and the rigorous Washbrook. Now, for pity's sake, Statham and Cowdrey.

For those of us of a certain age, when we were wide-eyed Jacks and they were giants, those distant mists through which strode England's cricketers of the 1950s will always be tinged with an auroral sparkle, a golden lustre. For summer after summer when we were young, a civilised, untroubled game rolled amiably along, genially cocooned in its own freemasonry. We in the grey, monochrome crowds, with our single-sheet unglossy scorecards and unfancy picnics, were illuminated to a rosy glow by these knights in what seemed shining white. I am not absolutely certain about cloudless skies but, golly, the grass really was greener then. And progress was a simple fact, not an order-in-council directive of cockeyed and manic decree.

Those luminaries of England's cricket were household names that tripped off the tongues not only of monarchs and peers and bishops and fathers and sons, but just as readily of wives and mothers, sisters, cousins and aunts. They were praetorian guardsmen of the very culture and lore. Serious poets wrote seriously heroic poems about them. Fore and aft of that mid-century decade, towering figures serenade the memory in a rhapsody of twosomes like love and marriage, horse and carriage: Hutton and Washbrook, Edrich and Compton, May and Cowdrey, Laker and Lock, Statham and Trueman.

Wretched life – or, rather, loss of it. Only a solitary one is left of that resonantly stirring five-brace constellation: only the last is alive still and shining, the man called Fred, good true-to-himself brass-tacks-and-bluster Fred. He was 70 this year, almost two years older than Cowdrey and some half a year younger than Statham. Colin [Cowdrey] dedicated his whole self to cricket, and in those terms his life of devotion, and achievement, was a mighty long one. He was thinking of the good of cricket on the day he died (and, I dare say, on the day he was born). Brian [Statham] devoted his life to bowling and so, in comparison, his was a short one. The phrase 'he bowled his boots off' was surely minted for, or even because of, him.

Cowdrey and Statham were of the same time, the same land, and both were garlanded for their deeds at the sharpest end of their game's two disciplines. But they had arrived from totally different, and distant, points of ken and culture. In background and outlook they were alpha and omega, sun and moon, or, while we are about it, chalk and cheese. Did Lord Cowdrey of Tonbridge choose that title because the lovelorn and lonely, but privileged, child had been happiest there at school under the familial canopy of its cloisters? Still in his school cap, the patrician princeling played first for Kent at windswept Derby. Welcome to the hard-graft workaday world, kid. Les Jackson, the former miner, shocked him by bowling a spiteful bouncer. The boy hurried off to enquire of Les Ames and Arthur Fagg the correct grip and technique for bouncers. He may have continued forever to fret over the intricacies of his talent, but there was never doubt about his valiance, or the touching gift of his quiet, sheepish, smile at triumph or disappointment alike.

Not many weeks before, in that precise midsummer of the century, the same staunch Arthur Fagg had opened Kent's innings at Old Trafford. He had followed on to that greenest of famed fields a Lancashire team that included for the first time, on his 20th birthday, a stringy uncoached colt who was being warned by his captain, Washbrook: 'Don't bowl short to Arthur, lad, else he'll flog you out of sight.' The cub, a natural, knew not what an outswinger was, nor a yorker, let alone which Kent opener answered to Arthur. So he shrugged, and reasoned that if he dropped one short – just one – he would soon find out and take it from there. Arthur went for the hook, but the rearing ball hurried on him: Fagg c Wharton b Statham 4.

Four years later Cowdrey and Statham were England teammates in Australia. For the next 10 summers and winters, there was an aura about their different skills, and an innate pride in us that we possessed such players. Creative invention and authentic artistry. Both Cowdrey and Statham were strong and courageous in their totally different, craft-versed ways. Cowdrey's power was concealed in his timing; his was the gentlest of strengths. As Alan Ross had it, Cowdrey's batsmanship was redolent of both 'the richest of ports and the lightest of soufflés'. For Statham, invariably up the hill and into the wind, line and length were inseparable companions. Maupassant wrote a tale of a circus knife-thrower who found, when he tried during their act to murder his unfaithful wife, that it was impossible to deviate from his ingrained and grooved pattern of hurling the daggers to miss her by fractions. Or as the bowler's Boswell, Eric Midwinter, bettered: 'Brian could no more bowl a bad ball than Paderewski could hit a wrong note.'

Even when, in later adult life, I was privileged to meet them, my sense of wonder in their presence never remotely diluted. Almost the sole published testament to his life's work that Statham uttered was, 'If they missed, I hit.' Enquire about details, and he'd shrug and say, with his unbothered half-grin, 'Look it up in the book, it's all in there somewhere.' And so it always will be. Indelibly. He lissomly bowled his last first-class delivery – his 100,955th, and the sixth ball of his fifth consecutive maiden – in the 1968 Roses match at Old Trafford, and then loped quietly away from the downstage limelight into more shadows. By happy fluke, all of seven summers on, I saw the very last of Cowdrey's 107 centuries, 119 undefeated against Procter and Graveney and Childs, and nicely at Cheltenham where the mellow, timeless, architecture of his drives, downhill all the way most of them, matched the slumbrous serenity of the College chapel in the golden evening of a heatwave.

In the winter before Colin Cowdrey died, when he was obviously none too well, I helped arrange for the now slippered, ermined eminence to make the journey all the long way westwards from Arundel to open a new technology wing at Hereford Cathedral School. And having done those honours, might he give an evening talk on cricket in Leominster? He would be privileged to do both, he said. Blimey! Squires and farmers' boys (and wives and sisters) packed the Corn Exchange to hear him. We were entranced, tight-squashed and some hanging off the rafters almost, till past 11 o'clock. Surely, he would stay the night? 'What a wonderful evening, but no,' the morrow was the House of Lords. And off he went, with that soft smile, into the dark, cold, night.

Stumps are drawn for the Brigadier
Peter Tinniswood
11 January 2003

The life and works of playwright Peter Tinniswood, who has died at 66, will be admiringly logged at more detailed length on other pages this weekend. Cricketing folk of a certain generation, however, will offer particular thanksgiving for the most consistently imaginative and droll dramatist in radio history, because he was also the only begetter of the Brigadier, the dotty, muddled reactionary whose series of nostalgic monologues and seethingly encrusted observations on the state of the modern game beguiled sporting literature more than two decades ago.

Tales from a Long Room was published in 1981, a snip at £1.50 for what at once was proclaimed an immediate classic of fertile and fantastical tomfoolery. Radio 4 released the audio tapes and in the next three years there were four ravishingly cranky little paperback sequels of irrefutable comic invention, one when the writer even accompanied the 1982–3 Ashes tour to Australia, before Tinniswood moved on to other creations.

Without apology he buried his Brigadier with, sadly, neither a last-post bugle nor muffled drum down at third man under the yews in the churchyard of St Robin and All the Marlars at Witney Scrotum. All we were left to imagine on the night before the funeral was Vicar Mole-Drably wrestling over the choice of text with which to introduce from the pulpit his requiem address. Would it be 'And behold, my brethren, the blessed Ron Saggers did tour England with the 1948 Australians and, lo, not a single Test match did he play in', or perhaps 'And lo, I say to you my children, if Gordon Garlick did smite such mighty sixes for Lancashire, why, of a sudden, was he so soon allowed a registration for Northamptonshire?'

I am aware new readers, young readers, neglectful readers, will not twig an earthly rhyme or reason from the foregoing. You might manage a glimpse at the picture if you can imagine the purple-faced Brigadier (retd.) being played by a cricket-loving, cricket-despairing, Victor Meldrew, padded up in his thatched Long Room appendage to his pretty Wessex cottage, nibbling chilled Zubes and quaffing mulled claret, issuing bombastic volleys of intimidatingly choleric dispatches (scripted in turn by James Joyce, John Betjeman, Woody Allen, and the *Sunday Sport*'s chief leader-writer) on the state of play and players. Or, as the case may be, moist-eyed sentiment on the good ol' days of yore – during which time the old soldier's demented reverie was occasionally interrupted by the entrance of his 'good lady wife, goddam 'er' in her voluminous Ken Higgs-autographed negligée and the fragrant hint of Eau de Washbrook about her presence.

If you are still there, you have surely got the picture by now. More than 20 years ago, when Tinniswood, the most engaging and companionable of self-proclaimed recluses, was toying with the idea of publishing the Brigadier's monographs as a relief from the novels and plays which the obituarists will be this morning celebrating elsewhere, he lived not far from a home of mine at the time in deepest Wiltshire. In Salisbury once, we had a memorably elongated supper in which, pre-prandially and in his cricketing mode, he tossed around possible menu options – duckworth à l'orange; roast tim lamb with tom graveney; dilley con carne; van geloven-ready chicken; followed by appleyard and bobberry pie or some very savoury jardines-on-toast.

Peter was a year older than me, but in a way we were kindred peas in a pod. His father was a printer on the old *Manchester Guardian*, and had imbued him with an eternal affection both for this newspaper and for Winston Place, Cyril Washbrook's unsung and faithful opening partner at Old Trafford. From Sale Grammar and Manchester University, he went to the *Sheffield Telegraph* as a reporter.

At last an opening came up on his beloved *Guardian*. The then editor, Alastair Hetherington, gravely asked the question: Who were his favourite writers on the paper? 'The chap who does the football and the lady who does Country Diary from Keswick,' said Peter with enthusing certainty. He didn't get the job, and was still sore decades later ('Ruddy blighter thought I was taking the piss'). Good job Hetherington did, or we would never have known the incomparable, unforgettable, truly immortal Brigadier from Witney Scrotum.

Farewell Grav, a small cog who became a big buddy

Ray Gravell

6 November 2007

Wales buries Ray Gravell next Thursday. To an outsider, the cascade of collective grief which followed the news of his death last week would seem astonishing. But the sadness and shock that reverberated far beyond the rugby world was understandable. For Grav was a phenomenon.

I cannot recall such anguish for the loss of a team-playing sportsman who, on his own admission, was 'just a minor cog and, actually, quite an ordinary player, let's be honest'. It was honesty, in fact, which embellished Ray's utter grandeur. On one sleeve he wore his insecurities; on the other, his God-given truth, valour and humanity.

Since their bright, fresh valleys changed from green to black, I fancy Wales honours differently its two species of native hero. Sure, there is a swank in, and esteem for, those achieving success and recognition in England and beyond. But the other is more rare, more treasured – those of the tribe who triumph greatly, yet unshakeably remain in the embracing pastures of home. They are the select few on which is bestowed the most cherished of partisan loyalty and love. One such was Gravell, not only hero as sportsman, but local hero as human being, the 'hard' man with the gentle, chivalrous, wholly self-sufficient nature.

For Ray, the litany and lore of Wales's saints and its language were those of his own soul, his heart and his hearth. In a moist-eyed eulogy in the *Times* on Friday, Carmarthenshire clansman Gerald Davies wrote: 'He was a man, as they say in Wales, of *y filltir sgwar* – the familiar square mile of the local community; for all his travelling, he never left his home.'

Gerald and Welsh rugby's most glistening confrères – Gareth and Barry, JJ, JPR and Benny – remain canonised immortals, and if they, as their poet Dylan said, were 'the boys of summer', honest cousin Gravell was the wintry fellow of flint and pitch, the hewer and carrier, the man shudderingly to knock down trespassers. Grav was supple, strong, resilient and close-grained as mountain ash. In defence he seemed impassable, in attack single-mindedly direct, generous. Could you imagine him playing in other than the scarlet of Llanelli or Wales – or, OK, in the darker strawberry-red of the Lions? Once I saw him in Barbarians' stripes, and it seemed sacrilege – he looked like a sheepish, defrocked sporting priest.

Thirty winters ago I took Grav to lunch in Carmarthen's posh hotel near the town's bridge. I was late: he was already at the table in a brooding gloom, his auburn beard burrowed into the red scarf and the lapels of his weatherbeaten old overcoat. He had been dropped that season by Wales and showed me a letter he planned to send the selectors asking never to be so much as considered in the future. Being dropped was too painful – 'and I could never face again this stigma of rejection by Wales. Doubtless my form deserved it, but it feels as though you've amputated my heart.' Don't dream of posting it, I said, he'd be reselected in no time (and so, of course, he was, triumphantly) – so now, I went on, take off those dark glasses, Grav, sit back and let's enjoy a slap-up meal at the *Guardian*'s expense.

Perked up, he asked: 'Are you sure the *Guardian*'s paying?' Undoubtedly, I said, flamboyantly calling for the wine list – at which Ray ran outside to the pavement and brought back a friend, Cliff, whom he'd obviously told to wait on the offchance. Cliff was a bent, threadbare, down-at-heel, out-of-work old Welsh miner colleague of Grav's beloved late father. And so the three of us tucked into a memorable banquet and the truly delightful ancient, Cliff (almost as sage a philosopher-poet as Ray himself), had second helpings of all five courses. It remains one of the meals of my life – and for years afterwards, wherever we met round the rugby world (which, happily, was often), Grav would saunter up and whisper: 'Saw Cliff last week, he sends the bonniest of felicitations to the *Guardian*.'

Grav's success as a broadcaster and actor was a given. Around a dozen years ago, I wrote a BBC Wales sports history doc in which, naturally, Grav starred. He had not long finished playing alongside Jeremy Irons in *Damage*, directed by the legendary Louis Malle, and he told me he'd nervously admitted at the audition: 'Monsieur Malle, I can only play myself, y'know.' 'Parfait, Raymond,' exclaimed the great director, 'I have worked with a thousand illustrious actors – and not one of them has been remotely good at playing themselves.'

Perfect casting, of course, because there has only ever – ever – been one, singular, one-and-only Ray Gravell.

A fond farewell to the good sage
John Rodda
10 March 2009

We bury John Rodda this Friday in the handsome village church alongside the Somerset home to which he retired in 1995. Celebration of, and gratitude for, the memory of the good sage and mentor will overcome much of the sadness.

All of 57 winters ago a short report of a London midweek rugby match between United Banks and Hampshire was printed in these sports pages – a freelance commission from a keen young cub on the *South London Press* and the first 250 words of what would be many millions written by Rodda for this newspaper. To be sure, older readers will recall that some mornings it seemed as if Rodda alone was writing the whole sports section.

Though fondly conversant with all games, through his prime John specialised in boxing and athletics; as well, he became fabled for keeping a beady weather-eye on all sporting politics, and his devotion to the purist ideals of the Olympic movement was to make him the most challengingly robust critic of that movement's oligarchic transgressions. It was an education to hear him prick the pomp and the protocol with the most forensic and well-briefed of inquiries.

Next year would have marked Rodda's half century of reporting the Olympics. He had joined the *Guardian* full-time in 1959 and within a year, on the sudden death at only 50 of legendary sports editor (and athletics correspondent) Larry Montague, the greenhorn was dispatched to Rome pronto to cover the Games of 1960. Those stirring, colourful 'innocent' Games were to remain seminal to him throughout his long career. In Rome, he chronicled the dramatic arrival on the stage of the Africans, by way of the astonishing marathon runner Abebe Bikila. And to the end John would always whoopingly log as his most thrilling and vivid Olympic memory the unbelievable 'eruption' down the back-straight of Herb Elliott which laid waste the field in the 1500 metres final: 'In a blink a pack of tremendous athletes, each coiled and gathered to win it themselves, became traumatised also-rans: it was unimaginable. Elliott won by a street, in a world-record time, and on a cinder track and in heavy leather shoes.'

News, of course, was Rodda's staple. Has any British sports-writer ever produced more three or four-par scoops? The bad guys all feared John. His aldermanic bearing only lent weight to his journalistic rectitude. He was never an in-my-day fogey nor crusty prude. He was inspiriting company at the end of a long day, always first to chortle at recall of his own apocalyptic, but off-beam prognostications in print, like his assured forecast after 1960 that the Olympic 800m for women would cause collapse, distress and even death – only to have Ann Packer so glisteningly breast the tape at Tokyo in 1964 with a sublime smile on her face. Or after Tokyo, where Lynn Davies and Mary Rand won the respective long jump gold medals, JR forecast the absolute certainty that every excited British child would demand a myriad of long jump pits to be built all over Britain. They weren't.

Likewise, four years later after Dick Fosbury with his back-flip 'Flop' won the 1968 high jump title – 'and I demanded that the technique should forthwith be banned because every emulating jumper would unquestionably suffer crippling back injuries. But guess what, in 50 years nobody has.'

Rodda witnessed all the figures of Olympic grandeur through half a century and was admired by most of them. John's final Olympics, his 10th, were at Atlanta in 1996. For half of them, it was a privilege, a luxury, a joy, to be alongside him high in the press tribune and sharing his phone and his wisdom. Same when covering boxing together. By the end, he was disillusioned by the 'showbiz' of pro boxing and although he described countless contests by such luminaries of the lore as Muhammad Ali, Ray Leonard and Mike Tyson, always the nonpareil exemplar was his cockney boyhood favourite George Daly of Blackfriars, a seeming journeyman of 150 fights and 31 defeats who John would say, 'brought artistry to a genuinely noble sport through balance, nimble feet and the way he mesmerised opponents with the feint'.

Once, in the raucous maelstrom of a pre-fight press conference I found myself asking said Ali his technique for outsmarting a southpaw opponent. Next to me, Rodda murmured approvingly: 'Good question.' I flushed, proud: as if I'd been awarded my colours by the esteemed Head of House.

The whistling postman
Arthur Milton
Foreword to *Arthur Milton: Last of the Double Internationals* by Mike Vockins, 2011

It was a dreadful shock to hear that Arthur Milton had died at 79 in the springtime of 2007. Yet how apt and telling, I thought, for good Arthur to die in the last week of April, the very calendar quintessence of the traditional changeover of the sporting seasons

– the week he would have bid adieu to the raucous wintry fever-pitch of Highbury and its stately marble halls, slung his football boots into his London landlady's cupboard and whistled expectantly to himself all the way across to Paddington and the train back to Temple Meads, home, and the mellow warm westerlies of another pastoral Gloucestershire summer.

Arthur Milton embodied that timeless ritual of the seasons. We shall never – ever – see his like, for Arthur was the very last of an exceptional line: only a dozen men have ever played for England at both football and cricket – Lyttelton, Gunn, Gay, Foster, Fry, Sharp, Makepeace, Hardinge, Ducat, Arnold, Watson and – finally and forever, and the last to go – Milton himself. It was an exceptional line; and Milton was an exceptional man.

Gentle Arthur was one of the giants of my boyhood. A giant he remained even when childhood's callow, eyes-wide worship grew into warm man-to-man friendship.

Is it just my generation? There was a lasting and valorous chivalry in the craft-versed cigarette-card heroes of our youth. They taught us urchins pride – and boy, oh boy, what pride we had in them. I recall vividly still the wondrous flush of it three-score years ago when, out of the blue, our favourite smiling young god of a natural cricketer was suddenly picked on the wing for England at Wembley (Matthews dropped, Tom Finney injured. Wow! Third in line!), and the same sort of local pride too, much later, when the England team came calling again, this time in the summer and, of course, Arthur answered the call with a chanceless debut century in the Headingley Test to seal the whole deal for history.

The small print logs all Milton's breathless 90-minute winter heroics and, to be sure, all his timeless long days of summer runs down to the last decimal point – as well as his fabled bag of catches, too: why, only seven men in the whole of cricket history held more catches – but to us behind the ropes all those years ago, with our pound of plums and our autograph books, it was

Arthur's congenially boyish one-of-us enjoyment and constancy which most appealed; that and the jaunty, feel-good zest of his inborn talent and authentic artistry and, of course, his friendly, foppish mop of buttercup hair.

Someone said that everyone was 11 in 1948. Well, everyone romantic, that is – which I most certainly was on both counts. The year saw the London Olympic Games, and the launching of that cultural sporting base-touching signpost *Sports Report* – on the BBC radio still on Saturday teatimes. It was the year of what many continue to reckon was Wembley's most sumptuously appealing FA Cup final ever (Manchester United 4 Blackpool 2); 1948 was the year Bradman's Immortals ruthlessly laid waste all England and its cricket shires.

And 1948 in late August was the first time us urchins in the north of the county came down from the hills to witness a one-off school-holiday fixture (Gloucestershire against the Combined Services) at the genial, grimy old Gloucester Wagon Works ground in which two brand new fresh-faced heroes blazed a trail into our consciousness for ever – when Tom Graveney scored his first 100 for Gloucestershire in a beguiling buddies' century stand in collaboration with (as the *GCCC Yearbook* called him) Clement Milton (58 not out) ... the former lanky, languid, elegant, princely; the latter shorter, more athletic, matier, more carefree and certainly more smiling. As Arthur remembered in his reverie not long before he died: 'I played because I loved it. It was born in me to play. I didn't make much money, but I was very happy always. They were, simply, wonderful days, wonderful days in the sun. They were days that were never long enough.'

Arthur was the wise innocent personified, the stupendous all-rounder whose deeds together with his chivalry and generosity added a shining lustre to the trade of professional sport.

Having finished with his football after blazing across the sky for all too short a time, Milton played another 20 seasons of cricket. Then he became a postman – up daily at dead of night and across the Downs at Clifton on his regulation GPO boneshaker bike: 'Sun up, dawn chorus, all alone, truly wonderful ... Best of all the winter mornings, snow or heavy frost, eerie silence, whiteness all around, not a footprint, not a tyre-tread and sometimes a great huge bulbous moon ... utter perfection.'

For some earlier happy summers the happy postman coached the dark-blue scholars of Oxford University's first XI. Sometime captain was Vic Marks, Test player and now a distinguished journalist, who remembers fondly what an inspired choice Arthur had been – 'not least because he could finish the *Daily Telegraph* crossword each morning before any of us' – and star batsman and classicist John Claughton (now equally distinguished Chief Master of King Edward's School Birmingham) recalls the done-it-all all-knowing coach's modesty by, as you'd expect, nicely paraphrasing Ovid: *Ars Arthur est celare artem* ('Art's art is to conceal his art').

From his Arsenal digs in north London, like all *Boys' Own* heroes should, Arthur had married the landlady's beautiful daughter. It was a blissful marriage. Happy families. Once the Post Office had insisted on him acknowledging their official retirement age, Arthur bagged the same district, sorted out every local newsagent and continued his dawn watch for another couple of decades. In 2002, in front of a packed house, harmonious choirs, Latin quotations, and the full purple-gowned works, Bristol University gave Milton an honorary MA. That morning he'd delivered the newspapers to the Common Room. How many other universities anywhere in the world have given an MA to their paperboy?

Oh, happy man. Oh, happy days.

15

STRANGE THINGS HAPPEN

For several years Keating edited the letters sent to the Guardian *sports page. The process was distinctly informal – he would weave extracts from readers' comments into a very readable column. It reflected the way readers regarded him as a personal friend, and also allowed them to express their enthusiasm for the quirkier aspects of sport. Sometimes he just had to launch an idea and it could fly for weeks. For instance, the time he asked for nominations for favourite sporting mannerisms. It produced what is now a feast of three-quarter forgotten memories, including that of Manchester United being relegated.*

These fidgets you have loved
18 December 1979

Continuing our everyday saga of mannered folk, many of you nominate Derek Randall's frenzied fidgeting for the ferret in his flannels, and no one puts his case better than the artist, Kevin Macey. Sir Geoffrey's contortions as he attempts to wipe the bald patch with the back of his right sweatband is also clocking up votes for the Mannerism of the Decade – as is his unaccountable habit of touching the ankle of his right foot when he's non-striker. Jack Lewis, of Bradford, says he did it 43 times in an innings of 28 minutes last season.

Pancho Gonzales and his obsession with his sweat-soaked eyebrows had a boost after the recent veterans' tourney on television, but leading the field still is what Jim Kevan, of Cheltenham, was inspired to call 'the Lancaster gait' of the former soccer manager of England. Martyn Stead, of Sale, elaborates: 'What mannerism more encapsulates the spirit of the decade than Mr Revie's trudge back to the Wembley dressing room – eyes pained, shoulders hunched, hands deep in the pockets of that awful overcoat?'

Martyn, who is a Leeds supporter, also offers 'Norman Hunter's bowed head, outstretched arms and supplicant's palms as he placated referees; Jan Kodes's mechanical angular rocking to and fro before service: and, if a team can have a mannerism, what about the way all Liverpool players seem to run alike, as in Keegan, Callaghan and Hall, for example?'

Dwight Stones, he of the spring heels, did it all for Tony Pembrooke, of Bracknell: 'The way he nodded out his imagined run up, looking to see where his feet would land, then raising his head as he "saw" himself flop over the bar was unique – though Phil Rogers, the US golfer, has also developed a similar slow nodding action as he acts out an imaginary ball falling into the hole, prior to putting.'

John Burridge's repertoire also gets an entry from Kevin Macey, but for Peter G Thornton, of Salford, there remains only one Law unto himself. 'Having passed over Ali's shuffle and Ovett's wave I turn to Denis Law who has inspired a thousand other imitators over the years, amongst them your own favourite Rodney.

'The shirt outside the shorts and the cuffs gripped in each hand to start with. But it was the Law salute that will be most remembered. After every goal, except his last one in the derby that sent United down, the arm would shoot skywards, the cuff would be clenched and the index finger would point to the sky.

'There has been no finer mannerism in football – Channon's windmill, Pearson's clenched fist and Jordan's toothless grin are poor compensation: and one day Burridge will do himself an injury. As a City fan I cherish the memory of the few salutes Denis Law did for us.'

Sometimes the tone was a bit different. 'A bundle of outraged letters from west of Offa's Dyke take the biscuit this week,' Keating wrote in February 1978 after the Welsh took exception to his description of their rugby pack as 'a bunch of coalface toughs'. 'Other than Arsenal supporters,' Frank asked, a bit sulkily, 'can there be a more collectively touchy lot than Welsh rugby folk?' Anyway, when he went out and about he was quite capable of spotting the weird and wonderful for himself, often involving the aforementioned Sir Geoffrey.

Geoff plays the prince
26 January 1979

SYDNEY: Our last few hours in Sydney went from the sublime to the ridiculous. A lunch in the blissful shade of Watson's Bay at Doyle's celebrated seafood restaurant meandered on past teatime. It was followed by a few gentle digesting swipes as a cooling breeze tinkled the gum leaves around the Royal Sydney Golf Club. Then, believe it or not, we went to a seedy, raucous little dive just off the city's red light area to see England's premier batsman be a disc jockey for half an hour and a hundred quid.

'And now, the moment you've all been waiting for,' said a spotty, pale, night owl with sweat stains in his armpits and pretentions to punk. 'Here he is, the new sound of Sydney from out of the west. Guys and gals, the Zoo Disco is proud to give you – Geoffrey Boycott!'

Our run-hero pranced on to the stage and gave his emperor's two-armed salute like when he hit the famous on-drive off Chappell at Headingley three years ago. Only this time the applause was, to put it kindly, not quite so enthusiastic. There were one or two amiable jeer-cheers from the back of the bar in this darkened dump, but most of the sad over-made-up little girls with slits up the side of their frocks looked gawpingly unimpressed, took a slug of Bacardi and coke, scratched themselves and itched for the next record.

In a corner of the cellar, unbeknown to our star of the show as the strobe lights surrounded him, sat Bairstow, Emburey, Dilley and Colonel Ken Barrington, absolutely creasing themselves with mirth.

Geoffrey wore tight black slacks and a frightful gaudy shirt of purply flowers. Not a hair of his hairpiece, preening and pommaded, was out of place. The lights kept changing – red, green, amber, you name it. His bright, blue-tinted contact lenses turned positively and glaringly green when the lights were on amber. The first record he put on was 'Baby Love' and he jived in time to it, sticking out his bottom and clicking his thumbs and middle fingers in the prescribed fashion.

It seemed he did not actually have to say anything for his £100. He and the punk just put one deafening record after another on to the turntable. Geoffrey's lopsided grin got wider and wonkier. He genuinely seemed to be enjoying himself. 'Come down and 'ave a dance,' asked a little black girl in a little black dress with golden glitter glued on her eyelids. 'I can't, luv,' said the greatest living Yorkshireman, 'I'm putting on the records you see.'

He especially enjoyed giving away the spot prizes just before the evening's grand finale when he and the punk played cricket with a child's plastic bat and ball. Afterwards he was elated as he signed one or two beer mats before collecting his little brown envelope.

'I were alright, weren't I?'

'Yes, Geoffrey, you were absolutely terrific; they really loved you,' I assured him.

'Yes, they did seem to didn't they?'

Sir Geoffrey sees the costume joke
28 December 1981

DELHI: The Indians were not quite sure about Christmas. Nor were we. One friend, in a taxi, passed a street-corner group in excitable haggle over some freshly-arrived goods at the market place. 'Turkeys?' he queried. 'No,' replied the taxi driver, 'they're Lebanese.'

The British Raj, mind you, had gone for Christmas in a big way. Santa Claus always made his entry on an elephant at the Viceroy's tea party. The holly and the ivy had long been sent from home in the hothouse-hold of the Royal Mail steamships. No refrigeration then, so the British had to make do with the dry, white meat of the Indian pea-hen as sub for goose or turkey.

In 1981, for these 16 high commissioners from the Old Country, the Oberoi Hotel went at Christmas with a will. The bewildered staff had been told to say 'Happy Christmas' to anything white that moved. There was interminable 'Hark the herald' music in lobbies and lifts. Real turkey, too, for lunch, and some few drops of the hard stuff, even though 25 December is officially a 'dry' day in Delhi.

Bob Taylor went to Mass at the Vatican-style chapel near the British High Commission. He said it was superb. Jack Richards and his wife Birgitta went to Midnight Mass in the tented 'overflow' nave of the Sacred Heart Cathedral, where you had to go in through a line of beggars. One of the carols was Amazing Grace, and we thought warmly for a fleeting moment of cold and frosty Portman Road in good old Ipswich town. In the wide, wide skies of India the stars of Christmas night seemed even more than usually bright.

The press gave a party for the players in the mid-morning. Earlier, Gooch and Emburey, sharing the room next to me, had hung up their cards on the wall, and then we'd had a Buck's Fizz, conned from the British Council, and talked of home and Botham's batting.

Lunch was taken in fancy dress. Some had been working on their costumes for weeks. Some hadn't, like Emburey who tore up a sheet and went as some sort of Ku Klux Klansman, I presume. The theme was 'heroes'. There was heavy betting that Boycott would come as himself, but he looked marvellous as a turbaned Prince Ranjitsinjhi.

Botham came as Boycott, wearing a tight, pink rubber swimming cap on his head, holed at random to allow a few sprigs of hair to poke out. He completed the costume with wire specs and Gandhi loincloth, and on his naked chest was emblazoned in lipstick '8,032', Sir Gary [Sobers]'s former run record that Sir Geoffrey had given himself for Christmas the day before. There was much mirth and Geoffrey took it well.

Dilley and Fletcher were outstanding as the long and the short of it from the TV series *It Ain't Half Hot, Mum*. Bob Taylor was a high-heeled Dick Emery. Gatting was Doctor Who, Cook a very fine Bertie Wooster and Willis, whose nickname is 'Goose', dressed up as the Indian Prime Minister, as in 'Goosey, Goosey ...' Original as ever, Gower came as the one-armed crocodile-keeper we met at Baroda, and Gooch's hero was Billy Bonds of West Ham – 'I would 'ave preferred to be Trevor, actually, but it would have meant me shavin' off me beard.'

After the crackers had been pulled there was a concert of sorts, and very much the star of the show was Dilley, who came out with Eamonn's big red book and perfect Irish brogue to do an impromptu, unexpurgated 'Ian Botham. This is Your Life.' It brought the house down. Then Prince Ranjitsinjhi turned back into the Prince of Plod and the two of us went out for a few digestive holes of golf. Geoffrey, as ever, played straight down the middle to his comfy 14 handicap. Mine was the unaccustomed drink and the hot sun.

I lost five balls in six holes, as the Voice of the Tyke droned on: 'Keep y'head down, Uncle Frank. Keep y'head down.' Trouble was, I couldn't keep my eyes open. Still, it was Christmas day in Delhi, wasn't it?

If Boycott's career was one rich seam, an unpromising-looking book that arrived unbidden one autumn day in 1979 gave Frank endless delight.

The unsporting side of writing
19 December 1979

A reader, Derek Kemp, of Bath, has posted me a slim volume. I was not quite sure how to take this. It is called *How to Become a Sporting Journalist*.

It is a classic read of the old-style pomp-and-bombast memoir manner by BJ Evans, who was a celebrated Fleet Street reporter between the wars. It is full of such advice as:

'Often I have arrived at a press box to be asked by a colleague if I could spare a pencil or a few sheets of paper. For my part, I never arrived there without having at least three pencils sharpened and enough paper to do treble as much work as originally planned ... I numbered the sheets in advance so I was never able to spare any to accommodate an improvident colleague. Later I caught a rude remark about my meanness in refusing paper when I had so much to spare, but being on the job I have no time for other people's opinions.'

And on and on he goes ...

BOXING: 'I don't consider any writer on boxing fully equipped for his job unless he can advise a trainer on how to prepare his man for the championship. He should be able to write on the exact physical condition of the man and suggest changes in the last week's work to secure perfect fitness for the big night.'

ROWING: 'On Boat Races I secure a new notebook with hard covers. On the inside of one cover only I draw a diagram of each boat, Oxford on the left and Cambridge on the right, with the stern at the bottom and the name of each oarsman jutting out from port or starboard as they sit. On the other cover is the same diagram, except that Oxford is on the right and Cambridge on the left. Thus whichever crew wins the Surrey station I am able to have a diagram showing them in proper position when the race started. I write my notes from that end of the book. Complete concentration is essential.'

But it is Evans on cricket that allowed me a laugh over the holiday. I came across mention of this author's name in EW Swanton's paperback book on MCC Australian tours. 'Evans's English in print and talk alike was almost more basic than anything I remember,' Jim growls, before telling the wonderful story of Evans dismissing the best of all cricket writers: 'Cardus? He's the bugger who pinches all my bleedin' epigrams.'

Did Cardus really spend his days eavesdropping BJ Evans? 'I have always tried to help colleagues in distress,' he says in the book, 'but refused to earn a living for them. The worst case I ever encountered of scrounging occurred during Essex cricket week at Brentwood ... My wife had come in the car with me: not to watch the cricket but to sit in a deckchair with her knitting ... I had gone off to talk to some of the players on their way to the pavilion to learn some facts about the morning's play.

'Seated in a deckchair next to my wife was this man engaged with a morning paper. He was pretending to do the *Times* crossword but my wife noticed he was jotting down in the margin of the paper all the data he had overheard in my story, which I had told my wife.

'On my return she told me about this. My first instinct was to punch him on the chin, but I thought better of it. So I went to the bar with some real journalists to warn them that a sneak was present. That gentleman never stole a cricket story from me again, but it must ever have been a mystery to him why he did not get another chance of doing so.

'I mention this to show newcomers to journalism that all writers are not sportsmen.'

16

FLASHES OF ANGER

Most journalism is ill-tempered by design. Some of it involves getting justifiably cross about the failings of politicians, sportsmen or whoever. Much of it involves getting unjustifiably, though theatrically, cross about the same people. The Keating style was to err on the side of forgiveness, which is what made his work so refreshing. It also ensured that, when he did get into a lather, it was quite startlingly effective.

And the band played on...
1 September 1980

At teatime the band played that tiddley-om theme tune from *Monty Python's Flying Circus*. Honest it did. The Royal Marines Band it was and they were conducted by a precise and very well turned-out chap called Hoskins, which is a very Pythonesque sort of name. So was the day.

A monumental cock-up. Lord's and all of cricket should be totally ashamed of itself. Someone should resign. No one will, of course. Their judgment of priorities is unbelievable. Apparently, last year an MCC member, nervously fingering his yellow-and-red tie, was hauled into the secretary's office and given a dressing down and final warning for eating an apple in the Long Room. 'The committee take a very dim view of this behaviour, Bloggins, a very dim view indeed ...' Shown the yellow card and red card.

Saturday of the Centenary Test, their day of days in a hundred years and they let the whole thing go to pot – from slight eccentricity to fairly decent charades to high farce to downright teeth-grinding tragedy.

Do you remember that day at the Oval a few years ago when we all helped mop up after a deluge? On Saturday the sun shone down and the breezes hummed but not a sack nor a sponge nor a pitchfork was in evidence. The groundsman had announced quite simply at elevenses that the match could start easily before lunch. The umpires said it could not. So did one captain. And all this time was the big boss wandering round with beady bloodshot eye as livid as his MCC tie keeping a lookout for some rotter who was daring to eat an apple in the Long Room?

At speeches all week guys fingering the same ties have got up to say how Lord's wanted us to remember this celebration shindig for the next hundred years. We will, sir, we will. Pray be upstanding ... especially those thousands who queued outside (some all night) who were not let in 'till the umpires announce play will start' because officialdom did not want to be involved in argy-bargy about refunded money.

A month ago in that bureaucratic hellhole in Olympic Russia (like a friend said at breakfast one Moscow morning when told the Shah was dead – 'good, perhaps this bloody hotel will now release my laundry') one of our main grouses was that, in the second week when we all wanted to go to the athletics stadium, the press buses to other venues would still be scheduled. Hundreds who could not find a hubcap or mudguard to hang on to would be left stranded while empty buses came and went to the pistol-shooting range or the egg-and-spoon stadium or whatever.

Buckpassing. Nobody at the depot could make a decision. Funk turned into ridiculous chaos. It could never happen in Britain, we said. Well, it can. It did on Saturday.

Late in the evening we cadging loiterers hung around Mick Jagger. The Mick Jagger. He summed it up. 'It's been a reasonable day for us boozers up here in private boxes. But what about the geezers queueing and those blokes munching their sandwiches up there at the Nursery End?' Mr Jagger agreed we might meet again on Monday – 'but we'll have to tune in to the weather forecast – I am not turning up to see the umpires inspect the wicket – when you've seen that once you've seen it all.' Quite.

Then, late into the evening as they announced in blissful sunshine that play had been abandoned, a handful of Australian players – Chappell, Lillee, Hughes and co – ironically compounded the day's disaster by jogging around the ground in tight little tights. 'C'mon Sebastian!' shouted Max Boyce. 'C'mon Steve!' said Ollie Milburn. And Lillee and Chappell took the joke and waved back. They looked cheesed off as well.

Even after all the rum happenings, the Centenary Test continues oblivious. Strange opposites – well, Jagger, Boyce, Milburn, me and a million others – still get together today in celebration. Cricket will still win – but, bugger me, cricket's administration still does not know a thing about cricket's adoration.

I was almost the last to leave Lord's. In the immortal phrase I was 'as sponsored as a newt'. Well, put it this way, we were thrown out of our box.

At the Nursery End car park a light went on in the corner. In a caravan, of all things. I was intrigued. Through the undrawn blinds I saw a haggard man with a thin moustache slumped down on a bench looking worried, at the end of his tether. He seemed to be saying: 'I'd just love a nice cup of tea, dear, it's been a hard day at the office.' Painted on the outside of this caravan was the legend 'Welton Caravan Supplied To D Constant, Umpire.'

He had certainly had a hard day at the office, hadn't he, dear? So had we all.

Pop sociology from the boardroom
25 October 1981

You must assume a serious face before reading this, because Desmond Morris takes himself and sport seriously. Very seriously indeed. Of the tens of thousands of names in the Rothmans soccer bible, his is the only one followed by the letters BSc., D.Phil.

279

He has been a director of Oxford United for four years, an honorary capacity which he has put to good use in the writing of a sumptuously illustrated and sumptuously priced new book *The Soccer Tribe*. It is already translated and selling in a dozen languages and looks certain to make Dr Morris as much money as *The Naked Ape* and *Manwatching*, his previous popular and overblown statements of the obvious.

It is written in the plonking tone which Stephen Potter defined as 'roundly, hollowly, and dogmatically' and might suit those of you who have a new coffee table with stainless steel legs and a glass top.

Of his own kind, that is league club directors, he writes: 'If a director seems to the outside world to be antiquated in his approach, it must be remembered that he is, in a very real sense, the chief guardian of the Tribal Traditions. If he resists progress it is because he intuitively feels the need to retain the age-old mood of rigid ritual that gives the soccer game much of its intensity ... Some may indeed be self-important and pretentious, but whether haughty or humble, magisterial or modest, they share an almost pathological love of the sport. To overlook this, as their critics prefer to do, is a grave injustice.'

Morris's 'pathological love' of soccer seems very much a sudden middle-aged affair, as dangerous and dramatic as Humbert's. I forgot to ask him what came first, his idea for a blockbusting book or his directorship into the inner sanctum of a football league club. At Dauntsey's, a minor public school in Wiltshire, he was taught geography by FNS Creek, last of the old Corinthian footballers, but he learned nothing from him about that, for in those days, the young Morris was not in the least bit excited by soccer. His father did want to take him to watch Swindon Town. 'All I can remember is that they wore red shirts,' he says.

He dresses in the powder blue of Coventry City himself – powder blue suit, powder blue shirt, powder blue socks. The effect is ruined by the hideously brash black bull's head of the Oxford

United tie. His hairstyle borrows from soccer tradition – the tufts around the ears worn extremely long, then wrapped across his bald pate à la Bobby Charlton. Something in that perhaps for an amateur anthropologist?

His luxuriously appointed Oxford office in the Banbury Road is not at all the sort of place you expect to come across a director of an extremely modest third division club. It is lined with ancient leather-bound books all about ancient Egypt, Greece and Papua New Guinea. The only giveaway is on the shelf holding video recordings: there, mixed up with such bold, no-messing titles as *The Human Race* or *The Origins of Everything* are 'Ox. vs Luton' and 'Ox. vs Shrewsbury' and 'DM on Parkinson Show'.

His son, Jason, was born in 1968. The new book is dedicated to him. When the boy was five and the family still living in tax exile in Malta, his parents took him to a football match. 'The game dissolved into a riot after a disallowed goal. Honestly, the crowd were really aiming to kill the referee. In minutes we were the only three left sitting in the stand.' It was a good start for a man looking to follow up *The Naked Ape*.

Back at Oxford, Jason's fascination with the game grew. His father promised to take him to watch the local team, Morris's university colleagues, he says, cocked a quizzical eye. 'They have to go off to New Guinea to study what makes tribal peoples tick. As an anthropologist I now realise there was just as elaborate, colourful and bizarre a ritual being played out for an hour or two every British Saturday afternoon.' That's fine for starters, but I'm afraid the book never really develops those flip sort of presumptions.

When a manager is sacked by the Board, Morris puts it down to 'getting rid of the witchdoctor by tribal elders to appease the God of soccer.' He has been through that when Oxford sacked a manager last season. 'He had to go but it was very distracting.' Now vice-chairman, he has yet to be on the wrong end of a boardroom split – 'For restraint and rational thinking it has all the qualities of the ousting of the leader of a pack of baboons.' Well, he said it.

He is good and sympathetic about 'the tribal followers'. He says the police 'drearily continue to arrest: surely it is not beyond their wit to go in and sort out the few leaders, the tiny criminal element of the head-bangers, possibly just one nutter whose thing is to rely on the loyalty of others.'

For the rest his premise is too pat, his whole 'tribal' thesis much too simplistic for anyone who knows anything about the game. You will read each beautifully produced paragraph and sigh 'So what?' Sure, maiden aunts with coffee tables might glean a bit of gen and realise what all the fuss has been about for a century. So what?

Games for Wellies planned by Wallies
2 August 1986

In the early morning yesterday a panic-stricken siren shriek of a nuclear air-raid warning was triggered off, by accident, design or demonstration. It woke the whole city to an early breakfast. I reckon it must have been set off by the sun, which had apparently chosen that moment to show its face for the first time – though not for long – after the soggiest succession of summer days even Scotland can have been blighted with.

When, years ago, they were deliberating on exact dates for these unlucky 13th Commonwealth Games, Mark Barker, marketing director of the organising consortium, telephoned various local meteorological centres to inquire about weather prospects hereabout for the last week of July. He was told that apart from a couple of weeks in January the drenchingest average rainfall for the year was – you've guessed it – the end of July. Choose September, the weather men insisted.

They stuck with July. That was their first mistake. There were many more to come, and there is a strong school of thought that had the boycott over South African sanctions not denuded the games by 50 per cent, then the botch-up may well have been worse. Nevertheless, while the 1986 Games will go down in history as being wretchedly wrecked by the boycott of 1,300 athletes from 31 of the original entry of 58 countries, most of us who attended them will recall only the cold and the rain. Macintosh really is the perfect Scottish surname.

Budgeting disasters early on had long meant these would be called the Games Without Frills. When they got under way they fast became the Games Without Thrills. Alas, I will always think of them myself as the Welly Games, run by Wallies.

At the stadium yesterday the journalists were given a form to fill in, yet another sponsor's gimmick, in which we were asked to select the 1-2-3 who had contributed most to the spirit of the Games. In my little area of the pressbox each gigglingly entered – 1. Daley Thompson (England); 2. Colin Shields (Scotland), the local official Thompson allegedly told to 'piss off'; 3. Robert Maxwell (Czechoslovakia), who says he is still manfully seeking to make the Games solvent in the name of Mirror Group Newspapers and the *Scottish Daily Record*.

For my money at least Mr Maxwell's vast presence enlivened the whole occasion – okay, I agree, 'enlivened' isn't quite the word; shall we say 'loomed over'? His press conferences were connoisseurs' classics of dogmatic, table-thumping flannel. He had 'rescued' the games and figures in millions were banded about with carefree zest, but nobody could remotely pin him down on actually how much it was costing him.

Before he goes back to select his squad for Oxford United's big kick-off, Edinburgh's shell-shocked city fathers might just be inclined to ask him to sort out the one and only princely and proud Princes Street. When I first came to the city in 1960 they were talking of opening it up exclusively to pedestrians. Yet still the traffic jams creep along in bad-tempered, exhaust-fumed fits and starts.

Heaven knows what it would have been like had two thousand more Gamesters crammed the badly paved pavements: when you weren't looking down to hopscotch the puddles like a Keith Connor, you were in fear of your eyeballs from the sabre-sharp umbrella points wielded in abandoned distraction by rainswept old ladies. And all the time your eardrums were being savaged by the wail of bagpipers. Rain does not stop play at the bagpipes. For the most part these Commonwealth Games have sounded like carving-knife time in an Isle of Man cattery.

It goes without saying that the BBC's credits start with a be-sporranned cheek-puffing caterwauler. Mind you, after that they have not had much else to show. By way of relief in the rain on Wednesday they even put in front of the cameras some flute-twiddling twit from the velodrome who had been driving everybody mad for days with his non-stop James Galways.

On and on went the raindrops and the moving wallpaper. The interest was not so much what the BBC might be showing, but how they were dragging out their long-scheduled aeons of air time. On day one they ran two unending hours of the high jump in the women's pentathlon; never can TV longeurs have been longer.

The bowlers bowled on and on in the wet and David Vine droned on and on in the dry. Tony Gubba unaccountably got as strainingly worked up as some of his weightlifters. Never can badminton have had such expoz-z-z-ure.

On Thursday morning honest David Moorcroft suggested to the smooth frontman Steve Ryder that without Coe the forthcoming 800m by Cram would be a one-horse race. 'Hang on a minute there, Dave,' said Steve, or words to that effect as he desperately zapped up his built-in promo hype, 'surely we've still got a classic on our hands with such as Elliott and McKean in the race?' In the event, McWho ran his fastest time ever but was still beaten by the length of a cricket pitch as Cram laid on even more of a procession than Shergar used to lead.

Cram, it must be said, was majestic. But it wasn't no race. The balding Ovett's rehabilitation was a thrill as well. But nor was that remotely a race. Thompson's two days were simply one-man exhibitions. The Sanderson-Whitbread cat fight was the very stuff of drama. Yet on their edited highlights on Thursday night the BBC primly edited out all but a few seconds of the attendant soul-baring and gnashing of big white teeth.

And the rain it raineth every day. Wellies and Wallies. If the Commonwealth itself still exists we will doubtless assemble again in four years' time at Auckland. It's been known to rain there too, not 'alf it hasn't. The marketing director of the Auckland consortium, Malcolm Beattie, did not mention his weather yesterday, but on all other counts he is unquietly confident – 'Our lot are professionals, Edinburgh's organisation was in the hands of a bunch of amateurs.'

But when Mark Barker had accepted his job as marketing director years ago, his first report to Edinburgh's consortium read: 'I do not wish to be thought a Jeremiah, only to be realistic about what marketing can raise in finance. We are operating in a totally new environment which places considerable restrictions on our ability to spend. We must make a virtue of our restricted means so that both the general public and the Federation are aware that if they wish major sporting competitions like this to continue, then the ever-escalating costs have got to be contained.'

He had based his warning on the following figures – Edinburgh's 1970 Games cost £615,867 in management and administration, and made a profit of £5,277. By Brisbane 1982 the costs had rocketed nearly thirtyfold, but that was heavily supported by government. Exact figures here are not at hand yet and Mr Maxwell, for one, is so far keeping them close to his ample chest. It depends who you talk to if you want to get exactitudes; everyone moves the goalposts to suit themselves.

It looks, however, as if the final budget of costs will be between £13 million and £16 million. Certainly the BBC's budget has been announced as in excess of £15 million. Could the TV operation end up as more expensive than the Games themselves? The BBC will get, say, around £11 million back in fees from overseas countries, but when it is costing more to put out the TV signal than it is to run the very event they are televising, it all seems a very cockeyed state of affairs.

Bowing down to the bleak business of sport
4 August 1986

Last summer, the Scottish Amateur Athletic Association banned from all further participation a schoolboy athlete who revealed he once won a bar of chocolate worth 10p in a junior event on the Highland Games professional circuit.

At the same time, we must presume, the stern members of that oligarchic committee, having banished the weeping waif, turned smugly to any other business, polished the badges and buttons on their blazers and continued the planning of the 13th Commonwealth Games, just as they had so successfully planned the ninth 16 years earlier.

They were not to know what was about to hit them. And then some more. For in that time athletics itself had shaken off its village fete folksiness and was hopping, stepping and (always via the bank) jumping into Mammon's 21st century – and those blazered volunteer worthies who administrated were, comparatively, still in the 19th.

The whole structured, sub-committeed edifice of a century caved in, I fancy, the exact moment that young Daley Thompson staunchly looked the former President of the Scottish AAA up and down and told him to 'piss off'. For 30 years and more Mr Colin Shields had toiled selflessly away at his hobby, giving up holidays, and expecting in return only an occasional shiny new blazer badge. Daley earns £300,000 for advertising somebody's plimsolls. When two such worlds collide, these days there can only be one winner.

Edinburgh's Games were organised by 400 such volunteers who doodled on their blotters in an incredible 40 subcommittees.

Those honest and faithful Colin Shieldses added up to – as Colin Liddell of Guinness put it – 'an amorphous mass of volunteers, 98 per cent of whom had no knowledge or understanding of sports sponsorship.' So now it is all sponsorship is it, and not enough to want earnestly to put back into sport what you got out of it in your youth? Balance in sport now is only to do with balancing books.

Money pervades all these festivals now and we had better get used to it. The upfront presence throughout this week of the London boxing promoter Mickey Duff, for instance, was not all to do with love of the amateur Corinthian sporting ethic. He even put himself about the athletics press box, and when challenged it was explained that he was working for the BBC, who had accredited him.

Nor was it enough that he brought up Frank Bruno to attempt, in the event jarringly and ineptly, to upstage the Games. The BBC, with insensitive gall, also accredited Bruno's manager, Terry Lawless. That outraged the England boxing coach, Kevin Hickey, whose fine little squad gave the outstanding Canadians such a run for their money.

Said Hickey: 'The BBC should not even have considered Mr Lawless as a commentator. It's just not right. He even said our headguards caused cuts: there's no way that can happen, it's a monstrous suggestion. Certainly it more than annoys me that these Commonwealth Games of ours are being used as a springboard for Bruno: it's terrible, it's mixing up two different sports and two different philosophies.

'Bruno will be coming round to my lads saying "What's all this amateur stuff then? C'mon son, learn your game and come and turn pro with us big boys! Lots of lovely lolly and all that" – it's very wrong. If someone wants to turn pro and he's well advised he has a chance, then it's absolutely fair enough.'

Hickey was resigned to the fact that welterweight gold medallist Darren Dyer would turn pro. 'Jolly good luck to him,'

Hickey said. 'He's a lovely lad, a real team boy – and I hope he makes a lot of money: though I hope, too, that he's not easily used or badly led and that he knows the difference between 10 per cent of a cut and 25 per cent.' Percentages – that's how they keep the score in sport these days.

For the rest as I am drying out, I know for years I will recall Edinburgh '86 for the sploshingest, galoshingest, most freezing wetness I can remember. The Athens of the North? No, as Stoppard re-defined, 'The Reykjavik of the South'. And also for the astonishing daily book-balancing gyrations of Mr Robert Maxwell.

For sheer brass neck, his last trick in pleading with a Japanese 'benefactor' to save the Commonwealth Games took the biggest cream cracker of all. At his every pronouncement and plonking assurance, I felt like that little girl of long ago when she observed Mr Randolph Churchill in full spate – 'Mummy, what exactly is that man for?'

Where is the Twickers of yesteryear?
30 October 1991

Suckers for nostalgia and tradition should concentrate longingly at Twickenham on Saturday. Things might be what they used to be for just one last time.

The majority of the throng should be smug and suited sponsors, corporate global bigwigs and all the world's rugby committeemen rounding off their freebie junkets. So it could just be that a modicum of hush will prevail when – as that endearing PA announcer at Lansdowne Road had it on Sunday – 'the place-kickers essay their place-kicks'. It could be ... though, on the whole, one doubts it.

In the past year or two at Twickenham not only has the ancient, lettucey-green and grand old stadium itself changed beyond all recognition but so have the make up and the manners of those who attend it. And the barrage of boos and jeers that attend any opponent's attempt at a penalty goal is only a minor manifestation of rugby union's radical, and youthful, new luggage. As a spectator sport the game has been detonated out of its snug, century-old, well-stoppered bottle of aspic. Lager is now the liquid – and here-we-go, here-we-go, we-shall-not-be-moved …

The streams of urine and the pools of vomit which England's supporters left behind them in Paris a fortnight ago were not a new rugby phenomenon, so one is not becoming priggish in old age. But at least the one-time rugby rowdy abroad attempted to look for a loo or a discreet corner as the night wore on. For one thing, he had enough instinct left to resist staining his cavalry twills or Northampton brogues. The modern Twickers twit presumes only the right to unload where he stands.

After England's two Five Nations internationals at Twickenham early this year, various national papers, including a few Home Counties 'Horrifieds' in *The Times*, printed letters about the suddenly deplorable yobbishness of rugby's new followers. One letter in *Rugby World* had a spectator complaining of being 'incessantly spat on from behind' during a match.

The England XV's successes of late seem to have fortified the implicit nationalism in these new supporters, and fired their xenophobic certainties. The niceties and tactical intrigues of a lovely game are neither here nor there – as long as We stuff the Bastard Foreigners. Special hate seems at present reserved for 'the Micks' and 'the Frogs'. Heaven help us when England in the next decade or two have a run of defeats against the likes of Italy or Western Samoa (or even Wales).

Like their soccer counterparts of the 1980s they seem as oblivious to alcohol's properties as they are to midwinter weather. They rampage in (and at) sixes and sevens, and each dresses scantily: faded jeans to a man and trainers; sometimes a flimsy anorak. 'Inn-ger-land, Inn-ger-land' is their cry. And like everyone else they have no comprehension of the second line of the spiritual 'Swing Low, Sweet Chariot'. Their elder brothers in Twickenham's downmarket north car park – as they struggle both to undo their hampers and champers and to impress their overmade-up molls and dolls – do not want to know these noisy marauding gangs of new rugger types.

Twickenham, only last month it seems, was all so different. Jeering at penalties? Perish the thought. Polite claps for the chaps of either side, and the best team always won. Then the uniform was, more often than not: an officer's 'tash; a British-warm greatcoat or a decently cut and toggled duffel; a hip-flask in one pocket, St Bruno in the other; with the good lady wife – 'Dorothy's been a real brick down the years' – haughtily head-scarved, powdered and rouged, and with fingernails as scarlet as bloody daggers, faithfully carrying the tartan travel-rug. Those were the days. C'mon England. Play up, chaps. C'mon, Nim, give the line a run. Oh, well played, sir.

'An international at Twickenham,' wrote Alec Waugh, 'is more than a mere spectacle: it is the gathering of the clan.' Ivor Brown revelled in Twickenham as 'the last fortress of the Forsytes'. Even a Welshman, John Morgan, handsome Dai-the-Box and journalist, understood perfectly when he described 'the caps, the coats, the accents that mark a man from Kuala Lumpur to Salisbury; in the carpark the Bentleys and the TR3s; and all along the touchline screaming boys in blazers, and in the stands the men with unmistakable faces and the pretty women in camelhair coats; how did the middle classes manage before Twickenham was built?' But now, perhaps, the most prescient of any might turn out to be Philip Toynbee. Over half a century ago he wrote: 'A bomb under Twickenham's West stand on an international day would end Fascism in England for a generation.'

Give or take another generation or two and old Professor Toynbee could yet be seen to have hit the very button.

A final futile blazer flourish
16 January 1996

It was a tragi-comic debacle all right when the committee of the RFU was ambushed, trussed up and held to ransom by its own backwoodsmen in Birmingham on Sunday.

Thus it was that, instead of smoothly spiriting through its blueprint for change and its far-seeing plans for a seamless and open game, the RFU was forced to convene another special meeting by the tribesmen in blazers at which the first vote will be on the bald and specific question of whether the clubs and counties of England want their game to stay amateur.

As they flounder, the rugger men of England at least want to go down with the satisfaction of sending a booming ya-boo which tells the international board what it can do with its new open rugby regulations. Such a result from the English shires would cause a far greater eruption of side-splitting jollity around the rest of the rugby world than did even Master Will's old farts' flatulence-in-a-teacup which so enlivened the gaiety of nations last spring.

At a stroke such a vote would have England's dozen or so senior clubs breaking away from the RFU. Already all of them are tooled up for full professionalism next season. And, if the inmates in checked caps did win the vote and take over the asylum, would they demand the England squad players pay back the handsome payments they have already pocketed?

Purity has its place in life; so does a romantic's turning back of clocks. But this thing is too far gone. These rank-and-file rugger blokes are in imminent danger of making the game a laughing stock. Athletics, golf, tennis and soccer are all games which have adapted to rampant professionalism at the top and the purity of amateurism at the bottom.

What irks these buffers? Or did revolution stir and hackles rise spontaneously on Sunday just because they suddenly found themselves in that vast conference-room 'clubhouse' with 800 like-minded souls and blood brothers? And was it one last despairing and doom-laden collective bray of anguish from this endangered herd?

There were, voiced with passion, three mentions of 'this great game of ours' in the first nine minutes of speeches on Sunday. Moreover, in proposing men for the highest office in the domestic game it was always the acme of regard and recommendation to say that he sold the raffle-tickets at his club every Saturday afternoon and that his wife and daughter-in-law made the clubhouse teas. The gathering of this clan used to happen regularly at Twickenham itself. But that was before those new grandstands were filled by the hordes of corporate-hospitality City slickers in suits. If there were 800 in the hall on Sunday, at least 750 were in the regulation blue club blazer with faded twirly-whirly wire badge at the breast. This was their last collective round-up and more than likely they knew it, too.

The brand new RFU administration at Twickenham is as changed as its stadium. It is now on the ball, slick, professional and even visionary as it looks with vigour to the next century. But in planning Sunday's meeting the officers misjudged totally their mass of blue-blazered footslogging counter-revolutionaries from the shires and ran slap-bang into a stirring mutiny.

But British officers have their methods. They are sly, cunning devils when roused and they know the score. Let the infantry rebel-rousers think they have made their point, butter them up with a couple of meaningless concessions, let them sleep on their one-off triumph – and put it to another vote in six weeks' time and, hey presto, with a shrug they will be marching to the leaders' drum again.

If not, mind you, what utter jollity lies ahead.

I think readers will know this story went on, and it was not back to amateurism.

Four-square answer to a one-sided war-dance
27 November 1997

The haka may evoke a folkloric culture of antiquity but why the hell, before a match kicks off, should the All Blacks be the only international rugby team allowed to glower at the opposition with eyeballing menace and seethingly to paw the earth in a blatantly intimidating manner?

Richard Cockerill's noisy, breast-beating challenge and generally prickly prattishness have got up the noses of most English club spectators in recent years but one had to smile as one also winced at the weekend pictures of the toothless Tiger doing the same to his All Black opposite number before the start of Saturday's match at Old Trafford. It apparently rattled the New Zealanders so much that their game became ragged in the desperation to mete out some retribution for such disrespect. Afterwards their coach John Hart remained in a tizz about the 'indignity to our ancient national culture'.

Well, what about our peaceable sporting culture, mate, when the words of this war dance of yours, 'Kamate kamate ka ora ka ora', translate into 'It is death. It is death. This is the strong one who makes the sun shine'. All Cockerill was miming, and why not, was his own version of 'Yeah, you and whose army?'

For the return contest next week, will Twickenham command Cockerill to back off, especially since Wales's coach Kevin Bowring has said his men this Saturday will 'treat the haka with the respect its tradition demands'? Or perhaps, if Cockerill does feel roused again, the RFU will order him to answer the bellicose Maori challenge only in the classical Latin, 'We who are about to die salute you.'

Hart said the tradition dated back to the first All Blacks' tour to Britain in 1905. Wrong. It was 17 years before that. The front page of the *Illustrated London News* of 13 October 1888 shows the New Zealand all Maori team enacting the haka in ostrich-feather capes to boot, and doffing their tasselled caps as they jumped, before winning their match against Surrey, 'a device of novelty and excitement to present to the sizeable gathering'.

Of course Cockerill's glowering *coup de théâtre* on Saturday, though a defiant one-man show, was not wholly original. In Dublin eight years ago Ireland's captain from Dungannon, Willie Anderson, gathered his 14 fellows in green and shuffled them with eyeballing bravado into the very heart of the enemy dance.

'I'd do it again,' said Anderson cheerfully. 'Sure it was premeditated. I had the idea myself and my friend Andy Leslie, who captained the All Blacks, said it was worth graphically showing them we weren't going to be intimidated. Okay, it's a "culture" thing for them but in translation it's not what you'd call a Sunday school song, is it? It's all about threats and killing and revenge at all costs.' After they had duly won 23-6, the All Blacks just laughed and said they were surprised no one else had done the same. Wayne Shelford, the captain, thought it promised a decent game of rugby.

Perhaps at Twickenham Cockerill should do his own war dance and write a few of his own lyrics. He has more than a week to learn them. That sort of thing was done by the South African team in the final match at Newlands of the All Blacks' first tour in 1928.

It went down well all round, although thereafter the haka was not danced on South African paddocks when New Zealand were there for the next 48 years, until Leslie's team were happily allowed to revive it in 1976. A *Cape Times* editorial noted: 'Although the haka dancers are never likely to be confused with Nijinsky or Nureyev, this rugby rumba provides a good deal of fun for performers and spectators alike ... and it takes from the proceedings some of the grim-faced solemnity that is such a tiresome aspect of first-class rugby. Those of us who believe rugby is a game, not a war, will say, "Hurrah for the haka."'

The reason why this famous 'rugby rumba' and Maori war dance was not performed on the All Black tours of South Africa of 1949 or 1960 was simple. The craven New Zealand rugby union had been happy to pander to the demands of the South African apartheid regime and, shamingly, did not include any 'coloured' Maori players in its teams. Leicester's Master Cockerill might have displayed, as Caucasian Mr Hart whinged righteously on Saturday, 'indignity to our ancient national culture' – but nothing like as much as did Hart's not-so-long-ago predecessors in the All Black blazer. Keep stickin' it up 'em, Richard.

William Hill must be brought to book
29 November 2011

The 'Bookie' for the best sports book of the year, sponsored by William Hill and awarded on Monday with tragically topical coincidence to *A Life Too Short*, the story of a professional footballer who killed himself, differs in a significant way from the long established Booker prize for literary fiction.

The same unchanging panel of five adjudicates each year for the Hill. So no wonder, I suppose, that the authors of the same sort of book gush up to the podium every 12 months. Has the prize become routinely stuck on a conveyor belt of winners depicting sport as a wearisome battle against mental, addictive or physical adversity? If so, alas, is sporting literature being defined by a wretchedly painful type of valour as opposed to wide-eyed fun, enlightenment and enjoyment?

With 2009's uplifting biography of cricket's Harold Larwood the only exception, four of the last five William Hill awards have gone to life stories of, successively: rugby's abused, adopted unhappy hooker Brian Moore (2010); the troubled cricketer Marcus Trescothick (2008); football's misunderstood maestro and alcoholic Brian Clough (2007); and the racially oppressed boxer Jack Johnson (2006). As the always spot-on John Dugdale remarked in the *Guardian*'s *Saturday Review*: 'It's apt that a prize sponsored by a bookie should typically portray sport as instructive misery.'

The permanent judging panel consists of the prize founder and bookseller John Gaustad, broadcaster John Inverdale, and three sporting journalists, Danny Kelly, Hugh McIlvanney and Alyson Rudd. The bookmakers are generous sponsors, certainly, but does not each year's sameness suggest a generally cosy laziness? The Booker fiction prize has completely fresh judges every year, each bringing new insights and enthusiasms. These never seem to vary when it comes to the 'Bookie'.

If you can count bullfighting as a tragic, distasteful activity, then five of the seven entries on Hill's shortlist this year made for uneasy reading. It was really no surprise when the harrowing winner was announced on Monday.

17

FINAL WORDS

Frank survived the Edinburgh Commonwealth Games, the Atlanta Olympics and Nigel Mansel – and worked through to his official retirement just before his 65th birthday, an occasion marked with the Guardian *equivalent of a 21-gun salute. This was his own formal valedictory column.*

They pitilessly cut my florid flam about autumn leaves
9 September 2002

The final piece in this space under this byline is an unashamedly self-indulgent one all right, but of all the acres of rhubarb served up to long-suffering *Guardian* readers by this reporter, none could have been more intemperately self-absorbed than the very first submission dispatched to these pages more than 44 years ago.

In the midwinter of 1957–8 I was a 20-year-old cub on the *Hereford Times*, and on Monday 6 January, two days after I had been responsible for representing the final digit in southern league Hereford United's (still) record home crowd of 18,114 for their third-round FA Cup tie against Sheffield Wednesday, I typed out on an ancient upright office Remington a breathlessly descriptive colour piece and posted it to the sports editor of the *Manchester Guardian*.

They never used it, of course, but a printed rejection slip thanking me for my trouble and signed by a Bill Taylor not only made my week but encouraged me a month later to submit another piece (a day late and again by post). This time it was grief-stricken sob stuff on how the monthly meeting I was covering at the Talbot hotel, Leominster, of the young bumpkins of North Hereford Young Farmers' Club had been abandoned in sympathy on the night of 6 February when news came through of the Manchester United air disaster in Munich. This juvenile stuff did not even warrant an official rejection. Mr Taylor obviously had other things on his mind, not least the death in that airport slush of his paper's celebrated football correspondent HD Davies, who wrote under the byline 'An Old International'.

Davies's folksy and descriptive ebullience had made him a hero of what I knew to be the 'writers' paper'. I may have been a trainee yokel reporter with straw in my hair but I knew I was the only person in on the act in all of cuddly cut-off Hereford, because I would walk each lunch hour to the railway station to collect from the parcel office, direct from that morning's Manchester train, the day before's *Manchester Guardian*. A solitary copy just for little me.

When the time came to dare the wider world, this Billy Liar's ambitions alternating headily between becoming its chief foreign corr, flowery drama critic or ace football writer, I continued to lap up the giants of *Guardian*ese during stints on local rags in Guildford and Bristol. Then, during the then obligatory 18 months' penniless bum around Africa, I continued sending back (in longhand and on flimsy airmail paper, which must have taken weeks to reach Manchester (but only seconds to hit the reject bin)) my cornily callow – but, oh, so grave – opinions on the Congo war, Roy Welensky, Dr Hastings Banda and Jomo Kenyatta.

Returning home, the *Slough Observer* gave me a job as sports editor. And so it was that the call finally came. Wow! Deo gratias. A commission – 350 words, please, and pronto on the full-time whistle, on the county hockey match between Bucks and Surrey down alongside the Slough rubbish tip.

They pitilessly cut all my florid flam about autumn leaves and Windsor Castle in the distance. But they actually printed the boring bits in between. 18 October 1962 – SURREY SLOW TO

FIND FORM said the headline while 'in their sporadic offensives Bucks relied overmuch on the telegraphed through-pass' said the copy. Hey, mum, I'm a *Guardian* writer.

By which time, of course, the *Guardian* had begun London printing and dropped the Manchester prefix. Sports editor was David Gray, who doubled as a pathfinding tennis writer. On the strength of my Slough hockey scoop, Gray told me, not very convincingly, there might a sports desk job 'some time' – but it was not long before the late Keith Harper, flatmate on the *Bristol Evening World* and my dearest friend in journalism, who was by then *Guardian* reporter in the West Country, had wheedled me an interview as a general sub-editor – '£25 per week rising by two guineas after a year's satisfactory service ... with membership of our pension scheme obligatory.' And so, at 65, is the latter stricture enacted.

I stayed long enough to qualify for my extra guineas before ITV signed me for three times as much loot for six crazy years laughing round the world and taking in two Olympics and two World Cups. From the latter, in Mexico in 1970, I sent back a daily piece of waffle to the *Times*, which, for some reason, inspired former subs-desk friend Brian Jones, by then the *Guardian*'s deputy editor, to hint it might be worth applying to the new sports editor, John Samuel, for a staff job.

Never has a wayward prodigal gone home more happy. In the early 70s it was a golden age to tiptoe into work with awe – Gray had been released to hand down his gospels daily to the tennis world, David Frost and John Rodda were the universal sages respectively for rugby and athletics, Pat Ward-Thomas and, later, Peter Dobereiner ditto for golf; Richard Baerlein was idolised in racing and so, obviously, was John Arlott in cricket. In the north was our ever-complaining craftsman Eric Todd, terrific successor to my first hero Davies, and in London David Lacey was starting his splendiferous reign as soccer correspondent.

For well over a quarter of a century I was privileged to get in the drinks for them and carry their typewriters the world over, and they not only put up with me but were all werry, werry good to me as their sidebar Sancho Panza. Just as, to a man, their luminous successors have been.

When our distinguished rugby columnist Carwyn James died in 1983 I was late for his funeral in the chapel at Cefneithen. Breathless, I barged through the huge throng who had not been able to get in and flung myself at the mercy of a sidesman-steward. 'I've come all the way from the *Guardian* to report the service,' I pleaded. Follow me, he said, and to accompanying discontent he led me through a side door and pushed me through the overflowing bodies cramming the tabernacle to the front row. 'Move up, make room for this very important man,' he ordered, 'he's from the *Ammanford Guardian*!'

A desperately sad day – dear Carwyn – but he would have been first to chortle that it put everything about an unlikely but happy career into contented and carefree perspective. Manchester or Ammanford, who cares? The sheer fun was the thing. For which much thanks.

It was very far from the end of Frank's career, though. He continued writing columns for more than another decade. Though increasingly immobile, his memory, enthusiasm and literary skill were undimmed. In late 2012 he was asked to switch from the Guardian *to its Sunday sister the* Observer; *the two were by now almost wholly integrated into a single operation. The association was sadly brief. His seventh and penultimate* Observer *column was a partial nod of appreciation to the members-in-perpetuity of the judging panel for the William Hill book prize (heaven knows why he was never asked to join it) for a somewhat less miserable short list than usual: 'Thankfully the judges seem in a happier place this year'. No one knew there would be only one more column. But he went out with a classic* cri de coeur *that echoed the thoughts of every footballing romantic.*

Romantics left feeling black and blue
2 December 2012

White tornadoes! Tradition having reasserted itself, England's rugby players turned up in an all-white strip to thrill Twickenham against the All Blacks yesterday. There had been a generally hearty outcry a fortnight ago when the kit sponsors – in another wretched device to sell replica shirts – dressed the England XV in garish plum-coloured purple before their hapless defeat by Australia, an outfit memorably described in these pages by Richard Williams as making them resemble 'nothing more than a bunch of damsons in distress'.

In recent seasons England have also sported strips of dark blue, vivid red or grey-black 'anthracite'. Will Twickenham ever realise that for romantic traditionalists the matter of ancient teams twinned with ancient colours remains a serious and un-jokey subject?

On the very same weekend as English rugby's purple splurge I cannot have been the only one who winced at the picture of a Cardiff City footballer sporting a bright robin-red shirt and not the club's blue of a century. The new Malaysian owners reckon red 'the more dynamic when it comes to marketing our merchandise in Asia'. So Wales's fabled Bluebirds are slaughtered at a stroke.

England rugby's narrow-eyed disrespect for traditional values is horribly modern. White, blue, red and green had been the timeless and inviolate robes that satisfied the four home unions since the first international contests in the early 1870s. It was the same at football – well, not quite and don't tell the SNP that the blue of the saltire was absent from the Scottish national football strip till as far into history as 1900. Before then the national team was adorned in primrose-and-pink hoops in feudal genuflection to the racing colours of the longtime Scottish FA president Lord Archibald Philip 'Primrose' Rosebery.

When it comes to romance, in fairness both Twickenham's and Cardiff's commercial regimes can legitimately ask: 'How long is a legend?' For instance, time immemorial's Red Devils of Manchester United have, since they were Newton Heath FC, played in the following kaleidoscope of colours: green and gold till 1896; white till 1902; red till 1923; white (1927); and for the first half of the 1934 season it was cherry hoops before they settled on plain red shirts. So when does tradition become history? Have Liverpool FC always been the Reds of Anfield and Everton the Blues of Goodison? For the first Merseyside derby in 1893 Liverpool wore royal blue and white quarters, Everton 'ruby' tops and black shorts. So there.

The black-and-yellow of Wasps and the red-and-black of Saracens are probably the most ancient surviving rugby colours of all while, for football, if Arsenal's bespoke and singular white sleeves on red body look as if they are pre-Victorian, it is only 80 years next spring since manager Herbert Chapman's whim and wheeze about the change.

The current rugby internationals have nicely reminded us how the first All Blacks arrived in 1905 with their 'dark blue guernseys' turning them from a distance into the collective name they happily retain. Two years earlier, on the first official tour by a British side, the South Africans played the first two Tests in white shirts, but for the third at Newlands they wore a set bequeathed them by a local club, the Old Diocesans, which had just folded, so handed over its basket of myrtle-green jerseys to the fledgling international side. And myrtle green it famously remains.

The Australian rugby union Wallabies arrived in Britain for a tour in 1928 with their skip of light blue shirts, but at once a horrified Twickenham informed their manager: 'Didn't you know, ol' boy? Cambridge are the only serious club to play in light blue.' And so they ordered up for them some 'yellow-ochre shirts with optional green piping'.

In football, patterns as well as colours remain severely under threat from the commercial greed of men who know the price of everything and the value of nothing. So be ready for a possible last glimpse of the legendary colours of generations – and each distinctively to their own. It is never the russety-yellow of Wolves but always the sacrosanct old gold; or only the canary of Norwich; it is never the orange but always the tangerine of Blackpool; never the blue of Coventry but only the sky blue; and never the dull red and soft blue of Burnley, Villa or the Hammers but always, always, only the claret and blue.

The same went for the patterns: the stripes of Stoke and the Sheffields; the blue 'halves' of Blackburn, the blue 'quarters' of Bristol Rovers, the blue hoops of Queens Park Rangers, the green ones of Celtic; the black verticals of good ol' Newcastle and prehistoric Notts County ...

One of the loveliest stories of recent times – with regular and happy reminders this autumn of the Italian club's stylish progress in the Champions League – was the invitation from that mighty institution Juventus to ancient but unlikely little Notts County, 150 last week and the world's oldest football club currently professional, to be guests of honour and opponents at last year's opening of their new stadium. County were the 1903 donors of a set of black-and-white-striped shirts to the boys' club which was to grow into the one and only, and massive Juve. Hooray for both of them.

And that was all he wrote: the last of several million gloriously distinctive words, only a small fraction of them contained in this book. He died just under two months later, and a huge crowd of family, friends and colleagues crowded into Belmont Abbey, just outside Hereford, for the funeral.

Eulogy

by Matthew Engel
7 February 2013

Ladies, Gentlemen, M'dears:

Two Fridays ago, I took the phone call that told me Frank had died, while I was in the hideous centre of Stevenage New Town, a bizarre disjunction I am still trying to process. That has made me extra conscious of the sense of place that surrounds Jane's choice of settings for today's events.

Here we are in the High Victorian, Catholic-Revival-Gothic of this Benedictine Abbey which was also the heart of Belmont Abbey School until the school closed in 1994. And it was here, in the frigid, half-starved second winter after the war that Keating, aged not quite nine I think, arrived to be walloped by the monks for bed-wetting, occasionally dangled from this tower by the older boys, and generally manned up.

There is an assumption that Frank always bathed the past in a rosy glow. His relationship with both his childhood and his faith was actually rather complex. How could it be anything else? It's the same with all great writers. But he never shunned the past, he embraced it. The whole first third of his life was central to his work and his being. And it is wholly appropriate that we should be here today. After this service, the family will cross Hereford to the churchyard at Marden, the village where Frank and Jane made their wonderful, warm, welcoming home for the final third of his life.

And they will meet the rest of us again at Lyde Arundell, where we will have what we might politely call the refreshments. But this is *Frank's* funeral and it is imperative that we laugh and tell stories in his honour. So let's say we'll have a bit of a party. Because he did love a party. Especially in that middle third.

And all of this is happening in Herefordshire. Which means, I know, that many of you have endured interminable journeys to get here. Welcome to *our* world. But being here is central to an understanding of Frank. This isn't like London. I don't want to be over-romantic about it. Can't think of *anyone* who would do such a thing. But I think in a city, when you meet new people, you trust them when you've learned to trust them. Here you trust them until you have a reason not to.

And up the road is the little town of Leominster, home of the Rankin Club: it's supposed to be the Conservative Club but no one takes much notice of that. And every winter month it holds a sports night. And over the years an astonishing array of sporting celebrities have made the journey to speak there. Very largely, in the old days, thanks to Frank's contacts. They certainly don't come for the money.

And every month the room is packed, and they love every minute. I'm the least famous of the 400-plus speakers in John Beamon's big book. And I was so bowled over by the reception I walked on air for weeks afterwards. The audience at the Rankin doesn't want to hear about the crookery of sport, the cynicism, the corruption, the fakery. Sport is their pleasure. It's not important but it *is* important. Frank understood that instinctively. It was fundamental to his work. This is also a place where you can't afford to get high-falutin'. The *Hereford Times* website. Friday 25 January 2013. 'A former *Hereford Times* journalist has died at the age of 75.' Point. New paragraph. He did a few other things too.

A funeral is a recognition that we are all unique. It is also a bridge. Between the rawness of grief and the slow fading towards the back of our memory. But some human beings are more unique than others. And there is no danger that any of us will ever begin to forget Frank Keating.

Of course he wasn't just Herefordshire. It takes a one-off background to produce a one-off like this one. Though he was born here, the Keatings soon moved into Gloucestershire, where his family settled down as absolutely bog-standard typical Irish Catholic cockney Christian socialist Labour activist Cotswold farmers – with a hint of Jewish.

Frank's education was Catholic. From here he went to Douai, another lost school. And there he flourished, in the most important respects. I've received a lot of messages in response to the appreciation that I wrote in the *Guardian* two weeks ago. One, from Charles Fox, went as follows: 'When I first went to Douai in 1955, Frank was in the first XV and I was deputed to keep his white shorts clean before matches. Needless to say I hero-worshipped him.' *Needless to say?* There must have been a lot of Catholic forbearance at Douai. Not sure cleaning another boy's rugby shorts would induce hero-worship in most kids. But we'll come back to that.

Frank arrived at Douai just at the end of the long headmastership of Father Ignatius Rice, who had actually played two matches for Warwickshire in 1920. According to Frank's autobiography, *Half-Time Whistle*, which I regard as a reliable source in outline, if not perhaps every single detail, Father Ignatius spoke to him just twice.

Once was to advise him never to call the maids skivvies, as was the school custom. The other was to tell him that, in life, as in cricket, he should play himself in a bit, and then 'get on the front foot at every opportunity. You'll have more fun that way.'

Well, he certainly heeded the second bit. An inability to pass exams saved him from the dead hand of academic advancement. A bit of fibbing got him out of national service. And then, as a young man could in those days, he made his way in journalism and life. He went via Stroud, the *Hereford Times*, where he lost his virginity and his job (neither fact mentioned in that website piece), Guildford, Southern Rhodesia (where he acquired his lifelong hatred of white South African attitudes), Bristol, and at some point Slough. Maybe even Stevenage was in the mix somewhere.

He got a job sub-editing on the *Guardian*. Then he left to go into television. Personally, I don't believe that Frank was ever quite so incompetent a TV executive as he liked to make out. If he were, ITV would have gone out of business. Then he came back to the *Guardian*. He claims to have written a freelance hockey piece for the paper from Slough in 1962. The first bylined piece I can find is dated 17 March 1971: 'Littlechild gives Durham victory', a seven-a-side universities rugby match between Durham and Liverpool. Very straight, very factual. Was that Frank obeying Father Ignatius' instructions and playing himself in? Evidently not. Sources suggest he turned in all kinds of flowery stuff that was duly red-pencilled by the subs.

But his sports editor John Samuel spotted something. And over the next couple of years he started to get a few more cover-drives past the fielders, including a piece I remember vividly: his reminiscence – in 1975, when they reached the cup final – of the days when Fulham had Johnny Haynes and the rest were hilariously no good. 'Haynes suffered 18 glorious, exasperated years for Fulham, carpeting out the world's most sumptuous passes to a motley crew of single-jointed unappreciative nuts: a Brylcreemed Schweitzer among the Pygmies.' Oh, m'dear; what an exquisite sentence.

There is something that keeps coming back to me that I can't quite pin down. It was Fred Titmus telling someone who asked him about playing with Denis Compton. 'I can't tell you how good he was,' said Fred. 'You'd never believe me.' I could try to explain how good Frank was. But the day is short, the seats are hard, the food and drink are waiting, and I hope there will be another occasion specifically to celebrate the works of Keating. I will give just a few examples of how our Schweitzer kept rolling out sentences like that that we journalistic pygmies could never match.

The hapless Yorkshireman Richard Dunn attempting to get off the canvas after being hit by Muhammad Ali 'like a drunken matelot trying to take off his waders under water.' John Conteh getting his teeth knocked out: 'a faint tinkle of crystal like a chandelier caught in a Waterford breeze.'

There was angry Frank, as at the Centenary Test at Lord's when the umpires kept inspecting the pitch and refusing to let play start. He began like this. 'At teatime the band played that tiddley-om theme tune from *Monty Python's Flying Circus*. Honest it did. The Royal Marines Band it was and they were conducted by a precise and very well turned-out chap called Hoskins, which is a very Pythonesque sort of name. So was the day.

'A monumental cock-up. Lord's and all of cricket should be totally ashamed of itself. Someone should resign. No one will, of course. Their judgment of priorities is unbelievable.'

Or Frank at his most Frankish, slipping away from an England tour in Calcutta to visit Mother Theresa, who starts miming cricket shots. 'You are not in awe any more. You are laughing with her and want to call her "Luv".' And so it went on. This was not nostalgia recollected in tranquility. This was live reporting executed with a sizzle and a panache that had simply never been achieved before. And it changed sports journalism. He broke the rules so successfully the rules had to be changed.

That wasn't all. There is an old story about some nobleman involved in a scrape being informed by his butler with some distaste: 'The press are here, m'lud. And the gentleman from the *Times*.' Well, in my day, it would be, 'The bloody press are here. And good old Frank.' He had that rapport, that easy manner, that belonged to every son of an Irish Catholic cockney Christian socialist Labour activist Cotswold farming family with a hint of Jewish that I've ever known. People in sport just took to him. That showed itself very clearly in the TV series, *Maestro*, when he interviewed ageing greats. His colleagues' attitude is shown by the turn-out here today. And then there were the readers.

He wrote for various publications: *The Times*, the *Sunday Tel*, *Punch*, the *Speccy*, the *Oldie*, the rugby mags, the cricket mags, at the end the *Observer*. But in the *Guardian* it was different. One old *Guardian* hand – not a sports person at all – said to me that the online tributes to Frank on the website were 'An outpouring of something a bit more than respect and affection, more like gratitude and love. I don't remember seeing anything before quite like it.' And I don't think you ever will. It was a unique relationship between a unique writer and a unique readership.

I imagine everyone here will have experienced the more exaggerated manifestations of Frank's good nature. Mention anyone you like. Silvio Berlusconi: 'For all that, I do love him.' Vladimir Putin: 'Oooh, he *is* a dear.' Of course it was largely an act. But then good manners and politeness are always an act. I am inclined to think he took it too far for his own good. Pretending that he didn't mind what the subs did to his copy was, in my judgment, a serious strategic error. He did mind, believe me.

And it was an act that enhanced the lives of dozens of young journalists who would come seeking advice from Dr Frank about how to make their career better. Very Herefordshire word: pilgrims. Much used by the SAS. But these were the real Herefordshire pilgrims, coming to the shrine in the hope that they might acquire a little of Frank's genius, and his beatitude. And if they couldn't imbibe his genius, they always imbibed his encouragement. And indeed just imbibed.

I return to Charles Fox, the Douai boy who had to keep Frank's shorts clean. Why on earth would that lead to hero-worship? 'Because,' said Fox, 'he was an incredibly nice guy then as always – gentle was a good description.'

After, let's say, a rumbustious kind of life in Holland Park, Frank married Jane in 1983 and they produced Paddy and Tess. Late fatherhood is generally accompanied by an extra sense of pride and also a certain mutual bemusement. In Frank's case this was multiplied by Paddy's choice of career. I have been known to tease people who know Frank but not the family, by asking if they know what his son does and offering two hundred guesses. But I can tell you this. He was enormously chuffed last August when Keating PFB, First Battalion, the Rifles, passed out of Sandhurst as a second lieutenant and a very fine young man.

And furthermore I sense in Paddy's determination to pursue his chosen course the same determination that his father had, but hid beneath layers of self-deprecation and bogus dilletantism. In Tess's case I think he was continually surprised by her beauty, forgetting perhaps that Jane's genes might have been largely responsible for that. But again he lived to see her starting to make her way at the BBC with every prospect of a career in broadcasting to outshine his own.

The most important person comes last. Throughout our own family trauma, when our son Laurie became ill and died, we were hugely grateful for the steadfast support of Frank and Jane. Frank was not in good health for a long time. Through it all, Jane supported him with devotion and heroism. Since the final crisis began in November, that has been doubled and redoubled. She must have been exhausted. Never once did she falter. Never once did we hear her be anything less than positive.

'The love that asks no questions
The love that stands the test.'

Their last day together, in the lovely surroundings of the Hereford hospice, was a very happy one. Frank was feeling better. He was talking of writing again. There was lots of jollity. He died quietly in his sleep that night. He was blessed, in many, many ways. Having Jane's love and support most of all.

One of my favourite Frank pieces is one he wrote in the *Guardian* at the end of September 1982 when the cricket season concluded with an old masters' match at the Oval including the likes of 61-year-old Ray Lindwall and Garry Sobers, a mere 46 but well gone from regular cricket. This was the height of the *Guardian*'s 'Grauniad' phase and the piece has to be translated from the original typesetter's gibberish. Some of us, however, are well practised.

The piece ends as follows: 'Sobers leaves. Lindwall nods goodbye. There is a sudden, awed, hush in the room as Sir Garfield Sobers eases his way out, down the stairs, and across the Oval concourse for, perhaps, the very last time. The lights go out. It is, in fact, the end of many, many summers.'

And so it is today. But Frank leaves behind a warm glow that will sustain Jane and Paddy and Tess and all of us, and which will never be extinguished.

18

TRIBUTES

Frank was one of the best sports writers of any generation, someone who spoke as he wrote. When you spent any time in his company, you knew laughter would be on the menu; he was a man not just with a deep knowledge of sport, but warmth and wit, revelling in anecdotes.

Barry John, Wales and Lions fly half

I wanted Frank to write my autobiography not because I wanted him to convey my words, but because I wanted him to tell my story in his words.

Graham Gooch, England cricket captain

He was a gentleman and a gentle man. If one was interviewed by Frank it was just a gentle pleasure. There was no sense of interrogation or anything else. He had wide-ranging interests – you were just as likely to learn something from him as he was from you. If you asked the likes of Mike Brearley, they would say he was very easy to get on with and someone with whom you could have what you might call a normal conversation. That might sound strange, but for any of us who've been on either side of the equation that's not always the case. Some people would try and force things out of you, Frank would just coax it out.

David Gower, England cricket captain turned broadcaster

His rare, special quality as a writer on sport was to understand that exceptional physical performance, occasionally exquisite, came largely from otherwise ordinary folk. He recognised their particular worth as people, rather than as the celebrities into which contemporary media can too hastily transform them. When they failed, his response was to wince sympathetically rather than condemn.

David Miller, former chief sports writer, Times

He saw the best in everyone. Given the right occasion – usually a confrontation with either a jobsworth or a charlatan, both of whom he loathed – he could be supremely and entertainingly angry, but at heart he was a fan and a fan of almost anything and everyone sporting.

Mike Averis, Guardian *writer and former sports editor*

I was travelling between my home in Yung Shue Wan and Hong Kong when my life changed for ever. My professional life, anyway. For I read Frank Keating for the first time. I had been given the *Guardian Weekly,* and naturally I turned to the sport first. And Frank. It was a piece about Lucinda Prior-Palmer, as she was at the time, the great eventer. It was full of affection and mischief and admiration. It celebrated her as a traditional English type, it celebrated her brilliance, filtering both through himself as a lovestruck groundling with the ironies all intact. It was a beautifully turned piece that celebrated Lucinda, sport, horses, England and the English language. It wasn't like reading a newspaper; it was like reading a novel. It was simply – and complexly – brilliant. I had never read anything like it in a newspaper. I hadn't realised journalists were allowed to write like that; they'd never have put up with it on the local papers I worked for, nor on the national newspapers I read. But that, I thought, is the way to write about sport.

Simon Barnes, chief sports writer, Times

Few modern sports writers have brought alive sporting people, past and present, champions and also-rans, as Keating did. Few have written with such sympathy, able to laugh with them, not at them, at the same time minting fresh, inventive phraseology. He created a new language for the nation's sporting press. He was unique, and beloved by contemporaries, who saw his writing skills and awards as a guiding path for their own.

John Samuel, former sports editor, Guardian

Our friendship went back to the mid-50s when Frank arrived in Bristol to join me on the *Evening World,* a paper full of humanity, good humour and emergent talent, though heading for fiscal decline. It was his first stab at evening paper journalism. He was visibly apprehensive, I remember ... He drifted, from choice or luck, more towards sport. By now he knew what his career was going to be. He also discovered that the *World* had a useful cricket team with a challenging midweek fixture list against the best of the local village sides. I would drive him on these 20-over matches, two off-spinners who kidded ourselves we were Lock and Laker when we could hardly turn the ball. At least Keating looked the part. He was never ostentatious but he did turn up for one fixture in an improvised cravat, perhaps shaped by his mother, though.

Subbing was all very well but it was writing, his own, he wanted to do. He always talked a good game and it looked for a time as if he was settling for sweet-tongued television. But he belonged to the by-ways of prose. He quickly became a distinctive voice, ever generous with his musical alliteration, mischievous with the adjectives he sprinkled like confetti. He didn't write too much about the game's technique or language. He wrote about its soul.

David Foot, Guardian *colleague*

'Glorious' is not too extravagant a term for Keating's talent. In more than 40 years at the *Guardian* he evolved a style and set a standard of writing about sport, and especially about cricket, which was easy to admire and impossible to emulate. It is one thing to love the game, another to convey that ardour in a whirligig of words, spinning across the printed page. And it is another thing entirely to unleash that whirligig in time for the first edition. Frank managed it on a daily basis.

Patrick Collins, chief sports writer, Mail on Sunday

Adjectives, verbs, adverbs sprang from pen to page, as if in a particularly dotty race, scattered with aplomb and great chunks of humanity. He loved sport and he loved the people who played it. Never malicious, sometimes fanciful, he would roar you along with whatever event he had been sent to. He did not have to be kind or interested, but he was: kind, interested, funny, big-hearted and dazzling. It was what made him so popular with readers. It was what made him so popular with sportsmen. It was what made him so popular with fellow journalists, young and old. And it was what made his writing what it was: erudite popping candy writ large upon the tongue.

Tanya Aldred, Daily Telegraph

... wonderfully evocative pieces infused with wit, joy, melancholy, mischief, romanticism, drama, well-channelled vitriol and a welcome sense of proportion.

Phil Shaw, Independent

A beautifully lyrical sportswriter for whom the press box was a window on the heart.

Paul Fitzpatrick, Guardian *colleague*

Frank's final column appeared in these pages on 2 December, about sporting kits, with a jibe or two at England for wearing purple against the Wallabies. On the day before publication England (in white) gave the All Blacks an unexpected thrashing, and as we were remaking the front pages I received an email – 'Urgent' – suggesting a tweak or two to his column. Nice one

Frank, I thought, and made the changes. Only later did we hear he had been seriously ill at home that afternoon and was admitted to hospital that evening. But he still kept in touch with the match and filed his correction. Professional to the end.

Matthew Hancock, sports editor, Observer

Dad often told us as kids that it was more important to be the happiest than to be the best. A phrase with which I once managed to send a Sandhurst colour sergeant into an apoplectic rage – an image Dad would have undoubtedly enjoyed. But Dad was lucky enough to be both the happiest and the best. Even as he lay in hospital earlier this year he managed to chuckle when I told him that he must be very proud to be in such excellent company as on that very day Margaret Thatcher had gone into hospital as well. He spent far more time asking about other people, joking with the hospital staff and instructing Mum to send champagne to far-flung friends and family than he did admitting any pain. That was Dad.

Lieutenant Paddy Keating, Frank's son

INDEX

(FK refers to Frank Keating)

Dugdale, John 295
Duke, Geoff 245
Dunn, Richard 105–8, 307
Durham CCC 52, 55
Dyer, Darren 287–8

Easby, Dennis 128
Edrich, Bill 234, 249, 255
Edwards, Gareth 120, 121, 251
Edwards, Vic 146
Elizabeth, Queen Mother 154
Ella, Mark 139
Elliott, Herb 263
Elliott, Peter 203
Elsworth, David 156
Emburey, John 271, 273
Emmett, George 234
Engel, Laurie 309
Engel, Matthew 303
England cricket team:
    Ashes won by 50, 56
    Bedser's record for 29
    in India 180–4
England rugby team 119–24,
    127–31, 218
England soccer team:
    in Oslo 80–2
    see also World Cup (soccer)
European Cup 220, 221–2
    1965 75
    1977 74–6
    1979 77–80
Eusébio 222
Evans, BJ 275–6
Evans, Eric 126
Evening Standard 21–2
Evening World 313
Evert-Lloyd, Chris 145
Everton FC 302

FA Cup:
    1948 20, 266
    1975 17–18
    1987 223
Facchetti, Giacinto 75
Fagg, Arthur 255–6
Faldo, Nick 103
Faulkner, Max 99, 101
Ferguson, John 139
Ferguson, Sarah 150
Fisher, Bob 196
Fitzpatrick, Paul 314
Five Nations 122, 289
Fix Your Life Now! (Goodhew,
    Hislop) 39
Fletcher, Keith 183, 274
Flynn, Errol 49
Foot, David 239–41, 313
Football League Review 230
football programmes 228–30
Foreman, George 143, 151
Fosbury, Dick 264
Fox, Charles 305–6, 309
fox hunting 159–64
Fragments of Idolatry (Foot) 240
France rugby side 122–7, 134–5
Francis, Trevor 78
Frazier, Joe 26, 143
French Without Tears 48
Frindall, Bill 139
Frost, David 299
Frys, Paul 10
Fulham FC 17–18, 23–4, 69–
    73, 89, 90–2, 218

Gabrichenko, Viktor 207
Garlick, Gordon 258
Garner, James 138
Gatting, Mike 132, 183, 184,
    274